Programming in
JAVA

Programming in JAVA

Harish Gupta

ANMOL PUBLICATIONS PVT. LTD.
NEW DELHI-110 002 (INDIA)

ANMOL PUBLICATIONS PVT. LTD.

Regd. Office: 4360/4, Ansari Road, Daryaganj,
New Delhi-110002 (India)
Tel.: 23278000, 23261597, 23286875, 23255577
Fax: 91-11-23280289
Email: anmolpub@gmail.com
Visit us at: www.anmolpublications.com

Branch Office: No. 1015, Ist Main Road, BSK IIIrd Stage
IIIrd Phase, IIIrd Block, Bangalore-560 085 (India)
Tel.: 080-41723429 • Fax: 080-26723604
Email: anmolpublicationsbangalore@gmail.com

Programming in JAVA

First Edition, 2010

ISBN 978-81-261-4368-9

PRINTED IN INDIA

Printed at Mehra Offset Press, Delhi.

Contents

Preface

Programming in JAVA: is an introductory textbook aimed at the traditional CS1 course.. The book avoids trendiness for its own sake by focusing on teaching students programming skills. The book emphasis on learning how to design, implements, and debug programs written in an object-oriented language. In this book the topics are introduced in a spiral fashion, with as little "magic" as possible. After using this book, students should be well-prepared to move on to C++ or more advanced courses in Java.

Programming In Java is an introductory computer programming textbook that uses Java as the language of instruction. It is suitable for use in an introductory programming course and for people who are trying to learn programming on their own. There are no prerequisites beyond a general familiarity with the ideas of computers and programs. There is enough material for a full year of college-level programming. Many of the examples in the book use features that were not present earlier.

Author

Chapter 1

Internet

NETWORK

DEFINITION

A group of computers & associated peripheral devices connected by a communicational channel, capable of sharing files & other resources between several users is known as networking. Networking provides us the facility to share distant resources such as database, processor or software.

It provides high reliability by having alternate resources for providing distribution of processing so that load sharing can be achieved. Networks are used to save money by using a network of computer, which is cheaper, that using a single mainframe. A Mainframe is 100 times faster than a PC but thousand times costlier than a PC.

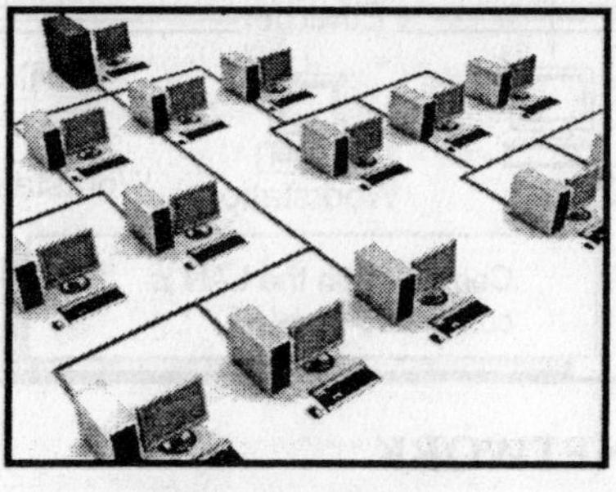

DESCRIPTION

If you have two or more computers, including laptops, Why not network them together and share music, pictures, files and folders, printers,scanners etc? The big advantage of your own network will be that all of your computers on the network can share one internet connection and view different pages at the same time. You can also link in your game console and play online. There are two main networks:

LOCAL AREA NETWORK (LAN)

LAN is a group of computers & associated peripheral devices connected by a communication channel, capable of sharing files & other resources between several users. Using LAN we can get the high speed the connections among computers but sacrificing the ability to cover long distance. LAN can operate between 10 Mbps (mega bit per second) to 2 Gbps.

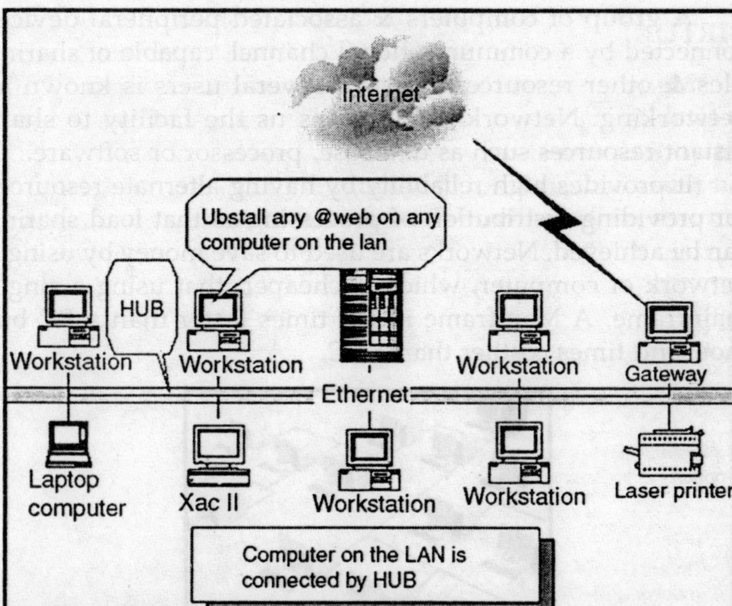

WIDE AREA NETWORK

A network that connects users across larger distances, often crossing geographical boundaries of cities, states, or countries is known as WAN. WANs normally use public telephone network & satellite links for data transmission. Data transmission rates are bellow 1 Mbps for WAN. It is normally owned by multiple organizations. The transmission time is more for WAN because of longer distances & different transmission medium used.

VIRTUAL PRIVATE NETWORK

Many organizations use virtual private networks (VPN) to establish to secure intranet & extranets. A VPN is a secure network that uses the internet as its main backbone network, but relies on network firewalls, encryption and other security features of its internet and intranet connection and those of participating organizations.

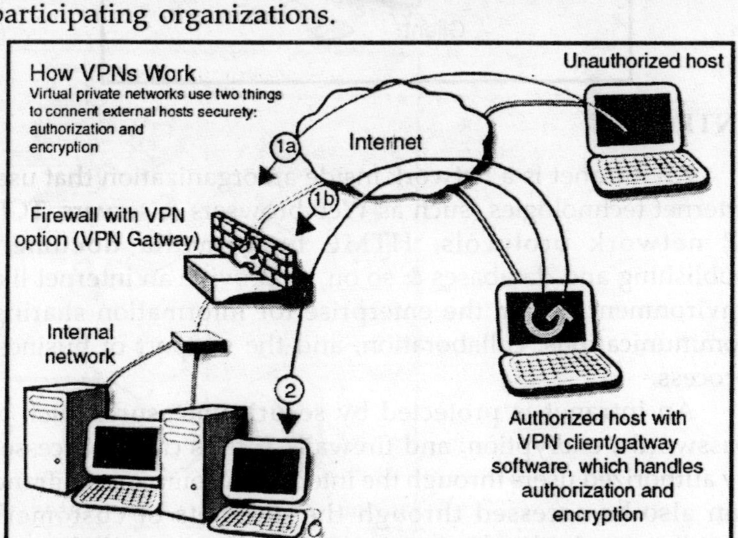

CLIENT SERVER NETWORKS

Client Sever have become the predominant information architecture of enterprise computing. In a client/server network, end user PC or NC work stations are the clients. They are interconnected by local area network & share application processing with network server, which also manage the network.

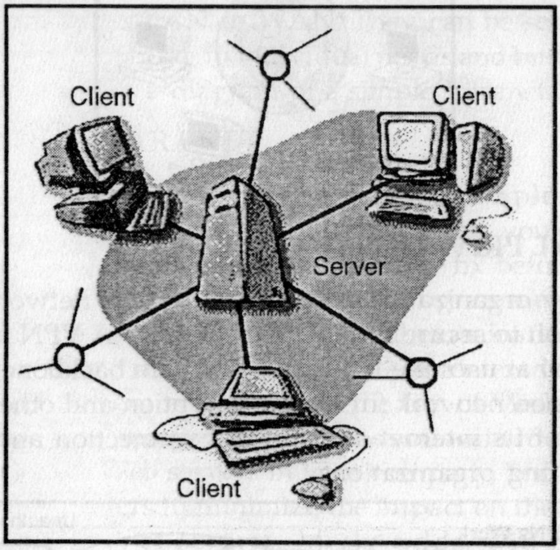

INTRANET

An intranet is a network inside an organization that uses internet technologies (such as Web browsers & servers, TCP/IP network protocols, HTML hypermedia document publishing and databases & so on, to provide an internet like environment within the enterprise for information sharing, communications, collaboration, and the support of business process.

An intranet is protected by security measures such as passwords, encryption, and firewalls & thus can be accessed by authorized users through the internet. A companies intranet can also be accessed through the internets of customers, suppliers, and other business partners via *extranet links*.

WIRED NETWORK

A wired network is the most reliable type but the only disadvantage is hiding the cables that network your computers together. However, with a little forward planning, this can be easily overcome.

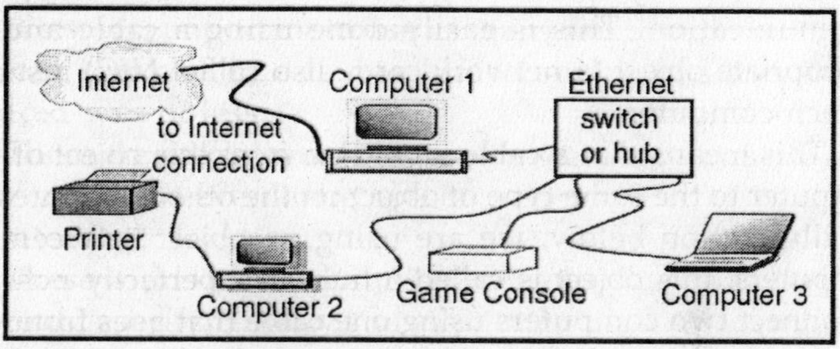

WIRELESS NETWORK

A wireless network operates on radio waves, so a lot depends on the environment the system is installed in. Other radio objects, such as cordless phones, can interfere with your network signal. But wireless is still a reliable system of networking.

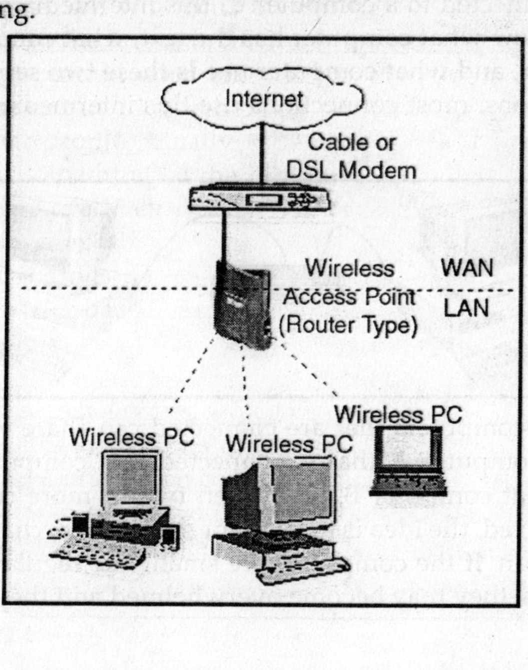

NETWORKING

Because a computer can never be complete, it can complement itself by using resources that other, also incomplete, computers have. In order for two computers to share what they have, they must establish some type of communication. This is easily done using a cable and an appropriate object (a network card, also called NIC) inserted in each computer.

This means that a cable would go from this object of one computer to the same type of object on the other computer (In the illustration below, we are using an object between the computers, this object is called a hub. It is perfectly possible to connect two computers using one cable that goes from one computer to the other but this works only if you have two computers.

If you have more than one computer, then you use a type of intermediary object whose job is to "direct traffic". For example, when one computer A requests to use or open a piece of text that is located in a computer B but to print it in a printer that is connected to a computer C, this intermediary object is able to know what computer has the text, what computer has the printer, and what computer needs these two services. For these reasons, most connections use this intermediary object: the hub):

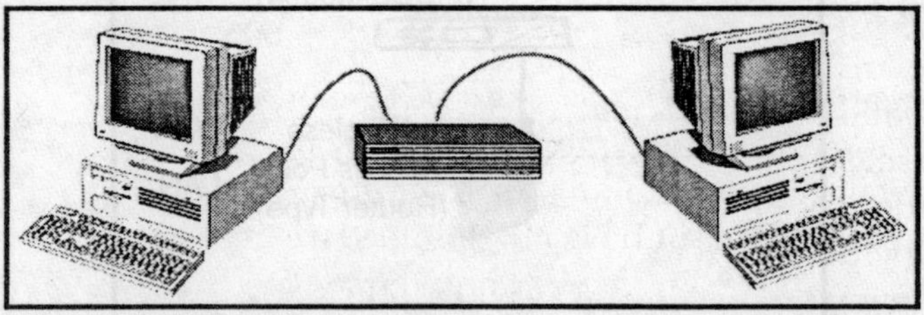

Only computers that are connected can share what they have. A computer A that is connected to a computer B can access what computer B has. When two or more computers are connected, the idea is to let them share and exchange what they contain. If the computers are small, like regular desktop computers, they may become overwhelmed and they may not have enough to share. The next step is to have a "bigger" central computer that holds even more things that other small computers would need (the word big here doesn't necessarily mean that this computer is physically big; it implies that this computer can do more things, for example it can perform more and faster calculations, than the other small computers). Such a central computer is called a server, because its job is to serve other computers (these other small computers are then called workstations):

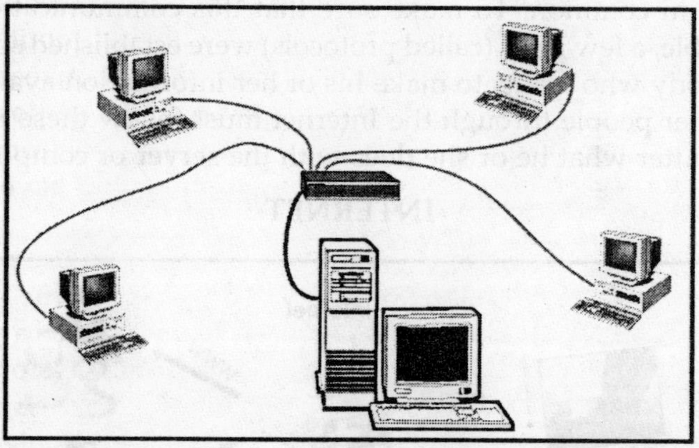

Once again, only a computer that is a member of this network can take advantage of what the network has to offer. If a computer is not connected to this network, it cannot access the information (and/or resources) of this network.

As information and resources (things to share) became more and more useful and in demand, servers of different companies started establishing types of connections among themselves, of course following some rules. In fact, in some situations, some big computers (servers) were made simply to provide information to other computers, without needing to know who owned these small computers, why these small computers needed this information, or what to do with them. The internet was born.

INTERNETWORKING

The Internet is a group of big computers connected to share the information they hold. Some of these computers belong to the government. Some of these computers belong to schools (mostly universities). Some of these computers belong to big companies (corporations). Some of these computers belong to small companies. And some of these computers belong to individuals (located in the basement of their mother). There are two things that may already come to your mind: This is wonderful, and this can be messy; right on both accounts.

The computers that are connected may not have anything at all in common. To make sure that this communication is possible, a few rules (called protocols) were established so that anybody who wants to make his or her information available to other people through the Internet must follow these rules, no matter what he or she does with the server or computer.

INTERNET

DEFINITION OF INTERNET

The Internet is a global network of computers. Every computer that is connected to the Internet is considered a part of that network. This means even your home computer. It's all a matter of degrees, you connect to your ISP's network, then your ISP connects to a larger network and so on. At the top of the tree is the high-capacity backbones, all of these interconnect at 'Network Access Points' 'NAPs' at important regions around the world.

The entire Internet is based on agreements between these backbone providers who set in place all the fibre optics lines and other technical aspects of the Internet. The first high speed backbone was created by the 'National Science Foundation' in 1987.

The Internet was first created by the Advanced Research Projects Agency (ARPA) of the U.S. government in 1960's, and was first known as the ARPANet. At this stage the Internet's first computers were at academic and government institutions. They were mainly used for accessing files and to send email. From 1983 onwards the Internet as we know it today started to form with the introduction of the communication protocol TCP/IP to ARPANet.

Since 1983 the Internet has accommodated alot of changes and continues to keep developing. The last two decades has seen the Internet accommodate such things as network LANs and ATM and frame switched services. The Internet continues to evolve with it becoming available on mobile phones and pagers and possibly on televisions in the future.

The actual term "Internet" was finally defined in 1995 by FNC (The Federal Networking Council). The resolution created by the The Federal Networking Council (FNC) agrees that the following language reflects our definition of the term "Internet". "Internet" refers to the global information system that,

EVOLUTION OF THE INTERNET

The underpinnings of the Internet are formed by the global interconnection of hundreds of thousands of otherwise independent computers, communications entities and information systems. What makes this interconnection possible is the use of a set of communication standards, procedures and formats in common among the networks and the various devices and computational facilities connected to them.

The procedures by which computers communicate with each other are called "protocols." While this infrastructure is steadily evolving to include new capabilities, the protocols initially used by the Internet are called the "TCP/IP" protocols, named after the two protocols that formed the principal basis for Internet operation.

On top of this infrastructure is an emerging set of

architectural concepts and data structures for heterogeneous information systems that renders the Internet a truly global information system. In essence, the Internet is an architecture, although many people confuse it with its implementation.

When the Internet is looked at as an architecture, it manifests two different abstractions. One abstraction deals with communications connectivity, packet delivery and a variety of end-end communication services. The other abstraction deals with the Internet as an information system, independent of its underlying communications infrastructure, which allows creation, storage and access to a wide range of information resources, including digital objects and related services at various levels of abstraction.

Interconnecting computers is an inherently digital problem. Computers process and exchange digital information, meaning that they use a discrete mathematical "binary" or "two-valued" language of 1s and 0s. For communication purposes, such information is mapped into continuous electrical or optical waveforms. The use of digital signaling allows accurate regeneration and reliable recovery of the underlying bits. We use the terms "computer," "computer resources" and "computation" to mean not only traditional computers, but also devices that can be controlled digitally over a network, information resources such as mobile programs and other computational capabilities.

For digital communications, packet switching is a better choice, because it is far better suited to the typically "burst" communication style of computers. Computers that communicate typically send out brief but intense bursts of data, then remain silent for a while before sending out the next burst. These bursts are communicated as packets, which are very much like electronic postcards. The postcards, in reality packets, are relayed from computer to computer until they reach their destination. The special computers that perform this forwarding function are called variously "packet switches" or "routers" and form the equivalent of many bucket brigades spanning continents and oceans, moving buckets of electronic postcards from one computer to another. Together these routers and the communication links between them form the underpinnings of the Internet.

Without packet switching, the Internet would not exist, as we now know it. Going back to the postcard analogy, postcards can get lost. They can be delivered out of order, and they can be delayed by varying amounts.

The same is true of Internet packets, which, on the Internet, can even be duplicated. The Internet Protocol is the postcard layer of the Internet. The next higher layer of protocol, TCP, takes care of re-sending the "postcards" to recover packets that might have been lost, and putting packets back in order if they have become disordered in transit.

Of course, packet switching is about a billion times faster than the postal service or a bucket brigade would be. It also has to operate over many different communications systems, or substrata. The authors designed the basic architecture to be so simple and undemanding that it could work with most communication services. Many organizations, including commercial ones, carried out research using the TCP/IP protocols in the 1970s. Email was steadily used over the nascent Internet during that time and to the present. It was not until 1994 that the general public began to be aware of the Internet by way of the World Wide Web application, particularly after Netscape Communications was formed and released its browser and associated server software.

ADVANTAGES OF INTERNET

There are many advantages of using the Internet, such as:

Global Audience

Content published on the World Wide Web is immediately available to a global audience of users. This makes the World Wide Web a very cost-effective medium to publish information. Reaching more than 190 countries.

Operates 24 Hours and 365 Days

You don't need to wait until resources are available to conduct business. From a consumer's perspective as well as a provider's business can be consummated at any time. The fact that the Internet is operational at all times makes it the most efficient business machine to date.

Relatively Inexpensive

It is relatively inexpensive to publish information on the Internet. At a fraction of the cost to publish information by traditional methods, various organizations and individuals can now distribute information to millions of users. It costs only a few thousand dollars to establish an Internet presence and publish content on the Internet.

Product Advertising

You can use the World Wide Web to advertise various products. Before purchasing a product, customers will be able to look up various product specification sheets and find out additional information. You can use the multimedia capabilities of the World Wide Web to make available not only various product specification sheets but also audio files, images, and even video clips of products in action. The beauty of the Web is that it allows customers to explore products in as much detail as they desire. If the client just wants a general overview, he or she can look at the advertising information. For those wanting more in depth information, you can provide white papers and product descriptions for download. The Web allows a business to provide timely information, you can simply place the information on the Web page and it is available immediately for your customers.

Distribute Product Catalogs

The World Wide Web is a very effective medium for distributing product catalogs. In the old days, putting together a product catalog used to be very costly in terms of time and money needed to publish and distribute it. The World Wide Web changes all this by allowing content developers to put together a sales catalog and make it available to millions of users immediately. Furthermore, unlike printed product catalogs that are usually updated around once a month, product catalogs on the World Wide Web can be updated as needed to respond to various changing market conditions.

Online Surveys

Traditional methods of performing surveys are often relatively slow and expensive compared to online surveys conducted on the Internet.

For example, in order to fill out various needs of customers or what they would like to see in a future product, it's often necessary to compile a list of address and mail a questionnaire to many customers. The success of such an attempt is not always guaranteed and can be very costly in terms of mailing the questionnaires and entering responses to a databases and analyzing it. On the other hand, you can use the World Wide Web to automate the whole process. For example, you can set up a CGI script to conduct online surveys. Results of such a survey can be automatically updated to a database. This database can then be used to keep a pulse on various opinions and needs of customers.

Announcements

With the World Wide Web, you can distribute various announcements to millions of users in a timely manner. Because there is virtually no time lag from the time it takes to publish information to making the information available to users, the Web is an ideal medium to publicize announcements.

As more people discover the virtues of the Web and get connected to the Internet, the Web will become the medium of choice for many organizations and individuals to publicize various announcements.

Provide Technical Support

You can also use Web site to provide technical support to users. Because Web pages can be updated immediately with new information, various technical support literature can be immediately modified in light of new findings and developments.

This can be accomplished without having to distribute changes to all users affected by any changes using traditional mediums of information distribution, which are often quite costly compared to the World Wide Web.

Create Online Discussion Forums

By using applications such as WebBoard, it's possible to set up online discussion forums on the Web.

Obtain Customer Feedback

The interactive nature of the World Wide Web is ideal for obtaining customer feedback. You can easily set up a CGI script to obtain customer feedback about a product or service.

Because customer feedback submitted by customers can be read immediately, it's possible to respond to various customer concerns in a timely manner, increasing customer satisfaction and quality of customer service.

Immediate Distribution of Information

When information is added to a Web site, it's immediately available for browsing by millions of Internet users. The World Wide Web is an ideal medium of information distribution because it takes away the time lag associated with publishing content and actually making it available to users

Easy Integration with Internal Information Systems

Internet information systems deployed on the Internet can be easily integrated with internal information systems managed with office productivity applications such as Microsoft Office.

Powerful Content Publishing Tools

A new breed of Internet aware applications will start emerging in software stores by the time you read this. These applications will enable users to develop content for the World Wide Web by simply saving as an HTML file.

In addition to software developers making existing

applications Internet aware, various new, powerful, and easy-to use Internet content publishing applications are also being developed. These applications will make the task of publishing content on the Internet even easier. Most of these applications are developed for Windows users.

Multimedia

The capability to incorporate multimedia into Web pages is a major advantage of using World Wide Web to publish information. For example, many Web sites use sounds and video clips to make the content easier and more interesting to browse.

Formatting Capabilities

Content published on the World Wide Web can be richly formatted by using various HTML tags and graphic formats. The capability to do this is a major reason for the success of the World Wide Web.

In addition to using HTML tags and various multimedia formats in Web pages, various interactive controls can also be added to a web page. This capability allows Web site content developers to create "active" Web sites.

DISADVANTAGES OF INTERNET

Many fear the Internet because of its disadvantages. They claim to not use the Internet because they are afraid of the possible consequences or are simply not interested. People who have yet connected to the Internet claim they are not missing anything. Today's technological society must realise, it is up to them to protect themselves on the Internet.

Children using the Internet has become a big concern. Most parents do not realise the dangers involved when their children log onto the Internet. When children are online, they can easily be lured into something dangerous. When children talk to others online, they do not realise they could actually be talking to a harmful person.

In addition, children may also receive pornography online by mistake; therefore, causing concern among parents everywhere. Whether surfing the Web, reading newsgroups, or using email, children can be exposed to extremely inappropriate material.

Pornographic sites tend to make sure they are the first sites to be listed in any search area. To keep children safe, parents and teachers must be aware of the dangers. They must actively guide and guard their children online.There are a number of tools available today that may help keep the Internet environment safer for children.

Another major disadvantage of the Internet is privacy. Electronic messages sent over the Internet can be easily snooped and tracked, revealing who is talking to whom and what they are talking about.

As people surf the Internet, they are constantly giving information to web sites.. Computers are mainly getting these viruses from the Internet; yet, viruses may also be transmitted through floppy disks.

However, people should mainly be concerned about receiving viruses from the Internet. Some of these dangerous viruses destroy the computer's entire hard drive, meaning that the user can no longer access the computer. The Internet is a very powerful tool. It has many advantages; however, people need to be extremely aware of the disadvantages as well.

INTRANET

DEFINITION

An Intranet is merely a network of computers that can share data with each other using existing standardized WWW protocols.

By storing information on an Internal Web Server and providing each computer on the network with browser software such as Internet Explorer, and a network data access application, anyone on the network can view information located on the Intranet Server.

This allows for easy and inexpensive distribution of internal corporate information, an essential ingredient in today's fast-moving competitive environment.

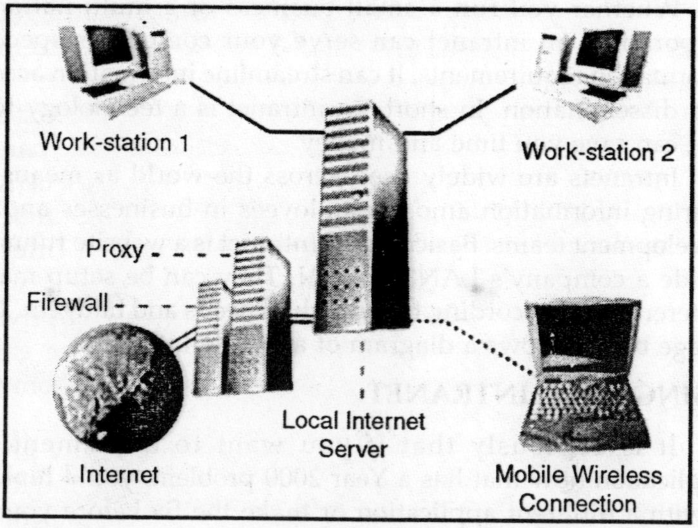

Fig. Intranet Basics

An intranet is a private communications system built on the infrastructure of the Internet that can increase employee productivity, build stronger ties with your customers and encourage more profitable relationships with vendors.

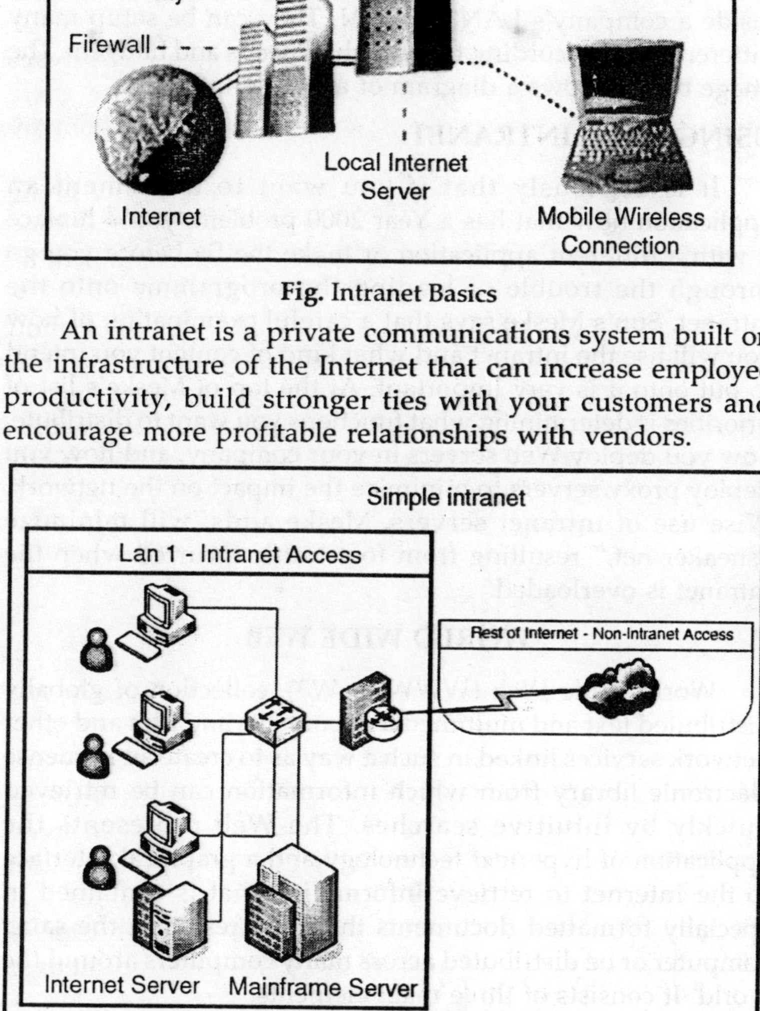

Whether you run a small business or a multi-national corporation, an intranet can serve your company's specific information requirements. It can streamline information access and dissemination. In short, an intranet is a technology tool that can save you time and money.

Intranets are widely used across the world as means of sharing information among employees in businesses and/or development teams. Basically, an Intranet is a website running inside a company's LAN or WAN. They can be setup many different ways according to individual needs and budgets. The image below shows a diagram of a simple Intranet.

USING YOUR INTRANET

It is obviously that if you want to implement an application now that has a Year 2000 problem; you'd replace it with a different application or make the fix before you go through the trouble of loading the programme onto the intranet. Sun's Meske says that a careful examination of how you will use the intranet and what kind of content you intend to put onto it is very important. At the top of Meske's list of priorities is determining what functions you want to distribute, how you deploy Web servers in your company, and how you deploy proxy servers to minimize the impact on the network. Wise use of intranet servers, Meske adds, will minimize "sneaker net," resulting from foot traffic incurred when the intranet is overloaded.

WORLD WIDE WEB

World Wide Web (WWW or W3), collection of globally distributed text and multimedia documents and files and other network services linked in such a way as to create an immense electronic library from which information can be retrieved quickly by intuitive searches. The Web represents the application of hypertext technology and a graphical interface to the Internet to retrieve information that is contained in specially formatted documents that may reside in the same computer or be distributed across many computers around the world. It consists of three main elements.

The Hypertext Markup Language (HTML) comprises the programming codes, or tags, that define fonts, layouts, embedded graphics, and links (hyperlinks) to other documents accessible via the Web.

The HyperText Transfer Protocol (HTTP) defines a set of standards for transmitting Web pages across the Internet. The Universal Resource Locator (URL) is a standardized naming convention for identifying a Web document or file, in a sense the address of a link. The result is called the Web because it is made up of many sites, all linked together, with users traveling from one site to the next by clicking a computer's pointing device on a hyperlink.

Web sites, also called Web pages, are really Internet sites that all use the same techniques and HTML tags to create multimedia documents with hypertext links. Each Web page can contain many screens or printed pages of text, graphics, audio, and even video, and the starting point for any Web site is called its home page.

Although each page is an Internet site, it must be accessed via a special programme called a Web browser, which can translate the HTML into the graphical images, text, and hypertext links intended by the creator of the page.

Interactive television is a generic term that encompasses a variety of Web-related television technologies and products. Typically, a home television receiver and a telephone line are connected through a small appliance that accesses the Internet through the telephone line and converts the downloaded Web pages into a form that can be displayed on the receiver. A remote control interface allows the user to navigate through the Web and select the information to be displayed.

Versions for the Windows and Macintosh operating systems followed in 1994, and acceptance of the World Wide Web blossomed quickly.

In the late 1990s the development of improved browsers with greater multimedia functionality, security, and privacy, as well as more powerful search engines capable of indexing the ever greater information on the Web, led to the commercialization of the Internet

EMAIL

DEFINITION

Email is simply the shortened form of electronic mail, a protocol for receiving, sending and storing electronic messages. Email has gained popularity with the spread of the Internet. In many cases, email has become the preferred method of communication.

Email is shothand term meaning Electronic Mail. Email much the same as a letter, only that it is exchanged in a different way. Computers use the TCP/IP protocol suite to send email messages in the form of packets. The first thing you need to send and recieve emails is an email address. When you create an account with a Internet Service Provider you are usually given an email address to send from and recieve emails. If this isn't the case you can create an email address/account at web sites such as yahoo, hotmail and lycos.

HOW DOES E-MAIL WORK?

Billions of electronic mail (e-mail) messages move across the Internet every year. Sending electronic letters, pictures and data files, either across a building or across the globe, has grown so popular that it has started to replace some postal mail and telephone calls. This universal medium is no longer restricted to exchange of simple text messages and is now regularly used to deliver voice mail, facsimiles and documents that may include images, sound and video.

Typically, a message becomes available to the recipient within seconds after it is sent—one reason why Internet mail has transformed the way that we are able to communicate.

MESSAGE SENDER

Uses mail software, called a client, to compose a document, possibly including attachments such as tables, photographs or even a voice or video recording. System software, called Transmission Control Protocol (TCP), divides the message into packets and adds information about how each packet should be handled-for instance, in what order packets were transmitted from the sender. Packets are sent to a mail submission server, a computer on the internal network of a company or an Internet service provider.

Internet Mail Addresses

Attached to each message are in the form "mailbox @domainname" - one specific example being "webmaster @seniorindian.com." The multipart domain name in the above example denotes a top-level domain (".com") following the second-level domain ("seniorindian"). A message is delivered to an individual or a group by the mailbox name ("webmaster").

Mail Submission Server

Converts the domain name of the recipient's mail address into a numeric Internet Protocol (IP) address. It does this by querying domain name servers interspersed throughout the Internet.

For example, the mail submission server can first request from the "root" name server the whereabouts of other servers that store information about ".com" domains,

- It can then interrogate the ".com" name server for the location of the specific "sciam.com" name server
- A final request to the "sciam.com" name server provides the IP address for the computer that

receives the mail for sciam.com, which is then attached to each message packet

ROUTERS

Dispersed throughout the Internet read the IP address on a packet and relay it toward its destination by the most efficient path. (Because of fluctuating traffic over data lines, trying to transmit a packet directly to its destination is not always the fastest way.) The packets of a single message may travel along different routes, shuttling through 10 or so routers before their journey's end.

Destination Mail Server

Places the packets in their original order, according to the instructions contained in each packet, and stores the message in the recipient's mailbox. The recipient's client software can then display the message.

SEARCH ENGINES

INTRODUCTION

Search engine as: 'a programme designed to help find information stored on a computer system such as the World Wide Web, or a personal computer.

The search engine allows one to ask for content meeting specific criteria (typically those containing a given word or phrase) and retrieving a list of references that match those criteria. Search engines use regularly updated indexes to operate quickly and efficiently.'

In other words, a search engine is a sophisticated piece of software, accessed through a page on a website that allows you to search the web by entering search queries into a search box. The search engine then attempts to match your search query with the content of web pages that is has stored, or cached, and indexed on its powerful servers in advance of your search.

Search engines are special tools that anyone can use. They are a database of web sites that contain information that is catalogued and indexed for easy reference. The secret of effective searching in knowing how to state what you want to search for.>

Most search engines allow you to use a group of words that narrow the search for you. If you use a general term like "history" for instance, you may get a listing of 3 or 4 MILLION web sites. It is important to use as many descriptive words as you can think of in order to limit your results to several hundred sites or less.

There are special words that some search engines use that allow you to be even more specific. They are called Boolean Operators.

These words include "and", "or", and "not". For example you could specify "history and revolution OR war not french" to search for all revolutions or wars in history that do not include the term French in the description. This would still be a broad search, but you can see how these special words can allow you to become very specific about your interests.

Note: many search engines allow you to search for things other than text: for example, images. However, for the purpose of this course, we will focus on text-based searches. As we pointed out in the last unit, SEO methods are largely (but not exclusively) centred upon text as they involve matching key parts of the text in your web pages with the keywords or key phrases that people actually type into search engines when looking for something on the internet.

There are two main types of search indexes we access when searching the web:

- Directories
- Crawler-based search engines

Directories

Unlike search engines, which use special software to locate and index sites, directories are compiled and maintained by humans. Directories often consist of a categorized list of links to other sites to which you can add your own site. Editors sometimes review your site to see if it is fit for inclusion in the directory.

Crawler-based Search Engines

Crawler-based search engines differ from directories in that they are not compiled and maintained by humans. Instead, crawler-based search engines use sophisticated pieces of software called spiders or robots to search and index web pages.

These spiders are constantly at work, crawling around the web, locating pages, and taking snapshots of those pages to be cached or stored on the search engine's servers. They are so sophisticated that they can follow links from one page to another and from one site to another.

Google is a prominent example of a crawler-based search engine. Some search systems are 'hybrid' systems as they combine both forms of index. Yahoo, for example, features both directories and search engines.

As we will see later in this course, the SEO process often involves optimizing your site in such a way that it allows search engine spiders to locate every page on your site quickly and easily.

Spidering vs Submitting your Site Manually

If you browse the web, you will notice that many companies will offer to submit your site to search engines for inclusion in their listings. The services these companies offer are largely unnecessary and can prove to be a waste of time and money.

It is important to remember that search engine spiders are constantly crawling the web, following links and indexing pages. Because spiders automatically index your pages when they find them, there is absolutely no need to submit your site manually to the major search engines.

Chapter 2

JAVA Programming Language

DEFINITION

The Java programming language is a general-purpose, concurrent, class-based, object-oriented language. It is designed to be simple enough that many programmers can achieve fluency in the language. The Java programming language is related to C and C++ but is organized rather differently, with a number of aspects of C and C++ omitted and a few ideas from other languages included. It is intended to be a production language, not a research language, and so, as C. A. R. Hoare suggested in his classic paper on language design, the design has avoided including new and untested features.

The Java programming language is strongly typed. This specification clearly distinguishes between the *compile-time errors* that can and must be detected at compile time, and those that occur at run time. Compile time normally consists of translating programs into a machine-independent byte code representation. Run-time activities include loading and linking of the classes needed to execute a programme, optional machine code generation and dynamic optimization of the programme, and actual programme execution.

The Java programming language is a relatively high-level language, in that details of the machine representation are not available through the language. It includes automatic storage management, typically using a garbage collector, to avoid the safety problems of explicit deallocation (as in C's **free** or C++'s **delete**). High-performance garbage-collected implementations can have bounded pauses to support systems programming and real-time applications. The language does not include any unsafe constructs, such as array accesses without index checking, since such unsafe constructs would cause a programme to behave in an unspecified way.

After initialization, class methods and class variables may be used. Some classes may be instantiated to create new objects of the class type. Objects that are class instances also contain an instance of each superclass of the class, and object creation involves recursive creation of these superclass instances.

When an object is no longer referenced, it may be reclaimed by the garbage collector. If an object declares a finalizer, the finalizer is executed before the object is reclaimed to give the object a last chance to clean up resources that would not otherwise be released. When a class is no longer needed, it may be unloaded.

Chapter describes binary compatibility, specifying the impact of changes to types on other types that use the changed types but have not been recompiled. These considerations are of interest to developers of types that are to be widely distributed, in a continuing series of versions, often through the Internet. Good programme development environments automatically recompile dependent code whenever a type is changed, so most programmers need not be concerned about these details.

Chapter describes blocks and statements, which are based on C and C++. The language has no **goto** statement, but includes labeled **break** and **continue** statements. Unlike C, the Java programming language requires **boolean** (or **Boolean**) expressions in control-flow statements, and does not convert types to **boolean** implicitly (except through unboxing), in the hope of catching more errors at compile time. A **synchronized** statement provides basic object-level monitor locking. A **try** statement can include **catch** and **finally** clauses to protect against non-local control transfers.

Chapter describes expressions. This document fully specifies the (apparent) order of evaluation of expressions, for increased determinism and portability. Overloaded methods and constructors are resolved at compile time by picking the most specific method or constructor from those which are applicable.

Chapter describes the precise way in which the language ensures that local variables are definitely set before use. While all other variables are automatically initialized to a default value, the Java programming language does not automatically initialize local variables in order to avoid masking programming errors.

Chapter describes the semantics of threads and locks, which are based on the monitor-based concurrency originally introduced with the Mesa programming language. The Java programming language specifies a memory model for shared-memory multiprocessors that supports high-performance implementations.

EXAMPLE PROGRAMS

Most of the example programmes given in the text are ready to be executed and are similar in form to:

```
class Test {
public static void main(String[] args) {
for (int i = 0; i < args.length; i++)
System.out.print(i == 0 ? args[i]: " " +
args[i]);
System.out.println();
}
}
```

On a Sun workstation using Sun's Java 2 Platform Standard Edition Develpment Kit software, this class, stored in the file **`Test.java`**, can be compiled and executed by giving the commands:

```
javac Test.java
java Test Hello, world.
producing the output:
Hello, world.
```

NOTATION

Throughout this book we refer to classes and interfaces

drawn from the Java and Java 2 platforms. Whenever we refer to a class or interface which is not defined in an example in this book using a single identifier N, the intended reference is to the class or interface named N in the package **java.lang**. We use the canonical name for classes or interfaces from packages other than **java.lang**.

CLASSES AND INTERFACES

As noted above, this specification often refers to classes of the Java and Java 2 platforms. In particular, some classes have a special relationship with the Java programming language. Examples include classes such as **Object**, **Class**, **ClassLoader**, **String**, **Thread**, and the classes and interfaces in package **java.lang.reflect**, among others. The language definition constrains the behaviour of these classes and interfaces, but this document does not provide a complete specification for them. The reader is referred to other parts of the Java platform specification for such detailed API specifications.

Thus this document does not describe reflection in any detail. Many linguistic constructs have analogues in the reflection API, but these are generally not discussed here. So, for example, when we list the ways in which an object can be created, we generally do not include the ways in which the reflective API can accomplish this. Readers should be aware of these additional mechanisms even though they are not mentioned in this text.

CONTEXT-FREE GRAMMARS

A context-free grammar consists of a number of productions. Each production has an abstract symbol called a nonterminal as its left-hand side, and a sequence of one or more nonterminal and terminal symbols as its right-hand side. For each grammar, the terminal symbols are drawn from a specified *alphabet*.

Starting from a sentence consisting of a single distinguished nonterminal, called the goal symbol, a given context-free grammar specifies a language, namely, the set of possible sequences of terminal symbols that can result from repeatedly replacing any nonterminal in the sequence with a right-hand side of a production for which the nonterminal is the left-hand side.

THE LEXICAL GRAMMAR

A lexical grammar for the Java programming language is given in. This grammar has as its terminal symbols the characters of the Unicode character set. It defines a set of productions, starting from the goal symbol Input, that describe how sequences of Unicode characters are translated into a sequence of input elements.

These input elements, with white space and comments discarded, form the terminal symbols for the syntactic grammar for the Java programming language and are called tokens. These tokens are the identifiers, keywords, literals, separators, and operators of the Java programming language.

SYNTACTIC GRAMMAR

The syntactic grammar for the Java programming language is given in later Chapters. This grammar has tokens defined by the lexical grammar as its terminal symbols. It defines a set of productions, starting from the goal symbol *CompilationUnit,* that describe how sequences of tokens can form syntactically correct programmes.

GRAMMAR NOTATION

Terminal symbols are shown in **fixed width** font in the productions of the lexical and syntactic grammars, and throughout this specification whenever the text is directly referring to such a terminal symbol. These are to appear in a programme exactly as written.

Nonterminal symbols are shown in *italic* type. The definition of a nonterminal is introduced by the name of the nonterminal being defined followed by a colon. One or more alternative right-hand sides for the nonterminal then follow on succeeding lines.

For example, the syntactic definition:

```
IfThenStatement:
if (Expression) Statement
```

states that the nonterminal *IfThenStatement* represents the token **if**, followed by a left parenthesis token, followed by an *Expression*, followed by a right parenthesis token, followed by a *Statement*.

```
As another example, the syntactic definition:
ArgumentList:
Argument
ArgumentList, Argument
```

states that an *ArgumentList* may represent either a single *Argument* or an *ArgumentList*, followed by a comma, followed by an *Argument*. This definition of *ArgumentList* is *recursive*, that is to say, it is defined in terms of itself. The result is that an *ArgumentList* may contain any positive number of arguments. Such recursive definitions of nonterminals are common. The subscripted suffix "opt", which may appear after a terminal or nonterminal, indicates an optional symbol. The alternative containing the optional symbol actually specifies two right-hand sides, one that omits the optional element and one that includes it.

This means that:

```
BreakStatement:
    break Identifieropt;
is a convenient abbreviation for:
BreakStatement:
    break;
    break Identifier;
and that:
BasicForStatement:
    for (ForInitopt; Expressionopt;
ForUpdateopt) Statement
is a convenient abbreviation for:
BasicForStatement:
    for (; Expressionopt; ForUpdateopt)
Statement:
    for (ForInit; Expressionopt; ForUpdateopt)
Statement:
```

```
which in turn is an abbreviation for:
BasicForStatement:
    for (;; ForUpdateopt) Statement
    for (; Expression; ForUpdateopt) Statement
    for (ForInit;; ForUpdateopt) Statement
    for (ForInit; Expression; ForUpdateopt)
Statement:
which in turn is an abbreviation for:
BasicForStatement:
    for (;;) Statement
    for (;; ForUpdate) Statement
    for (; Expression;) Statement
    for (; Expression; ForUpdate) Statement
    for (ForInit;;) Statement
    for (ForInit;; ForUpdate) Statement
    for (ForInit; Expression;) Statement
    for (ForInit; Expression; ForUpdate)
Statement
```

so the nonterminal *BasicForStatement* actually has eight alternative right-hand sides.

A very long right-hand side may be continued on a second line by substantially indenting this second line, as in:

ConstructorDeclaration:

`ConstructorModifiersopt ConstructorDeclarator`

Throwsopt ConstructorBody: Which defines one right-hand side for the nonterminal *ConstructorDeclaration*.

When the words "one of" follow the colon in a grammar definition, they signify that each of the terminal symbols on the following line or lines is an alternative definition. For example, the lexical grammar contains the production:

ZeroToThree: one of

0 1 2 3

which is merely a convenient abbreviation for:

ZeroToThree:

0 1 2 3

When an alternative in a lexical production appears to be a token, it represents the sequence of characters that would make up such a token.

Thus, the definition:

BooleanLiteral: one of

true false

in a lexical grammar production is shorthand for:

BooleanLiteral:

t r u e

f a l s e

The right-hand side of a lexical production may specify that certain expansions are not permitted by using the phrase "but not" and then indicating the expansions to be excluded, as in the productions for *InputCharacter* and *Identifier*

InputCharacter: UnicodeInputCharacter but not CR or LF

Identifier: IdentifierName but not a Keyword or BooleanLiteral or NullLiteral

Finally, a few nonterminal symbols are described by a descriptive phrase in roman type in cases where it would be impractical to list all the alternatives:

RawInputCharacter: any Unicode character

UNICODE

Programmes are written using the Unicode character set. Information about this character set and its associated character encodings. The Java platform tracks the Unicode specification as it evolves. The precise version of Unicode used by a given release is specified in the documentation of the class **Character**.

Versions of the Java programming language prior to 1.1 used Unicode version 1.1.5. Upgrades to newer versions of the Unicode Standard occurred in JDK 1.1 (to Unicode 2.0), JDK 1.1.7 (to Unicode 2.1), J2SE 1.4 (to Unicode 3.0), and J2SE 5.0. The Unicode standard was originally designed as a fixed-width 16-bit character encoding. It has since been changed to allow for characters whose representation requires more than 16 bits. The range of legal code points is now U+0000 to U+10FFFF, using the hexadecimal U+n notation. Characters whose code points are greater than U+FFFF are called supplementary characters. To represent the complete range of characters using only 16-bit units, the Unicode standard defines an encoding called UTF-16. In this encoding, supplementary characters are represented as pairs of 16-bit code units, the first from the high-surrogates range, (U+D800 to U+DBFF), the second from the low-surrogates range (U+DC00 to U+DFFF). For characters in the range U+0000 to U+FFFF, the values of code points and UTF-16 code units are the same.

The Java programming language represents text in sequences of 16-bit code units, using the UTF-16 encoding. A few APIs, primarily in the **Character** class, use 32-bit integers to represent code points as individual entities. The Java platform provides methods to convert between the two representations.

This book uses the terms code point and UTF-16 code unit where the representation is relevant, and the generic term character where the representation is irrelevant to the discussion.

Except for comments, identifiers, and the contents of character and string literals, all input elements in a programme are formed only from ASCII characters (or Unicode escapes which result in ASCII characters). ASCII (ANSI X3.4) is the American Standard Code for Information Interchange. The first 128 characters of the Unicode character encoding are the ASCII characters.

LEXICAL TRANSLATIONS

A raw Unicode character stream is translated into a sequence of tokens, using the following three lexical translation steps, which are applied in turn:

- A translation of Unicode escapes in the raw stream of Unicode characters to the corresponding Unicode character. A Unicode escape of the form \u*xxxx*, where *xxxx* is a hexadecimal value, represents the UTF-16 code unit whose encoding is *xxxx*. This translation step allows any programme to be expressed using only ASCII characters.
- A translation of the Unicode stream resulting from step 1 into a stream of input characters and line terminators.

- A translation of the stream of input characters and line terminators resulting from step 2 into a sequence of input elements which, after white space and comments are discarded, comprise the tokens that are the terminal symbols of the syntactic grammar.

The longest possible translation is used at each step, even if the result does not ultimately make a correct programme while another lexical translation would. Thus the input characters **a--b** are tokenized as **a**, **--**, **b**, which is not part of any grammatically correct programme, even though the tokenization **a**, **-**, **-**, **b** could be part of a grammatically correct programme.

UNICODE ESCAPES

Implementations first recognize *Unicode escapes* in their input, translating the ASCII characters **\u** followed by four hexadecimal digits to the UTF-16 code unit with the indicated hexadecimal value, and passing all other characters unchanged. Representing supplementary characters requires two consecutive Unicode escapes. This translation step results in a sequence of Unicode input characters:

```
UnicodeInputCharacter:
    UnicodeEscape
    RawInputCharacter
UnicodeEscape:
    \ UnicodeMarker HexDigit HexDigit HexDigit
    HexDigit
UnicodeMarker:
    u
    UnicodeMarker u
RawInputCharacter:
    any Unicode character
HexDigit: one of
0 1 2 3 4 5 6 7 8 9 a b c d e f A B C D E
F
```

The \, u, and hexadecimal digits here are all ASCII characters.

In addition to the processing implied by the grammar, for

each raw input character that is a backslash \, input processing must consider how many other \ characters contiguously precede it, separating it from a non-\ character or the start of the input stream. If this number is even, then the \ is eligible to begin a Unicode escape; if the number is odd, then the \ is not eligible to begin a Unicode escape. For example, the raw input "\\u2297=\u2297" results in the eleven characters " \\ u 2 2 9 7 = ⊗ " (\u2297 is the Unicode encoding of the character "⊗").

If an eligible \ is not followed by u, then it is treated as a *RawInputCharacter* and remains part of the escaped Unicode stream. If an eligible \ is followed by u, or more than one u, and the last u is not followed by four hexadecimal digits, then a compile-time error occurs.

The character produced by a Unicode escape does not participate in further Unicode escapes. For example, the raw input \u005cu005a results in the six characters \ u 0 0 5 a, because 005c is the Unicode value for \. It does not result in the character Z, which is Unicode character 005a, because the \ that resulted from the \u005c is not interpreted as the start of a further Unicode escape.

The Java programming language specifies a standard way of transforming a programme written in Unicode into ASCII that changes a programme into a form that can be processed by ASCII-based tools. The transformation involves converting any Unicode escapes in the source text of the programme to ASCII by adding an extra u-for example, \u*xxxx* becomes \uu*xxxx*-while simultaneously converting non-ASCII characters in the source text to Unicode escapes containing a single u each.

This transformed version is equally acceptable to a compiler for the Java programming language ("Java compiler") and represents the exact same programme. The exact Unicode source can later be restored from this ASCII form by converting each escape sequence where multiple u's are present to a sequence of Unicode characters with one fewer u, while simultaneously converting each escape sequence with a single **u** to the corresponding single Unicode character.

Implementations should use the **\u***xxxx* notation as an output format to display Unicode characters when a suitable font is not available.

LINE TERMINATORS

Implementations next divide the sequence of Unicode input characters into lines by recognizing *line terminators*. This definition of lines determines the line numbers produced by a Java compiler or other system component. It also specifies the termination of the// form of a comment.

```
LineTerminator:
the ASCII LF character, also known as
    "newline"
the ASCII CR character, also known as "return"
the ASCII CR character followed by the ASCII
    LF character
```

InputCharacter:

```
UnicodeInputCharacter but not CR or LF
```

Lines are terminated by the ASCII characters **CR**, or **LF**, or **CR LF**. The two characters **CR** immediately followed by **LF** are counted as one line terminator, not two.

The result is a sequence of line terminators and input characters, which are the terminal symbols for the third step in the tokenization process.

INPUT ELEMENTS AND TOKENS

The input characters and line terminators that result from escape processing and then input line recognition are reduced to a sequence of *input elements*. Those input elements that are not white space or comments are *tokens*. The tokens are the terminal symbols of the syntactic grammar.

This process is specified by the following productions:

```
Input:
    InputElementsopt Subopt
InputElements:
    InputElement
    InputElements InputElement
InputElement:
```

```
    WhiteSpace
    Comment
    Token
Token:
    Identifier
    Keyword
    Literal
    Separator
    Operator
Sub:
the ASCII SUB character, also known as
"control-Z"
```

White space and comments can serve to separate tokens that, if adjacent, might be tokenized in another manner. For example, the ASCII characters - and = in the input can form the operator token -= only if there is no intervening white space or comment.

As a special concession for compatibility with certain operating systems, the ASCII SUB character (\u001a, or control-Z) is ignored if it is the last character in the escaped input stream.

Consider two tokens *x* and *y* in the resulting input stream. If *x* precedes *y*, then we say that *x* is *to the left of y* and that *y* is *to the right of x*.

For example, in this simple piece of code:

```
class Empty {
}
```

we say that the} token is to the right of the {token, even though it appears, in this two-dimensional representation on paper, downward and to the left of the {token. This convention about the use of the words left and right allows us to speak, for example, of the right-hand operand of a binary operator or of the left-hand side of an assignment.

WHITE SPACE

White space is defined as the ASCII space, horizontal tab, and form feed characters, as well as line terminators.

```
WhiteSpace:
```

```
the ASCII SP character, also known as
   "space"
the ASCII HT character, also known as
   "horizontal tab"
   the ASCII FF character, also known as
"form feed"
   LineTerminator
```

COMMENTS

There are two kinds of *comments*:

`/* text */`	A traditional comment: all the text from the ASCII characters/* to the ASCII characters */ is ignored (as in C and C++).
`// text`	A end-of-line comment: all the text from the ASCII characters// to the end of the line is ignored (as in C++).

These comments are formally specified by the following productions:

```
Comment:
   TraditionalComment
   EndOfLineComment
TraditionalComment:
   / * CommentTail
EndOfLineComment:
   // CharactersInLineopt
CommentTail:
   * CommentTailStar
   NotStar CommentTail
CommentTailStar:
   /
   * CommentTailStar
   NotStarNotSlash CommentTail
NotStar:
   InputCharacter but not *
```

```
    LineTerminator
NotStarNotSlash:
    InputCharacter but not * or/
    LineTerminator
CharactersInLine:
    InputCharacter
    CharactersInLine InputCharacter
```

These productions imply all of the following properties:

- Comments do not nest.
- /* and */ have no special meaning in comments that begin with//.
- // has no special meaning in comments that begin with/* or/**.

As a result, the text:

```
/* this comment/*///** ends here: */
```

is a single complete comment.

The lexical grammar implies that comments do not occur within character literals or string literals.

IDENTIFIERS

An *identifier* is an unlimited-length sequence of *Java letters* and *Java digits,* the first of which must be a Java letter. An identifier cannot have the same spelling (Unicode character sequence) as a keyword, boolean literal, or the null literal.

```
Identifier:
    IdentifierChars but not a Keyword or
    BooleanLiteral or NullLiteral
IdentifierChars:
    JavaLetter
    IdentifierChars JavaLetterOrDigit
JavaLetter:
    any Unicode character that is a Java
    letter
JavaLetterOrDigit:
    any Unicode character that is a Java
    letter-or-digit.
```

Letters and digits may be drawn from the entire Unicode

character set, which supports most writing scripts in use in the world today, including the large sets for Chinese, Japanese, and Korean. This allows programmers to use identifiers in their programmes that are written in their native languages.

A "Java letter" is a character for which the method Character.is JavaIdentifierStart(int) returns true. A "Java letter-or-digit" is a character for which the method Character isJavaIdentifierPart(int) returns true.

The Java letters include uppercase and lowercase ASCII Latin letters A-Z (\u0041-\u005a), and a-z (\u0061-\u007a), and, for historical reasons, the ASCII underscore (_, or \u005f) and dollar sign ($, or \u0024). The $ character should be used only in mechanically generated source code or, rarely, to access preexisting names on legacy systems.

The "Java digits" include the ASCII digits 0-9 (\u0030-\u0039). Two identifiers are the same only if they are identical, that is, have the same Unicode character for each letter or digit. Identifiers that have the same external appearance may yet be different.

For example, the identifiers consisting of the single letters LATIN CAPITAL LETTER A (A, \u0041), LATIN SMALL LETTER A (a, \u0061), GREEK CAPITAL LETTER ALPHA (A, \u0391), CYRILLIC SMALL LETTER A (a, \u0430) and MATHEMATICAL BOLD ITALIC SMALL A (a, \ud835\udc82) are all different.

Unicode composite characters are different from the decomposed characters. For example, a LATIN CAPITAL LETTER A ACUTE (Á, \u00c1) could be considered to be the same as a LATIN CAPITAL LETTER A (A, \u0041) immediately followed by a NON-SPACING ACUTE (´, \u0301) when sorting, but these are different in identifiers.

```
String i3 αρετη MAX_VALUE isLetterOrDigit
```

KEYWORDS

The following character sequences, formed from ASCII letters, are reserved for use as *keywords* and cannot be used as identifiers:

Keyword: one of:

abstract	continue	for	new	switch
assert	default	if	package	synchronized
boolean	do	goto	private	this
break	double	implements	protected	throw
byte	else	import	public	throws
case	enum	instanceof	return	transient
catch	extends	int	short	try
char	final	interface	static	void
class	finally	long	strictfp	volatile
const	float	native	super	while

The keywords const and goto are reserved, even though they are not currently used. This may allow a Java compiler to produce better error messages if these C++ keywords incorrectly appear in programmes.

While true and false might appear to be keywords, they are technically Boolean literals.Similarly, while null might appear to be a keyword, it is technically the null literal.

LITERALS

A *literal* is the source code representation of a value of a primitive type, the **String** type, or the null type:

```
Literal:
    IntegerLiteral
    FloatingPointLiteral
    BooleanLiteral
    CharacterLiteral
    StringLiteral
    NullLiteral
```

INTEGER LITERALS

For a general discussion of the integer types and values.

An *integer literal* may be expressed in decimal (base 10), hexadecimal (base 16), or octal (base 8):

```
IntegerLiteral:
    DecimalIntegerLiteral
    HexIntegerLiteral
    OctalIntegerLiteral
```

```
DecimalIntegerLiteral:
    DecimalNumeral IntegerTypeSuffixopt
HexIntegerLiteral:
    HexNumeral IntegerTypeSuffixopt
OctalIntegerLiteral:
    OctalNumeral IntegerTypeSuffixopt
IntegerTypeSuffix: one of
    l L
```

An integer literal is of type **long** if it is suffixed with an ASCII letter **L** or **l** (ell); otherwise it is of type **int**. The suffix **L** is preferred, because the letter **l** (ell) is often hard to distinguish from the digit **1** (one).

A decimal numeral is either the single ASCII character **0**, representing the integer zero, or consists of an ASCII digit from **1** to **9**, optionally followed by one or more ASCII digits from **0** to **9**, representing a positive integer:

```
DecimalNumeral:
    0
    NonZeroDigit Digitsopt
Digits:
    Digit
    Digits Digit
Digit:
    0
    NonZeroDigit
NonZeroDigit: one of
    1 2 3 4 5 6 7 8 9
```

A hexadecimal numeral consists of the leading ASCII characters **0x** or **0X** followed by one or more ASCII hexadecimal digits and can represent a positive, zero, or negative integer. Hexadecimal digits with values 10 through 15 are represented by the ASCII letters **a** through **f** or A through **F**, respectively; each letter used as a hexadecimal digit may be uppercase or lowercase.

```
HexNumeral:
    0 x HexDigits
    0 X HexDigits
HexDigits:
```

```
        HexDigit
        HexDigit HexDigits
```

The following production from is repeated here for clarity:

```
    HexDigit: one of
    0 1 2 3 4 5 6 7 8 9 a b c d e f A B C D E F
```

An octal numeral consists of an ASCII digit 0 followed by one or more of the ASCII digits 0 through 7 and can represent a positive, zero, or negative integer.

```
OctalNumeral:
    0 OctalDigits
OctalDigits:
    OctalDigit
    OctalDigit OctalDigits
OctalDigit: one of
0 1 2 3 4 5 6 7
```

Note that octal numerals always consist of two or more digits; 0 is always considered to be a decimal numeral-not that it matters much in practice, for the numerals 0, 00, and 0x0 all represent exactly the same integer value.

The largest decimal literal of type int is 2147483648 (2^{31}). All decimal literals from 0 to 2147483647 may appear anywhere an int literal may appear, but the literal 2147483648 may appear only as the operand of the unary negation operator -.

The largest positive hexadecimal and octal literals of type int are 0×7fffffff and 017777777777, respectively, which equal 2147483647 (2^{31}-1). The most negative hexadecimal and octal literals of type int are 0 × 80000000 and 020000000000, respectively, each of which represents the decimal value -2147483648 (-2^{31}). The hexadecimal and octal literals 0xffffffff and 037777777777, respectively, represent the decimal value -1. A compile-time error occurs if a decimal literal of type int is larger than 2147483648 (2^{31}), or if the literal 2147483648 appears anywhere other than as the operand of the unary - operator, or if a hexadecimal or octal int literal does not fit in 32 bits.

Examples of int literals:

```
0 2 0372 0xDadaCafe 1996 0x00FF00FF
```

The largest decimal literal of type long is 9223372036854775808L (2^{63}). All decimal literals from 0L to

9223372036854775807L may appear anywhere a long literal may appear, but the literal 9223372036854775808L may appear only as the operand of the unary negation operator -.

The largest positive hexadecimal and octal literals of type long are 0 × 7fffffffffffffffL and 0777777777777777777777L, respectively, which equal 9223372036854775807L (2^{63}-1). The literals 0x8000000000000000L and 01000000000000000000000L are the most negative long hexadecimal and octal literals, respectively. Each has the decimal value -9223372036854775808L (-2^{63}). The hexadecimal and octal literals 0 × ffffffffffffffffL and 01777777777777777777777L, respectively, represent the decimal value -1L.

A compile-time error occurs if a decimal literal of type long is larger than 9223372036854775808L (2^{63}), or if the literal 9223372036854775808L appears anywhere other than as the operand of the unary - operator, or if a hexadecimal or octal long literal does not fit in 64 bits.

Examples of long literals:

```
0l 0777L 0x100000000L 2147483648L 0xC0B0L
```

FLOATING-POINT LITERALS

A *floating-point literal* has the following parts: a whole-number part, a decimal or hexadecimal point (represented by an ASCII period character), a fractional part, an exponent, and a type suffix. A floating point number may be written either as a decimal value or as a hexadecimal value. For decimal literals, the exponent, if present, is indicated by the ASCII letter **e** or **E** followed by an optionally signed integer. For hexadecimal literals, the exponent is always required and is indicated by the ASCII letter **p** or **P** followed by an optionally signed integer.

For decimal floating-point literals, at least one digit, in either the whole number or the fraction part, and either a decimal point, an exponent, or a float type suffix are required. All other parts are optional. For hexadecimal floating-point literals, at least one digit is required in either the whole number or fraction part, the exponent is mandatory, and the float type suffix is optional.

A floating-point literal is of type **float** if it is suffixed with an ASCII letter **F** or **f**; otherwise its type is **double** and it can optionally be suffixed with an ASCII letter **D** or **d**.

```
FloatingPointLiteral:
    DecimalFloatingPointLiteral
    HexadecimalFloatingPointLiteral
DecimalFloatingPointLiteral:
    Digits. Digitsopt ExponentPartopt
FloatTypeSuffixopt
    . Digits ExponentPartopt
FloatTypeSuffixopt
    Digits ExponentPart FloatTypeSuffixopt
    Digits ExponentPartopt FloatTypeSuffix
ExponentPart:
    ExponentIndicator SignedInteger
ExponentIndicator: one of
    e E
SignedInteger:
    Signopt Digits
Sign: one of
    + -
FloatTypeSuffix: one of
    f F d D
HexadecimalFloatingPointLiteral:
    HexSignificand BinaryExponent
FloatTypeSuffixopt
HexSignificand:
    HexNumeral
    HexNumeral.
    0x HexDigitsopt. HexDigits
    0X HexDigitsopt. HexDigits
BinaryExponent:
    BinaryExponentIndicator SignedInteger
BinaryExponentIndicator:one of
    p P
```

The elements of the types **float** and **double** are those values that can be represented using the IEEE 754 32-bit single-precision and 64-bit double-precision binary floating-point formats, respectively. The details of proper input conversion from a Unicode string representation of a floating-point number to the internal IEEE 754 binary floating-point representation are described for the methods valueOf of class Float and class Double of the package java.lang.

The largest positive finite float literal is 3.4028235e38f. The smallest positive finite nonzero literal of type float is 1.40e-45f. The largest positive finite double literal is 1.7976931348623157e308. The smallest positive finite nonzero literal of type double is 4.9e-324.

A compile-time error occurs if a nonzero floating-point literal is too large, so that on rounded conversion to its internal representation it becomes an IEEE 754 infinity. A programme can represent infinities without producing a compile-time error by using constant expressions such as 1f/0f or -1d/0d or by using the predefined constants POSITIVE_INFINITY and NEGATIVE_INFINITY of the classes Float and Double.

A compile-time error occurs if a nonzero floating-point literal is too small, so that, on rounded conversion to its internal representation, it becomes a zero. A compile-time error does not occur if a nonzero floating-point literal has a small value that, on rounded conversion to its internal representation, becomes a nonzero denormalized number.

Predefined constants representing Not-a-Number values are defined in the classes Float and Double as Float.NaN and Double.NaN.

*Examples of **float** literals*:

```
1e1f 2.f.3f 0f 3.14f 6.022137e+23f
```

*Examples of **double** literals*:

```
1e1 2..3 0.0 3.14 1e-9d 1e137
```

Besides expressing floating-point values in decimal and hexadecimal, the method intBitsToFloat of class Float and method longBitsToDouble of class Double provide a way to express floating-point values in terms of hexadecimal or octal integer literals.

For example, the value of:

```
Double.longBitsToDouble(0 × 400921FB54442D18L)
```

is equal to the value of `Math.PI`.

BOOLEAN LITERALS

The boolean type has two values, represented by the literals true and false, formed from ASCII letters.

A boolean literal is always of type boolean:

```
BooleanLiteral: one of
true false
```

CHARACTER LITERALS

A *character literal* is expressed as a character or an escape sequence, enclosed in ASCII single quotes. (The single-quote, or apostrophe, character is \u0027.) Character literals can only represent UTF-16 code units, i.e., they are limited to values from \u0000 to \uffff. Supplementary characters must be represented either as a surrogate pair within a char sequence, or as an integer, depending on the API they are used with.

A character literal is always of type char.

```
CharacterLiteral:
' SingleCharacter '
' EscapeSequence '
SingleCharacter:
InputCharacter but not ' or \
```

The escape sequences are described in.

As specified in, the characters CR and LF are never an *InputCharacter*; they are recognized as constituting a *LineTerminator*.

It is a compile-time error for the character following the *SingleCharacter* or *EscapeSequence* to be other than a '.

It is a compile-time error for a line terminator to appear after the opening ' and before the closing '.

The following are examples of **char** literals:

```
'a'
'%'
'\t'
'\\'
'\''
'\u03a9'
'\uFFFF'
```

```
'\177'
'W'
'Ä'
```

Because Unicode escapes are processed very early, it is not correct to write '\u000a' for a character literal whose value is linefeed (LF); the Unicode escape \u000a is transformed into an actual linefeed in translation step 1 and the linefeed becomes a LineTerminator in step 2, and so the character literal is not valid in step 3. Instead, one should use the escape sequence '\n'.Similarly, it is not correct to write '\u000d' for a character literal whose value is carriage return (CR). Instead, use '\r'. In C and C++, a character literal may contain representations of more than one character, but the value of such a character literal is implementation-defined. In the Java programming language, a character literal always represents exactly one character.

STRING LITERALS

A *string literal* consists of zero or more characters enclosed in double quotes. Characters may be represented by escape sequences - one escape sequence for characters in the range U+0000 to U+FFFF, two escape sequences for the UTF-16 surrogate code units of characters in the range U+010000 to U+10FFFF. A string literal is always of type **String.** A string literal always refers to the same instance of class **String.**

```
StringLiteral:
" StringCharactersopt "
StringCharacters:
StringCharacter
StringCharacters StringCharacter
StringCharacter:
InputCharacter but not " or \
EscapeSequence
```

The escape sequences are described in.

As specified in, neither of the characters CR and LF is ever considered to be an *InputCharacter;* each is recognized as constituting a *LineTerminator.*

It is a compile-time error for a line terminator to appear

after the opening " and before the closing matching ". A long string literal can always be broken up into shorter pieces and written as a (possibly parenthesized) expression using the string concatenation operator +.

The following are examples of string literals:

```
""// the empty string
"\""// a string containing " alone
"This is a string"// a string containing 16
characters
"This is a " +// actually a string-valued
constant expression,
"two-line string"// formed from two string
literals
```

Because Unicode escapes are processed very early, it is not correct to write "\u000a" for a string literal containing a single linefeed (LF); the Unicode escape \u000a is transformed into an actual linefeed in translation step 1 and the linefeed becomes a *LineTerminator* in step 2, and so the string literal is not valid in step 3. Instead, one should write "\n". Similarly, it is not correct to write "\u000d" for a string literal containing a single carriage return (CR). Instead use "\r".

Each string literal is a reference to an instance of class String. String objects have a constant value. String literals-or, more generally, strings that are the values of constant expressions -are "interned" so as to share unique instances, using the method String.intern.

Thus, the test programme consisting of the compilation unit:

```
package testPackage;
class Test {
public static void main(String[] args) {
String hello = "Hello", lo = "lo";
System.out.print((hello == "Hello") + " ");
System.out.print((Other.hello == hello) + "
");
System.out.print((other.Other.hello == hello)
+ " ");
System.out.print((hello == ("Hel"+"lo")) + "
");
```

```
System.out.print((hello == ("Hel"+lo)) + "
");
System.out.println(hello == ("Hel"+lo).
intern());
}
}
class Other {static String hello = "Hello";}
and the compilation unit:
package other;
public class Other {static String hello =
"Hello";}
produces the output:
true true true true false true
```

This example illustrates six points:

- Literal strings within the same class in the same package represent references to the same **String** object.
- Literal strings within different classes in the same package represent references to the same **String** object.
- Literal strings within different classes in different packages likewise represent references to the same **String** object.
- Strings computed by constant expressions are computed at compile time and then treated as if they were literals.
- Strings computed by concatenation at run time are newly created and therefore distinct.

The result of explicitly interning a computed string is the same string as any pre-existing literal string with the same contents.

ESCAPE SEQUENCES FOR CHARACTER AND STRING LITERALS

The character and string *escape sequences* allow for the representation of some nongraphic characters as well as the single quote, double quote, and backslash characters in character literals and string literals.

```
EscapeSequence:
\ b/* \u0008: backspace BS */
\ t/* \u0009: horizontal tab HT */
\ n/* \u000a: linefeed LF */
\ f/* \u000c: form feed FF */
\ r/* \u000d: carriage return CR */
\ "/* \u0022: double quote " */
\ '/* \u0027: single quote '*/
\ \/* \u005c: backslash \ */
OctalEscape/* \u0000 to \u00ff: from octal
value */
OctalEscape:
\ OctalDigit
\ OctalDigit OctalDigit
\ ZeroToThree OctalDigit OctalDigit
OctalDigit: one of
0 1 2 3 4 5 6 7
ZeroToThree: one of
0 1 2 3
```

It is a compile-time error if the character following a backslash in an escape is not an ASCII `b`, `t`, `n`, `f`, `r`, `"`, `'`, `\`, `0`, `1`, `2`, `3`, `4`, `5`, `6`, or `7`. The Unicode escape `\u` is processed earlier. (Octal escapes are provided for compatibility with C, but can express only Unicode values `\u0000` through `\u00FF`, so Unicode escapes are usually preferred.)

THE NULL LITERAL

The null type has one value, the null reference, represented by the literal `null`, which is formed from ASCII characters. A *null literal* is always of the null type.

```
NullLiteral:
null
```

SEPARATORS

The following nine ASCII characters are the *separators* (punctuators):

```
Separator: one of
```

```
() {} [];.
```

OPERATORS

The following 37 tokens are the *operators*, formed from ASCII characters:

```
Operator: one of
=  >   <   !   ~   ?   :
== <=  >=  !=  &&  ||  ++  --
+  -   *   /   &   |   ^   %   <<  >>  >>>
+= -=  *=  /=  &=  |=  ^=  %=  <<= >>= >>>=
```

The Java programming language is a *strongly typed* language, which means that every variable and every expression has a type that is known at compile time. Types limit the values that a variable can hold or that an expression can produce, limit the operations supported on those values, and determine the meaning of the operations. Strong typing helps detect errors at compile time.

The types of the Java programming language are divided into two categories: primitive types and reference types. The primitive types are the **boolean** type and the numeric types. The numeric types are the integral types **byte, short, int, long,** and **char**, and the floating-point types **float** and **double**. The reference types are class types, interface types, and array types. There is also a special null type. An object is a dynamically created instance of a class type or a dynamically created array. The values of a reference type are references to objects. All objects, including arrays, support the methods of class **Object**. String literals are represented by **String** objects.

Types exist at compile-time. Some types correspond to classes and interfaces, which exist at run-time. The correspondence between types and classes or interfaces is incomplete for two reasons:

- At run-time, classes and interfaces are loaded by the Java virtual machine using class loaders. Each class loader defines its own set of classes and interfaces. As a result, it is possible for two loaders to load an identical class or interface definition but produce distinct classes or interfaces at run-time.

- Type arguments and type variables are not reified at run-time. As a result, different parameterized types are implemented by the same class or interface at run time. Indeed, all invocations of a given generic type declaration share a single run-time implementation.

A consequence of is the possibility of heap pollution. Under certain conditions, it is possible that a variable of a parameterized type refers to an object that is not of that parameterized type. The variable will always refer to an object that is an instance of a class that implements the parameterized type.

THE KINDS OF TYPES AND VALUES

There are two kinds of *types* in the Java programming language: primitive types and reference types. There are, correspondingly, two kinds of data values that can be stored in variables, passed as arguments, returned by methods, and operated on: primitive values and reference values.

```
Type:
PrimitiveType
ReferenceType
```

There is also a special *null type*, the type of the expression **null**, which has no name. Because the null type has no name, it is impossible to declare a variable of the null type or to cast to the null type. The null reference is the only possible value of an expression of null type. The null reference can always be cast to any reference type. In practice, the programmer can ignore the null type and just pretend that **null** is merely a special literal that can be of any reference type.

PRIMITIVE TYPES AND VALUES

A *primitive type* is predefined by the Java programming language and named by its reserved keyword:

```
PrimitiveType:
NumericType
boolean
NumericType:
```

```
IntegralType
FloatingPointType
IntegralType: one of
byte short int long char
FloatingPointType: one of
float double
```

Primitive values do not share state with other primitive values. A variable whose type is a primitive type always holds a primitive value of that same type. The value of a variable of primitive type can be changed only by assignment operations on that variable including increment and decrement operators.

The *numeric types* are the integral types and the floating-point types. The *integral types* are **byte**, **short**, **int**, and **long**, whose values are 8-bit, 16-bit, 32-bit and 64-bit signed two's-complement integers, respectively, and **char**, whose values are 16-bit unsigned integers representing UTF-16 code units.

The *floating-point types* are **float**, whose values include the 32-bit IEEE 754 floating-point numbers, and **double**, whose values include the 64-bit IEEE 754 floating-point numbers. The **boolean** type has exactly two values: **true** and **false.**

INTEGRAL TYPES AND VALUES

The values of the integral types are integers in the following ranges:

- For byte, from -128 to 127, inclusive
- For short, from -32768 to 32767, inclusive
- For int; from -2147483648 to 2147483647, inclusive
- For long, from -9223372036854775808 to 922337203 6854775807, inclusive
- For char, from '\u0000' to '\uffff' inclusive, that is, from 0 to 65535

INTEGER OPERATIONS

The Java programming language provides a number of operators that act on integral values:

- The comparison operators, which result in a value of type boolean:
- The numerical comparison operators <, <=, >, and >=

- The numerical equality operators == and !=
- The numerical operators, which result in a value of type int or long:
  - The unary plus and minus operators + and -
  - The multiplicative operators *,/, and %
  - The additive operators + and -
  - The increment operator ++, both prefix and postfix
  - The decrement operator –, both prefix and postfix
  - The signed and unsigned shift operators <<, >>, and >>>
  - The bitwise complement operator ~
  - The integer bitwise operators &, |, and ^
- The conditional operator ?:
- The cast operator, which can convert from an integral value to a value of any specified numeric type
- The string concatenation operator + which, when given a String operand and an integral operand, will convert the integral operand to a String representing its value in decimal form, and then produce a newly created String that is the concatenation of the two strings

Other useful constructors, methods, and constants are predefined in the classes **Byte, Short, Integer, Long**.

If an integer operator other than a shift operator has at least one operand of type **long**, then the operation is carried out using 64-bit precision, and the result of the numerical operator is of type **long**. If the other operand is not **long**, it is first widened to type **long** by numeric promotion. Otherwise, the operation is carried out using 32-bit precision, and the result of the numerical operator is of type **int**. If either operand is not an **int**, it is first widened to type **int** by numeric promotion.

The built-in integer operators do not indicate overflow or underflow in any way. Integer operators can throw a **NullPointerException** if unboxing conversion of a null reference is required. Other than that, the only integer operators that can throw an exception are the integer divide operator/ and the integer remainder operator %, which throw an **ArithmeticException** if the right-hand operand is zero, and the increment and decrement operators ++ and – which can throw an **OutOfMemoryError** if boxing conversion is required and there is not sufficient memory available to perform the conversion.

The example:

```
class Test {
public static void main(String[] args) {
      int i = 1000000;
      System.out.println(i * i);
      long l = i;
      System.out.println(l * l);
      System.out.println(20296/ (l - i));
      }
}
produces the output:
-727379968
1000000000000
```

and then encounters an ArithmeticException in the division by l - i, because l - i is zero. The first multiplication is performed in 32-bit precision, whereas the second multiplication is a long multiplication.

The value -727379968 is the decimal value of the low 32 bits of the mathematical result, 1000000000000, which is a value too large for type int. Any value of any integral type may be cast to or from any numeric type. There are no casts between integral types and the type **boolean.**

FLOATING-POINT TYPES, FORMATS, AND VALUES

The floating-point types are **float** and **double,** which are conceptually associated with the single-precision 32-bit and double-precision 64-bit format IEEE 754 values and operations as specified in *IEEE Standard for Binary Floating-Point Arithmetic,* ANSI/IEEE Standard 754-1985 (IEEE, New York).

The IEEE 754 standard includes not only positive and

negative numbers that consist of a sign and magnitude, but also positive and negative zeros, positive and negative *infinities*, and special *Not-a-Number* values (hereafter abbreviated NaN).

A NaN value is used to represent the result of certain invalid operations such as dividing zero by zero. NaN constants of both **float** and **double** type are predefined as **Float.NaN** and **Double.NaN**.

Every implementation of the Java programming language is required to support two standard sets of floating-point values, called the *float value set* and the *double value set*. In addition, an implementation of the Java programming language may support either or both of two extended-exponent floating-point value sets, called the *float-extended-exponent value set* and the *double-extended-exponent value set*. These extended-exponent value sets may, under certain circumstances, be used instead of the standard value sets to represent the values of expressions of type **float** or **double**.

The finite nonzero values of any floating-point value set can all be expressed in the form $s \cdot m \cdot 2^{(e-N+1)}$, where s is +1 or -1, m is a positive integer less than 2^N, and e is an integer between $E_{min} = -(2^{K-1}-2)$ and $E_{max} = 2^{K-1}-1$, inclusive, and where N and K are parameters that depend on the value set. Some values can be represented in this form in more than one way; for example, supposing that a value v in a value set might be represented in this form using certain values for s, m, and e, then if it happened that m were even and e were less than 2^{K-1}, one could halve m and increase e by 1 to produce a second representation for the same value v.

A representation in this form is called *normalized* if $m \geq 2^{(N-1)}$; otherwise the representation is said to be *denormalized*. If a value in a value set cannot be represented in such a way that $m \geq 2^{(N-1)}$, then the value is said to be a *denormalized value*, because it has no normalized representation.

The constraints on the parameters N and K (and on the derived parameters E_{min} and E_{max}) for the two required and two optional floating-point value sets are summarized in Table.

Parameter	Float	Float-extended -exponent	double	Double-extended -exponent
N	24	24	53	53
K	8	≥ 11	11	≥ 15
E_{max}	+127	$\geq +1023$	+1023	$\geq +16383$
E_{min}	-126	≤ -1022	–1022	≤ -16382

Where one or both extended-exponent value sets are supported by an implementation, then for each supported extended-exponent value set there is a specific implementation-dependent constant *K*, whose value is constrained by above Table; this value *K* in turn dictates the values for E_{min} and E_{max}.

Each of the four value sets includes not only the finite nonzero values that are ascribed to it above, but also NaN values and the four values positive zero, negative zero, positive infinity, and negative infinity.

Note that the constraints in above Table are designed so that every element of the float value set is necessarily also an element of the float-extended-exponent value set, the double value set, and the double-extended-exponent value set. Likewise, each element of the double value set is necessarily also an element of the double-extended-exponent value set. Each extended-exponent value set has a larger range of exponent values than the corresponding standard value set, but does not have more precision.

The elements of the float value set are exactly the values that can be represented using the single floating-point format defined in the IEEE 754 standard. The elements of the double value set are exactly the values that can be represented using the double floating-point format defined in the IEEE 754 standard. Note, however, that the elements of the float-extended-exponent and double-extended-exponent value sets defined here do *not* correspond to the values that can be represented using IEEE 754 single extended and double extended formats, respectively.

The float, float-extended-exponent, double, and double-extended-exponent value sets are not types. It is always correct for an implementation of the Java programming language to use an element of the float value set to represent a value of type **float**; however, it may be permissible in certain regions of code for an implementation to use an element of the float-extended-exponent value set instead. Similarly, it is always correct for an implementation to use an element of the double value set to represent a value of type **double**; however, it may be permissible in certain regions of code for an implementation to use an element of the double-extended-exponent value set instead.

Except for NaN, floating-point values are *ordered*; arranged from smallest to largest, they are negative infinity, negative finite nonzero values, positive and negative zero, positive finite nonzero values, and positive infinity.

IEEE 754 allows multiple distinct NaN values for each of its single and double floating-point formats. While each hardware architecture returns a particular bit pattern for NaN when a new NaN is generated, a programmer can also create NaNs with different bit patterns to encode, for example, retrospective diagnostic information.

For the most part, the Java platform treats NaN values of a given type as though collapsed into a single canonical value (and hence this specification normally refers to an arbitrary NaN as though to a canonical value). However, version 1.3 the Java platform introduced methods enabling the programmer to distinguish between NaN values: the Float.floatToRawIntBits and Double.doubleToRawLongBits methods. The interested reader is referred to the specifications for the Float and Double classes for more information.

Positive zero and negative zero compare equal; thus the result of the expression 0.0==–0.0 is true and the result of 0.0>–0.0 is false. But other operations can distinguish positive and negative zero; for example, 1.0/0.0 has the value positive infinity, while the value of 1.0/–0.0 is negative infinity.

NaN is *unordered*, so the numerical comparison operators <, <=, >, and >= return false if either or both operands are NaN. The equality operator == returns false if either operand is NaN, and the inequality operator != returns true if either operand is

NaN. In particular, x!=x is true if and only if x is NaN, and (x<y) == !(x>=y) will be false if x or y is NaN.

Any value of a floating-point type may be cast to or from any numeric type. There are no casts between floating-point types and the type **boolean**.

FLOATING-POINT OPERATIONS

The Java programming language provides a number of operators that act on floating-point values:

- The comparison operators, which result in a value of type boolean:
  - The numerical comparison operators <, <=, >, and >=
  - The numerical equality operators == and !=
- The numerical operators, which result in a value of type float or double:
  - The unary plus and minus operators + and -
  - The multiplicative operators *,/, and %
  - The additive operators + and -
  - The increment operator ++, both prefix and postfix
  - The decrement operator –, both prefix and postfix
- The conditional operator ?:
- The cast operator, which can convert from a floating-point value to a value of any specified numeric type)
- The string concatenation operator + which, when given a String operand and a floating-point operand, will convert the floating-point operand to a String representing its value in decimal form (without information loss), and then produce a newly created String by concatenating the two strings

Other useful constructors, methods, and constants are predefined in the classes **Float**, **Double**, and **Math**.

If at least one of the operands to a binary operator is of floating-point type, then the operation is a floating-point operation, even if the other is integral. If at least one of the operands to a numerical operator is of type **double**, then the operation is carried out using 64-bit floating-point arithmetic, and the result of the numerical operator is a value of type **double**.

If the other operand is not a **double**, it is first widened to type **double** by numeric promotion Otherwise, the operation is carried out using 32-bit floating-point arithmetic, and the result of the numerical operator is a value of type **float.** If the other operand is not a **float**, it is first widened to type **float** by numeric promotion.

Operators on floating-point numbers behave as specified by IEEE 754 (with the exception of the remainder operator. In particular, the Java programming language requires support of IEEE 754 *denormalized* floating-point numbers and *gradual underflow*, which make it easier to prove desirable properties of particular numerical algorithms. Floating-point operations do not "flush to zero" if the calculated result is a denormalized number.

The Java programming language requires that 'floating-point arithmetic behave as if every floating-point operator rounded its floating-point result to the result precision. *Inexact* results must be rounded to the representable value nearest to the infinitely precise result; if the two nearest representable values are equally near, the one with its least significant bit zero is chosen. This is the IEEE 754 standard's default rounding mode known as *round to nearest*.

The language uses *round toward zero* when converting a floating value to an integer, which acts, in this case, as though the number were truncated, discarding the mantissa bits. Rounding toward zero chooses at its result the format's value closest to and no greater in magnitude than the infinitely precise result.

Floating-point operators can throw a **NullPointer Exception** if unboxing conversion of a null reference is required. Other than that, the only floating-point operators that can throw an exception are the increment and decrement operators ++ and –, which can throw an **OutOfMemoryError** if boxing conversion is required and there is not sufficient memory available to perform the conversion.

An operation that overflows produces a signed infinity, an operation that underflows produces a denormalized value or a signed zero, and an operation that has no mathematically definite result produces NaN. All numeric operations with NaN as an operand produce NaN as a result. As has already been described, NaN is unordered, so a numeric comparison operation involving one or two NaNs returns **false** and any **!=** comparison involving NaN returns **true**, including **x!=x** when **x** is NaN.

The example programme:

```
class Test {
public static void main(String[] args) {
    // An example of overflow:
    double d = 1e308;
    System.out.print("overflow produces
    infinity: ");
          System.out.println(d  +  "*10=="  +
d*10);
    // An example of gradual underflow:
    d = 1e-305 * Math.PI;
    System.out.print("gradual underflow: " +
    d + "\n ");
    for (int i = 0; i < 4; i++)
    System.out.print(" " + (d/= 100000));
    System.out.println();
    // An example of NaN:
    System.out.print("0.0/0.0 is Not-a-Number:
    ");
    d = 0.0/0.0;
    System.out.println(d);
    // An example of inexact results and
    rounding:
    System.out.print("inexact results with
    float:");
    for (int i = 0; i < 100; i++) {
          float z = 1.0f/ i;
          if (z * i != 1.0f)
    System.out.print(" " + i);
```

```
    }
    System.out.println();
    // Another example of inexact results and
    rounding:
    System.out.print("inexact results with
    double:");
    for (int i = 0; i < 100; i++) {
        double z = 1.0/ i;
        if (z * i != 1.0)
              System.out.print(" " + i);
    }
    System.out.println();
    // An example of cast to integer rounding:
    System.out.print("cast to int rounds
    toward 0: ");
    d = 12345.6;
    System.out.println((int)d + " " + (int)(-
    d));
    }
}
```

produces the output:

```
overflow produces infinity: 1.0e+308*10=
=Infinity
gradual underflow: 3.141592653589793E-305
3.1415926535898E-310 3.141592653E-315 3.142E-
320 0.0
0.0/0.0 is Not-a-Number: NaN
inexact results with float: 0 41 47 55 61 82
83 94 97
inexact results with double: 0 49 98
cast to int rounds toward 0: 12345 -12345
```

This example demonstrates, among other things, that gradual underflow can result in a gradual loss of precision. The results when **i** is **0** involve division by zero, so that **z** becomes positive infinity, and **z * 0** is NaN, which is not equal to **1.0**.

THE BOOLEAN TYPE AND BOOLEAN VALUES

The **boolean** type represents a logical quantity with two possible values, indicated by the literals **true** and **false**. The boolean operators are:

- The relational operators == and !=
- The logical-complement operator !
- The logical operators &, ^, and |
- The conditional-and and conditional-or operators && and ||
- The conditional operator ?:
- The string concatenation operator +, which, when given a String operand and a boolean operand, will convert the boolean operand to a String (either "true" or "false"), and then produce a newly created String that is the concatenation of the two strings.

Boolean expressions determine the control flow in several kinds of statements:

- The if statement
- The while statement
- The do statement
- The for statement

A boolean expression also determines which subexpression is evaluated in the conditional ?: operator. Only boolean or Boolean expressions can be used in control flow statements and as the first operand of the conditional operator ?:. An integer x can be converted to a boolean, following the C language convention that any nonzero value is true, by the expression x!=0. An object reference obj can be converted to a boolean, following the C language convention that any reference other than null is true, by the expression obj!=null.

A cast of a boolean value to type boolean or Boolean is allowed; no other casts on type boolean are allowed. A boolean can be converted to a string by string conversion.

REFERENCE TYPES AND VALUES

There are three kinds of *reference types*: class types, interface types, and array types. Reference types may be parameterized with type arguments.

```
ReferenceType:
    ClassOrInterfaceType
    TypeVariable
    ArrayType
ClassOrInterfaceType:
    ClassType
    InterfaceType
ClassType:
    TypeDeclSpecifier TypeArgumentsopt
InterfaceType:
    TypeDeclSpecifier TypeArgumentsopt
TypeDeclSpecifier:
    TypeName
    ClassOrInterfaceType. Identifier
TypeName:
    Identifier
    TypeName. Identifier
TypeVariable:
    Identifier
ArrayType:
    Type []
```

A class or interface type consists of a type declaration specifier, optionally followed by type arguments (in which case it is a parameterized type). Type arguments are described in.

A type declaration specifier may be either a type name, or a class or interface type followed by "." and an identifier. In the latter case, the specifier has the form *T.id*, where *id* must be the simple name of an accessible member type of *T*, or a compile-time error occurs. The specifier denotes that member type.

The sample code:

```
class Point {int[] metrics;}
interface Move {void move(int deltax, int
deltay);}
```

declares a class type **`Point`**, an interface type **`Move`**, and uses an array type **`int[]`** (an array of **`int`**) to declare the field **`metrics`** of the class **`Point`**.

OBJECTS

An *object* is a *class instance* or an array.

The reference values (often just *references*) are *pointers* to these objects, and a special null reference, which refers to no object. A class instance is explicitly created by a class instance creation expression. An array is explicitly created by an array creation expression.

A new class instance is implicitly created when the string concatenation operator + is used in a non-constant expression, resulting in a new object of type **String**. A new array object is implicitly created when an array initializer expression is evaluated; this can occur when a class or interface is initialized, when a new instance of a class is created, or when a local variable declaration statement is executed. New objects of the types Boolean, Byte, Short, Character, Integer, Long, Float and Double may be implicitly created by boxing conversion.

Many of these cases are illustrated in the following example:

```
class Point {
    int x, y;
    Point() {System.out.println("default");}
    Point(int x, int y) {this.x = x; this.y
    = y;}
    // A Point instance is explicitly created
    at class initialization time:
    static Point origin = new Point(0,0);
    // A String can be implicitly created by
    a + operator:
    public String toString() {
        return "(" + x + "," + y + ")";
    }
}
class Test {
    public static void main(String[] args) {
        // A Point is explicitly created
        using newInstance:
        Point p = null;
        try {
        p =
```

```
(Point)Class.forName("Point").newInstance();
  } catch (Exception e) {
  System.out.println(e);
  }
  // An array is implicitly created by an
  array constructor:
  Point a[] = {new Point(0,0), new
  Point(1,1)};
  // Strings are implicitly created by +
  operators:
  System.out.println("p: " + p);
  System.out.println("a: {" + a[0] + ", "
                      + a[1] + "}");
  // An array is explicitly created by an
  array creation expression:
  String sa[] = new String[2];
  sa[0] = "he"; sa[1] = "llo";
  System.out.println(sa[0] + sa[1]);
  }
}
```

which produces the output:

```
default
p: (0,0)
a: {(0,0), (1,1)}
hello
```

The operators on references to objects are:

- Field access, using either a qualified name or a field access expression
- Method invocation
- The cast operator
- The string concatenation operator + which, when given a String operand and a reference, will convert the reference to a String by invoking the to String method of the referenced object (using "null" if either the reference or the result of to String is a null reference), and then will produce a newly created String that is the concatenation of the two strings
- The **`instanceof`** operator

- The reference equality operators == and !=
- The conditional operator ?:.

There may be many references to the same object. Most objects have state, stored in the fields of objects that are instances of classes or in the variables that are the components of an array object.

If two variables contain references to the same object, the state of the object can be modified using one variable's reference to the object, and then the altered state can be observed through the reference in the other variable.

The example programme:

```
class Value {int val;}
class Test {
    public static void main(String[] args) {
        int i1 = 3;
        int i2 = i1;
        i2 = 4;
        System.out.print("i1==" + i1);
        System.out.println(" but i2==" + i2);
        Value v1 = new Value();
        v1.val = 5;
        Value v2 = v1;
        v2.val = 6;
        System.out.print("v1.val==" +
        v1.val);
        System.out.println(" and v2.val==" +
        v2.val);
    }
}
produces the output:
i1==3 but i2==4
v1.val==6 and v2.val==6
```

because **v1.val** and **v2.val** reference the same instance variable in the one **Value** object created by the only **new** expression, while **i1** and **i2** are different variables.

for examples of the creation and use of arrays.

Each object has an associated lock, which is used by **synchronized** methods and the **synchronized** statement to provide control over concurrent access to state by multiple threads.

THE CLASS OBJECT

The class **Object** is a superclass of all other classes. A variable of type **Object** can hold a reference to the null reference or to any object, whether it is an instance of a class or an array All class and array types inherit the methods of class **Object**, which are summarized here:

```
package java.lang;
public class Object {
    public final Class<?> getClass() {...}
    public String toString() {...}
    public boolean equals(Object obj) {...}
    public int hashCode() {...}
    protected Object clone()
        throws CloneNotSupportedException
        {...}
    public final void wait()
        throws IllegalMonitorStateException,
        InterruptedException {...}
public final void wait(long millis)
    throws IllegalMonitorStateException,
            InterruptedException {...}
public final void wait(long millis, int nanos)
{...}
        throws IllegalMonitorStateException,
            InterruptedException {...}
public final void notify() {...}
        throws IllegalMonitorStateException
    public final void notifyAll() {...}
        throws IllegalMonitorStateException
protected void finalize()
        throws Throwable {...}
}
```

The members of **Object** are as follows:

- The method getClass returns the Class object that represents the class of the object. A Class object exists for each reference type. It can be used, for example, to discover the fully qualified name of a class, its members, its immediate superclass, and any interfaces that it implements. A class method that is declared synchronized synchronizes on the lock associated with the Class object of the class. The method Object.getClass() must be treated specially by a Java compiler. The type of a method invocation e.getClass(), where the expression e has the static type T, is Class<? extends |T|>.

- The method toString returns a String representation of the object.
- The methods equals and hashCode are very useful in hashtables such as java.util.Hashtable. The method equals defines a notion of object equality, which is based on value, not reference, comparison.
- The method clone is used to make a duplicate of an object.
- The methods wait, notify, and notifyAll are used in concurrent programming using threads, as described in.
- The method finalize is run just before an object is destroyed and is described in.

THE CLASS STRING

Instances of class **String** represent sequences of Unicode characters. A **String** object has a constant (unchanging) value. String literals are references to instances of class **String**.

The string concatenation operator + implicitly creates a new **String** object when the result is not a compile-time constant.

WHEN REFERENCE TYPES ARE THE SAME

Two reference types are the *same compile-time type* if they have the same binary name and their type parameters, if any, are the same, applying this definition recursively. When two reference types are the same, they are sometimes said to be the *same class* or the *same interface*.

At run time, several reference types with the same binary name may be loaded simultaneously by different class loaders. These types may or may not represent the same type declaration. Even if two such types do represent the same type declaration, they are considered distinct.

Two reference types are the same run-time type if:

- They are both class or both interface types, are defined by the same class loader, and have the same binary name, in which case they are sometimes said to be the *same run-time class* or the *same run-time interface.*
- They are both array types, and their component types are the same run-time type.

TYPE VARIABLES

A type variable is an unqualified identifier. Type variables are introduced by generic class declarations generic interface declarations generic method declarations and by generic constructor declarations.

```
TypeParameter:
    TypeVariable TypeBoundopt
TypeBound:
extends ClassOrInterfaceType
AdditionalBoundListopt
AdditionalBoundList:
    AdditionalBound AdditionalBoundList
    AdditionalBound
AdditionalBound:
    & InterfaceType
```

Type variables have an optional bound, T & $I_1 ... I_n$. The bound consists of either a type variable, or a class or interface type T possibly followed by further interface types $I_1 ..., I_n$. If no bound is given for a type variable, **Object** is assumed. It is a compile-time error if any of the types $I_1 ... I_n$ is a class type or type variable. The erasures of all constituent types of a bound must be pairwise different, or a compile-time error occurs. The order of types in a bound is only significant in that the erasure of a type variable is determined by the first type in its bound, and that a class type or type variable may only appear in the first position.

A type variable may not at the same time be a subtype of two interface types which are different parameterizations of the same generic interface.

The members of a type variable X with bound $T \,\&\, I_1 \ldots I_n$ are the members of the intersection type $T \,\&\, I_1 \ldots I_n$ appearing at the point where the type variable is declared.

Discussion: The following example illustrates what members a type variable has.

```
package TypeVarMembers;
    class C {
          void mCDefault() {}
          public void mCPublic() {}
          private void mCPrivate() {}
          protected void mCProtected() {}
    }
    class CT extends C implements I {}
    interface I {
          void mI();}
          <T extends C & I> void test(T t) {
                t.mI();// OK
                t.mCDefault();// OK
                t.mCPublic();// OK
                t.mCPrivate();// compile-time
  error
                t.mCProtected();// OK
          }
    }
```

The type variable T has the same members as the intersection type C & I, which in turn has the same members as the empty class CT, defined in the same scope with equivalent supertypes.

The members of an interface are always public, and therefore always inherited (unless overridden). Hence mI is a member of CT and of T. Among the members of C, all but mCPrivate are inherited by CT, and are therefore members of both CT and T.

If C had been declared in a different package than T, then the call to mCDefault would give rise to a compile-time error, as that member would not be accessible at the point where T is declared.

PARAMETERIZED TYPES

A parameterized type consists of a class or interface name *C* and an actual type argument list $<T_1..., T_n>$. It is a compile time error if *C* is not the name of a generic class or interface, or if the number of type arguments in the actual type argument list differs from the number of declared type parameters of C. In the following, whenever we speak of a class or interface type, we include the generic version as well, unless explicitly excluded. Throughout this section, let $A_1..., A_n$ be the formal type parameters of *C*, and let be B_i be the declared bound of A_i. The notation $[A_i := T_i]$ denotes substitution of the type variable A_i with the type T_i, for $1 \leq i \leq n$, and is used throughout this specification.

Let $P = G<T_1..., T_n>$ be a parameterized type. It must be the case that, after *P* is subjected to capture conversion resulting in the type *G<X1..., Xn>*, for each actual type argument X_i, $1 \leq i \leq n$, $X_i <: B_i[A_1 := X_1..., A_n := X_n]$, or a compile time error occurs.

Discussion:

```
Example: Parameterized types.
Vector<String>
Seq<Seq<A>>
Seq<String>.Zipper<Integer>
Collection<Integer>
Pair<String,String>
// Vector<int> — illegal, primitive types
cannot be arguments
// Pair<String> — illegal, not enough
arguments
// Pair<String,String,String> — illegal, too
many arguments
```

Two parameterized types are provably distinct if either of the following conditions hold:

- They are invocations of distinct generic type declarations.
- Any of their type arguments are provably distinct.

TYPE ARGUMENTS AND WILDCARDS

Type arguments may be either reference types or wildcards.

```
TypeArguments:
    < ActualTypeArgumentList >
ActualTypeArgumentList:
    ActualTypeArgument
ActualTypeArgumentList, ActualTypeArgument
    ActualTypeArgument:
ReferenceType
Wildcard
Wildcard:
? WildcardBoundsOpt
WildcardBounds:
extends ReferenceType
super ReferenceType
```

Discussion:

```
Examples:
    void printCollection(Collection<?> c) {/
    / a   wildcard collection
    for (Object o: c) {
    System.out.println(o);
    }
    }
```

Note that using Collection<Object> as the type of the incoming parameter, c, would not be nearly as useful; the method could only be used with an actual parameter that had type Collection<Object>, which would be quite rare. In contrast, the use of an unbounded wildcard allows any kind of collection to be used as a parameter.

Wildcards are useful in situations where only partial knowledge about the type parameter is required.

Discussion:

Example: Wildcard parameterized types as component types of array types.

```
public Method getMethod(Class<?>[]
    parameterTypes) {...}
```

Wildcards may be given explicit bounds, just like regular type variable declarations. An upper bound is signified by the syntax:

```
? extends B
```

, where *B* is the bound.

Discussion:

Example: Bounded wildcards.

```
boolean addAll(Collection<? extends E> c)
```

Here, the method is declared within the interface Collection<E>, and is designed to add all the elements of its incoming argument to the collection upon which it is invoked. A natural tendency would be to use Collection<E> as the type of c, but this is unnecessarily restrictive. An alternative would be to declare the method itself to be generic:

```
<T> boolean addAll(Collection<T> c)
```

This version is sufficiently flexible, but note that the type parameter is used only once in the signature. This reflects the fact that the type parameter is not being used to express any kind of interdependency between the type(s) of the argument(s), the return type and/or throws type. In the absence of such interdependency, generic methods are considered bad style, and wildcards are preferred.

Unlike ordinary type variables declared in a method signature, no type inference is required when using a wildcard. Consequently, it is permissible to declare lower bounds on a wildcard, using the syntax:

```
? super B
```

, where *B* is a lower bound.

Discussion:

Example: Lower bounds on wildcards.

```
Reference(T referent, ReferenceQueue<? super
T> queue);
```

Here, the referent can be inserted into any queue whose

element type is a super type of the type T of the referent. Two type arguments are provably distinct if neither of the arguments is a type variable or wildcard, and the two arguments are not the same type.

Discussion:

The relationship of wildcards to established type theory is an interesting one, which we briefly allude to here.

Wildcards are a restricted form of existential types. Given a generic type declaration *G<T extends B>*, *G<?>* is roughly analogous to *Some X <: B. G<X>*. Readers interested in a more comprehensive discussion should refer to *On Variance-Based Subtyping for Parametric Types* by Atsushi Igarashi and Mirko Viroli, in the proceedings of the 16th European Conference on Object Oriented Programming (ECOOP 2002).

Historically, wildcards are a direct descendant of the work by Atsushi Igarashi and Mirko Viroli. This work itself builds upon earlier work by Kresten Thorup and Mads Torgersen ("Unifying Genericity", ECOOP 99), as well as a long tradition of work on declaration based variance that goes back to Pierre America's work on POOL (OOPSLA 89)

TYPE ARGUMENT CONTAINMENT AND EQUIVALENCE

A type argument TA_1 is said to contain another type argument TA_2, written $TA_2 <= TA_1$, if the set of types denoted by TA_2 is provably a subset of the set of types denoted by TA_1 under the following rules (where <: denotes subtyping:

- ? extends T <= ? extends S if *T <: S*
- ? super T <= ? super S if *S <: T*
- T <= T
- T <= ? extends T
- T <= ? super T

MEMBERS AND CONSTRUCTORS OF PARAMETERIZED TYPES

Let C be a class or interface declaration with formal type parameters $A_1 ..., A_n$, and let $C<T_1 ..., T_n>$ be an invocation of C, where, for $1 \leq i \leq n$, T_i are types (rather than wildcards).

Then:

- Let *m* be a member or constructor declaration in *C*, whose type as declared is *T*. Then the type of *m* in the type $C<T_1...,T_n>$, is $T[A_1:= T_1..., A_n:= T_n]$.
- Let *m* be a member or constructor declaration in *D*, where *D* is a class extended by *C* or an interface implemented by *C*. Let $D<U_1...,U_k>$ be the supertype of $C<T_1...,T_n>$ that corresponds to *D*. Then the type of *m* in $C<T_1...,T_n>$ is the type of *m* in $D<U_1...,U_k>$.

If any of the type arguments to a parameterized type are wildcards, the type of its members and constructors is undefined.

Discussion: This is of no consequence, as it is impossible to access a member of a parameterized type without performing capture conversion, and it is impossible to use a wildcard type after the keyword new in a class instance creation expression

TYPE ERASURE

Type erasure is a mapping from types (possibly including parameterized types and type variables) to types (that are never parameterized types or type variables). We write $|T|$ for the erasure of type *T*. The erasure mapping is defined as follows.

- The erasure of a parameterized type $G<T_1...,T_n>$ is $|G|$.
- The erasure of a nested type *T.C* is $|T|.C$.
- The erasure of an array type *T[]* is $|T|[]$.
- The erasure of a type variable is the erasure of its leftmost bound.
- The erasure of every other type is the type itself.

The erasure of a method signature *s* is a signature consisting of the same name as *s*, and the erasures of all the formal parameter types given in *s*.

REIFIABLE TYPES

Because some type information is erased during compilation, not all types are available at run time. Types that are completely available at run time are known as *reifiable types*. A type is reifiable if and only if one of the following holds:

- It refers to a non-generic type declaration.
- It is a parameterized type in which all type arguments are unbounded wildcards.
- It is a raw type.
- It is a primitive type.
- It is an array type whose component type is reifiable.

Discussion: The decision not to make all generic types reifiable is one of the most crucial, and controversial design decisions involving the language's type system.

Ultimately, the most important motivation for this decision is compatibility with existing code.

Naively, the addition of new constructs such as genericity has no implications for pre-existing code. The programming language per se, is compatible with earlier versions as long as every programme written in the previous versions retains its meaning in the new version. However, this notion, which may be termed language compatibility, is of purely theoretical interest. Real programmes (even trivial ones, such as "Hello World") are composed of several compilation units, some of which are provided by the Java platform (such as elements of **java.lang** or **java.util**).

In practice then, the minimum requirement is platform compatibillity - that any programme written for the prior version of the platform continues to function unchanged in the new platform.

One way to provide platform compatibillity is to leave existing platform functionality unchanged, only adding new functionality. For example, rather than modify the existing Collections hierarchy in **java.util**, one might introduce a new library utilizing genericity.

The disadvantages of such a scheme is that it is extremely difficult for pre-existing clients of the Collection library to migrate to the new library. Collections are used to exchange data between independently developed modules; if a vendor decides to switch to the new, generic, library, that vendor must also distribute two versions of their code, to be compatible with their clients. Libraries that are dependent on other vendors code cannot be modified to use genericity until the supplier's library is updated. If two modules are mutually dependent, the changes must be made simultaneously.

Clearly, platform compatibility, as outlined above, does not provide a realistic path for adoption of a pervasive new feature such as genericity. Therefore, the design of the generic type system seeks to support migration compatibility. Migration compatibiliy allows the evolution of existing code to take advantage of generics without imposing dependencies between independently developed software modules.

The price of migration compatibility is that a full and sound reification of the generic type system is not possible, at least while the migration is taking place.

RAW TYPES

To facilitate interfacing with non-generic legacy code, it is also possible to use as a type the erasure of a parameterized type. Such a type is called a *raw type.*

More precisely, a raw type is define to be either:

- The name of a generic type declaration used without any accompanying actual type parameters.
- Any non-static type member of a raw type *R* that is not inherited from a superclass or superinterface of *R*.

Discussion: The latter point may not be immediately self evident. Presenting for your consideration, then, the following example:

```
class Outer<T>{
   T t;
   class Inner {
         T setOuterT(T t1) {t = t1;return t;}
   }
}
```

The type of the member(s) of **Inner** depends on the type parameter of **Outer**. If **Outer** is raw, **Inner** must be treated as raw as well, as their is no valid binding for **T**. This rule applies only to type members that are not inherited. Inherited type members that depend on type variables will be inherited as raw types as a consequence of the rule that the supertypes of a raw type are erased, described later in this section.

Discussion: Another implication of the rules above is that a generic inner class of a raw type can itself only be used as a raw type:

```
class Outer<T>{
    class Inner<S> {
        S s;
    }
}
it is not possible to access Inner as
partially raw type (a "rare" type)
Outer.Inner<Double> x = null;// illegal
Double d = x.s;
```

because **Outer** itself is raw, so are all its inner classes, including **Inner**, and so it is not possible to pass any type parameters to it.

The use of raw types is allowed only as a concession to compatibility of legacy code. The use of raw types in code written after the introduction of genericity into the Java programming language is strongly discouraged. It is possible that future versions of the Java programming language will disallow the use of raw types.

It is a compile-time error to attempt to use a type member of a parameterized type as a raw type.

Discussion: This means that the ban on "rare" types extends to the case where the qualifying type is parameterized, but we attempt to use the inner class as a raw type:

```
Outer<Integer>.Inner x = null;// illegal
```

This is the opposite of the case we discussed above. There is no practical justification for this half baked type. In legacy code, no type parameters are used. In non-legacy code, we should use the generic types correctly and pass all the required actual type parameters.

Discussion: Variables of a raw type can be assigned from values of any of the type's parametric instances.

For instance, it is possible to assign a **Vector<String>** to a

Vector, based on the subtyping rules. The reverse assignment from **Vector** to **Vector<String>** is unsafe (since the raw vector might have had a different element type), but is still permitted using unchecked conversion in order to enable interfacing with legacy code. In this case, a compiler will issue an unchecked warning.

The superclasses (respectively, superinterfaces) of a raw type are the erasures of the superclasses (superinterfaces) of any of its parameterized invocations.

The type of a constructor, instance method, or non-static field *M* of a raw type *C* that is not inherited from its superclasses or superinterfaces is the erasure of its type in the generic declaration corresponding to *C*. The type of a static member of a raw type *C* is the same as its type in the generic declaration corresponding to *C*.

It is a compile-time error to pass actual type parameters to a non-static type member of a raw type that is not inherited from its superclasses or superinterfaces.

To make sure that potential violations of the typing rules are always flagged, some accesses to members of a raw type will result in warning messages. The rules for generating warnings when accessing members or constructors of raw types are as follows:

- An invocation of a method or constructor of a raw type generates an unchecked warning if erasure changes any of the types of any of the arguments to the method or constructor.
- An assignment to a field of a raw type generates an unchecked warning if erasure changes the field's type.

No unchecked warning is required for a method call when the argument types do not change (even if the result type and/or throws clause changes), for reading from a field, or for a class instance creation of a raw type. The supertype of a class may be a raw type. Member accesses for the class are treated as normal, and member accesses for the supertype are treated as for raw types. In the constructor of the class, calls to super are treated as method calls on a raw type.

Discussion:

```
Example: Raw types.
class Cell<E>
    E value;
    Cell (E v) {value=v;}
    A get() {return value;}
    void set(E v) {value=v;}
}
Cell x = new Cell<String>("abc");
x.value;// OK, has type Object
x.get();// OK, has type Object
x.set("def");// unchecked warning
```

Discussion:

For example,

```
import java.util.*;
class NonGeneric {
    Collection<Number> myNumbers(){return
null;}
}
abstract class RawMembers<T> extends
NonGeneric implements Collection<String> {
    static Collection<NonGeneric> cng =
new ArrayList<NonGeneric>();
    public static void main(String[] args) {
        RawMembers rw = null;
        Collection<Number> cn =
rw.myNumbers();// ok
        Iterator<String> is = rw.iterator();/
/ unchecked warning
        Collection<NonGeneric> cnn = rw.cng;/
/ ok - static member
    }
}
RawMembers<T> inherits the method
Iterator<String> iterator()
```

from the **Collection<String>** superinterface. However, the type **RawMembers** inherits **iterator()** from the erasure of its superinterface, which means that the return type of the member **iterator()** is the erasure of **Iterator<<String>, Iterator**. As a result, the attempt to assign to **rw.iterator()** requires an unchecked conversion from **Iterator** to **Iterator<String>**, causing an unchecked warning to be issued.

In contrast, the static member **cng** retains its full parameterized type even when accessed through a object of raw type (note that access to a static member through an instance is considered bad style and is to be discouraged). The member **myNumbers** is inherited from the **NonGeneric** (whose erasure is also **NonGeneric**) and so retains its full parameterized type.

Discussion: Raw types are closly related to wildcards. Both are based on existential types. Raw types can be thought of as wildcards whose type rules are deliberately unsound, to accommodate interaction with legacy code.

Historically, raw types preceded wildcards; they were first introduced in GJ, and described in the paper *Making the future safe for the past: Adding Genericity to the Java Programming Language* by Gilad Bracha, Martin Odersky, David Stoutamire, and Philip Wadler, in Proc. of the ACM Conf. on Object-Oriented Programming, Systems, Languages and Applications, (OOPSLA 98) October 1998.

INTERSECTION TYPES

An intersection type takes the form T_1 &... & T_n, $n>0$, where T_i, $1 \leq i \leq n$, are type expressions. Intersection types arise in the processes of capture conversion and type inference.It is not possible to write an intersection type directly as part of a programme; no syntax supports this. The values of an intersection type are those objects that are values of all of the types T_i, for $1 \leq i \leq n$.

The members of an intersection type T_1 &... & T_n are determined as follows:

- For each T_i, $1 \leq i \leq n$, let C_i be the most specific class or array type such that $T_i <: C_i$ Then there must be some $T_k <: C_k$ such that $C_k <: C_i$ for any i, $1 \leq i \leq n$, or a compile-time error occurs.
- For $1 \leq j \leq n$, if T_j is a type variable, then let IT_j be an

interface whose members are the same as the public members of T_j; otherwise, if T_j is an interface, then let IT_j be T_j.

- Then the intersection type has the same members as a class type with an empty body, direct superclass C_k and direct superinterfaces $IT_1 \ldots, IT_n$, declared in the same package in which the intersection type appears.

Discussion: It is worth dwelling upon the distinction between intersection types and the bounds of type variables. Every type variable bound induces an intersection type. This intersection type is often trivial (i.e., consists of a single type).

The form of a bound is restricted (only the first element may be a class or type variable, and only one type variable may appear in the bound) to preclude certain awkward situations coming into existence. However, capture conversion can lead to the creation of type variables whose bounds are more general (e.g., array types).

SUBTYPING

The subtype and supertype relations are binary relations on types. The *supertypes* of a type are obtained by reflexive and transitive closure over the direct supertype relation, written $S >_1 T$, which is defined by rules given later in this section. We write $S :> T$ to indicate that the supertype relation holds between S and T. S is a proper supertype of T, written $T < S$, if $S :> T$ and $S \neq T$.

The *subtypes* of a type T are all types U such that T is a supertype of U, and the null type. We write $T <: S$ to indicate that that the subtype relation holds between types T and S. T is a *proper subtype* of S, written $T < S$, if $T <: S$ and $S \neq T$. T is a *direct subtype* of S, written $T <_1 S$, if $S >_1 T$.

Subtyping does not extend through generic types: $T <: U$ does not imply that $C<T> <: C<U>$.

SUBTYPING AMONG PRIMITIVE TYPES

The following rules define the direct supertype relation among the primitive types:

```
double >1 float
float >1 long
long >1 int
int >1 char
int >1 short
short >1 byte
```

SUBTYPING AMONG CLASS AND INTERFACE TYPES

Let C be a type declaration with zero or more type parameters $F_1..., F_n$ which have corresponding bounds $B_1...,$ B_n. That type declaration defines a set of parameterized types $C_2 <T_1...,T_n>$, where each argument type T_i ranges over all types that are subtypes of all types listed in the corresponding bound. That is, for each bound type S_i in B_i, T_i is a subtype of $S_i[F_1 := T_1..., F_n := T_n]$.

Given a type declaration for $C<F_1...,F_n>$, the *direct supertypes* of the parameterized type $C<F_1...,F_n>$ are all of the following:

- The direct superclasses of C.
- The direct superinterfaces of C.
- The type Object, if C is an interface type with no direct superinterfaces.
- The raw type C.

The direct supertypes of the type $C<T_1...,T_n>$, where $T_i, 1 \leq i \leq n$, is a type, are $D<U_1$ *theta*..., U_k *theta*>, where

- $D<U_1...,U_k>$ is a direct supertype of $C<F_1...,F_n>$, and *theta* is the substitution $[F_1 := T_1..., F_n := T_n]$.
- $C<S_1...,S_n>$ where S_i contains T_i for $1 \leq i \leq n$.

The direct supertypes of the type $C<R_1...,R_n>$, where at least one of the R_i, $1 \leq i \leq n$, is a wildcard type argument, are the direct supertypes of $C<X_1...,X_n>$, where

$C<X_1...,X_n>$ is the result of applying capture conversion to $C<R_1...,R_n>$.

The direct supertypes of an intersection type T_1 &... & T_n, are T_i, $1 \leq i \leq n$.

The direct supertypes of a type variable are the types listed in its bound.

The direct supertypes of the null type are all reference types other than the null type itself.

In addition to the above rules, a type variable is a direct supertype of its lower bound.

SUBTYPING AMONG ARRAY TYPES

The following rules define the direct subtype relation among array types:

- If *S* and *T* are both reference types, then *S[]* $>_1$ *T[]* iff *S* $>_1$ *T*.
- Object $>_1$ Object[]
- Cloneable $>_1$ Object[]
- java.io.Serializable $>_1$ Object[]
- If *p* is a primitive type, then:
  - Object $>_1$ p[]
  - Cloneable $>_1$ p[]
  - java.io.Serializable $>_1$ p[]

WHERE TYPES ARE USED

Types are used when they appear in declarations or in certain expressions. The following code fragment contains one or more instances of most kinds of usage of a type:

```
import java.util.Random;
class MiscMath<T extends Number>{
    int divisor;
    MiscMath(int divisor) {
        this.divisor = divisor;
    }
    float ratio(long l) {
        try {
            l/= divisor;
        } catch (Exception e) {
        if (e instanceof ArithmeticException)
                l = Long.MAX_VALUE;
            else
                l = 0;
        }
            return (float)l;
```

```
        }
        double gausser() {
                Random r = new Random();
                double[] val = new double[2];
                val[0] = r.nextGaussian();
                val[1] = r.nextGaussian();
                return (val[0] + val[1])/ 2;
}
Collection<Number> fromArray(Number[] na) {
        Collection<Number> cn = new
  ArrayList<Number>();
        for (Number n: na) {
                cn.add(n)
}
return cn;
}
    void <S> loop(S s){this.<S>loop(s);}
}
```

In this example, types are used in declarations of the following:

- Imported types; here the type Random, imported from the type java.util.Random of the package java.util, is declared
- Fields, which are the class variables and instance variables of classes, and constants of interfaces; here the field divisor in the class MiscMath is declared to be of type int
- Method parameters; here the parameter l of the method ratio is declared to be of type long
- Method results; here the result of the method ratio is declared to be of type float, and the result of the method gausser is declared to be of type double
- Constructor parameters; here the parameter of the constructor for MiscMath is declared to be of type int
- Local variables the local variables r and val of the method gausser are declared to be of types Random and double[] (array of double)

- Exception handler parameters here the exception handler parameter e of the catch clause is declared to be of type Exception
- Type variables; here the type variable T has Number as its declared bound.

and in expressions of the following kinds:

- Class instance creations; here a local variable r of method gausser is initialized by a class instance creation expression that uses the type Random
- Generic class instance creations here Number is used as a type argument in the expression new ArrayList<Number>()
- Array creations here the local variable val of method gausser is initialized by an array creation expression that creates an array of double with size 2
- Generic method or constructor invocations here the method loop calls itself with an explicit type argument S
- Casts; here the return statement of the method ratio uses the float type in a cast
- The instanceof operator here the instanceof operator tests whether e is assignment compatible with the type ArithmeticException

Types are also used as arguments to parameterized types; here the type Number is used as an argument in the parameterized type Collection<Number>.

VARIABLES

A variable is a storage location and has an associated type, sometimes called its *compile-time type*, that is either a primitive type or a reference type. A variable's value is changed by an assignment or by a prefix or postfix ++ (increment) or — (decrement) operator.

Compatibility of the value of a variable with its type is guaranteed by the design of the Java programming language, as long as a programme does not give rise to unchecked warnings. Default values are compatible and all assignments to a variable are checked for assignment compatibility, usually at compile time, but, in a single case involving arrays, a run-time check is made.

VARIABLES OF PRIMITIVE TYPE

A variable of a primitive type always holds a value of that exact primitive type.

VARIABLES OF REFERENCE TYPE

A variable of a class type *T* can hold a null reference or a reference to an instance of class *T* or of any class that is a subclass of *T*. A variable of an interface type can hold a null reference or a reference to any instance of any class that implements the interface.

Discussion

Note that a variable is not guaranteed to always refer to a subtype of its declared type, but only to subclasses or subinterfaces of the declared type. This is due to the possibility of heap pollution discussed below.

If *T* is a primitive type, then a variable of type "array of *T*" can hold a null reference or a reference to any array of type "array of *T*"; if *T* is a reference type, then a variable of type "array of *T*" can hold a null reference or a reference to any array of type "array of *S*" such that type *S* is a subclass or subinterface of type *T*. In addition, a variable of type **Object[]** can hold an array of any reference type. A variable of type **Object** can hold a null reference or a reference to any object, whether class instance or array.

HEAP POLLUTION

It is possible that a variable of a parameterized type refers to an object that is not of that parameterized type. This situation is known as heap pollution. This situation can only occur if the programme performed some operation that would give rise to an unchecked warning at compile-time.

Discussion: For example, the code:

```
List l = new ArrayList<Number>();
List<String> ls = l;// unchecked warning
```

gives rise to an unchecked warning, because it is not

possible to ascertain, either at compile-time (within the limits of the compile-time type checking rules) or at run-time, whether the variable l does indeed refer to a **List<String>**.

If the code above is executed, heap pollution arises, as the variable ls, declared to be a **List<String>**, refers to a value that is not in fact a **List<String>**.

The problem cannot be identified at run-time because type variables are not reified, and thus instances do not carry any information at run-time regarding the actual type parameters used to create them.

In a simple example as given above, it may appear that it should be straightforward to identify the situation at compile-time and give a compilation error. However, in the general (and typical) case, the value of the variable l may be the result of an invocation of a separately compiled method, or its value may depend upon arbitrary control flow.

The code above is therefore very atypical, and indeed very bad style.

Assignment from a value of a raw type to a variable of a parameterized type should only be used when combining legacy code which does not make use of parameterized types with more modern code that does.

If no operation that requires an unchecked warning to be issued takes place, heap pollution cannot occur. Note that this does not imply that heap pollution only occurs if an unchecked warning actually occurred. It is possible to run a programme where some of the binaries were compiled by a compiler for an older version of the Java programming language, or by a compiler that allows the unchecked warnings to suppressed. This practice is unhealthy at best.

Conversely, it is possible that despite executing code that could (and perhaps did) give rise to an unchecked warning, no heap pollution takes place. Indeed, good programming practice requires that the programmer satisfy herself that despite any unchecked warning, the code is correct and heap pollution will not occur.

The variable will always refer to an object that is an instance of a class that implements the parameterized type.

Discussion: For instance, the value of **l** in the example above is always a **List**.

KINDS OF VARIABLES

There are seven kinds of variables:

1. A *class variable* is a field declared using the keyword static within a class declaration, or with or without the keyword static within an interface declaration. A class variable is created when its class or interface is prepared and is initialized to a default value. The class variable effectively ceases to exist when its class or interface is unloaded.
2. An *instance variable* is a field declared within a class declaration without using the keyword static. If a class *T* has a field *a* that is an instance variable, then a new instance variable *a* is created and initialized to a default value as part of each newly created object of class *T* or of any class that is a subclass of *T*. The instance variable effectively ceases to exist when the object of which it is a field is no longer referenced, after any necessary finalization of the object has been completed.
3. *Array components* are unnamed variables that are created and initialized to default values whenever a new object that is an array is created. The array components effectively cease to exist when the array is no longer referenced. for a description of arrays.
4. *Method parameters* name argument values passed to a method. For every parameter declared in a method declaration, a new parameter variable is created each time that method is invoked. The new variable is initialized with the corresponding argument value from the method invocation. The method parameter effectively ceases to exist when the execution of the body of the method is complete.
5. *Constructor parameters* name argument values passed to a constructor. For every parameter declared in a constructor declaration, a new parameter variable is

created each time a class instance creation expression or explicit constructor invocation invokes that constructor. The new variable is initialized with the corresponding argument value from the creation expression or constructor invocation. The constructor parameter effectively ceases to exist when the execution of the body of the constructor is complete.

6. An *exception-handler parameter* is created each time an exception is caught by a catch clause of a try statement. The new variable is initialized with the actual object associated with the exception The exception-handler parameter effectively ceases to exist when execution of the block associated with the catch clause is complete.
7. *Local variables* are declared by local variable declaration statements. Whenever the flow of control enters a block or for statement, a new variable is created for each local variable declared in a local variable declaration statement immediately contained within that block or for statement. A local variable declaration statement may contain an expression which initializes the variable. The local variable with an initializing expression is not initialized, however, until the local variable declaration statement that declares it is executed. (The rules of definite assignment prevent the value of a local variable from being used before it has been initialized or otherwise assigned a value.) The local variable effectively ceases to exist when the execution of the block or for statement is complete.

Were it not for one exceptional situation, a local variable could always be regarded as being created when its local variable declaration statement is executed. The exceptional situation involves the **switch** statement, where it is possible for control to enter a block but bypass execution of a local variable declaration statement. Because of the restrictions imposed by the rules of definite assignment, however, the local variable declared by such a bypassed local variable declaration statement cannot be used before it has been definitely assigned a value by an assignment expression.

```
The following example contains several
different kinds of variables:
class Point {
    static int numPoints;// numPoints is a
    class variable
int x, y;// x and y are instance variables
    int[] w = new int[10];// w[0] is an array
        component
    int setX(int x) {// x is a method
        parameter
    int oldx = this.x;// oldx is a local
        variable
    this.x = x;
    return oldx;
    }
}
```

FINAL VARIABLES

A variable can be declared **final**. A final variable may only be assigned to once. It is a compile time error if a final variable is assigned to unless it is definitely unassigned immediately prior to the assignment. A blank final is a final variable whose declaration lacks an initializer.

Once a **final** variable has been assigned, it always contains the same value. If a **final** variable holds a reference to an object, then the state of the object may be changed by operations on the object, but the variable will always refer to the same object. This applies also to arrays, because arrays are objects; if a **final** variable holds a reference to an array, then the components of the array may be changed by operations on the array, but the variable will always refer to the same array.

Declaring a variable **final** can serve as useful documentation that its value will not change and can help avoid programming errors.

In the example:

```
class Point {
```

```
    int x, y;
    int useCount;
    Point(int x, int y) {this.x = x; this.y
    = y;}
    final static Point origin = new Point(0,
    0);
}
```

the class **Point** declares a final class variable **origin**. The **origin** variable holds a reference to an object that is an instance of class **Point** whose coordinates are (0, 0). The value of the variable **Point.origin** can never change, so it always refers to the same **Point** object, the one created by its initializer. However, an operation on this **Point** object might change its state-for example, modifying its **useCount** or even, misleadingly, its **x** or **y** coordinate.

We call a variable, of primitive type or type **String**, that is final and initialized with a compile-time constant expression a *constant variable*. Whether a variable is a constant variable or not may have implications with respect to class initialization, binary compatibility and definite assignment.

INITIAL VALUES OF VARIABLES

Every variable in a programme must have a value before its value is used:

- Each class variable, instance variable, or array component is initialized with a *default value* when it is created:
  - For type byte, the default value is zero, that is, the value of (byte)0.
  - For type short, the default value is zero, that is, the value of (short)0.
  - For type int, the default value is zero, that is, 0.
  - For type long, the default value is zero, that is, 0L.
  - For type float, the default value is positive zero, that is, 0.0f.
  - For type double, the default value is positive zero, that is, 0.0d.

– For type char, the default value is the null character, that is, '\u0000'.
– For type boolean, the default value is false.
– For all reference types, the default value is null.

- Each method parameter is initialized to the corresponding argument value provided by the invoker of the method.
- Each constructor parameter is initialized to the corresponding argument value provided by a class instance creation expression or explicit constructor invocation.
- An exception-handler parameter is initialized to the thrown object representing the exception.
- A local variable must be explicitly given a value before it is used, by either initialization or assignment, in a way that can be verified by the compiler using the rules for definite assignment.

The example programme:

```
class Point {
    static int npoints;
    int x, y;
    Point root;
}
class Test {
    public static void main(String[] args) {
            System.out.println("npoints="+
   Point.npoints);
            Point p = new Point();
            System.out.println("p.x=" + p.x + ",
   p.y=" + p.y);
            System.out.println("p.root=" +
   p.root);
    }
}
prints:
npoints=0
p.x=0, p.y=0
p.root=null
```

illustrating the default initialization of npoints, which occurs when the class Point is prepared, and the default initialization of x, y, and root, which occurs when a new Point is instantiated. A full description of all aspects of loading, linking, and initialization of classes and interfaces, plus a description of the instantiation of classes to make new class instances.

TYPES, CLASSES, AND INTERFACES

In the Java programming language, every variable and every expression has a type that can be determined at compile time. The type may be a primitive type or a reference type. Reference types include class types and interface types. Reference types are introduced by type declarations, which include class declarations and interface declarations. We often use the term *type* to refer to either a class or an interface.

Every object belongs to some particular class: the class that was mentioned in the creation expression that produced the object, the class whose **Class** object was used to invoke a reflective method to produce the object, or the **String** class for objects implicitly created by the string concatenation operator +. This class is called the *class of the object*. (Arrays also have a class, as described at the end of this section.) An object is said to be an instance of its class and of all superclasses of its class.

Sometimes a variable or expression is said to have a "run-time type". This refers to the class of the object referred to by the value of the variable or expression at run time, assuming that the value is not **null**.

The compile time type of a variable is always declared, and the compile time type of an expression can be deduced at compile time.

The compile time type limits the possible values that the variable can hold or the expression can produce at run time. If a run-time value is a reference that is not **null**, it refers to an object or array that has a class, and that class will necessarily be compatible with the compile-time type.

Even though a variable or expression may have a compile-time type that is an interface type, there are no instances of interfaces. A variable or expression whose type is an interface type can reference any object whose class implements that interface.

Here is an example of creating new objects and of the distinction between the type of a variable and the class of an object:

```
public interface Colorable {
      void setColor(byte r, byte g, byte b);
}
class Point {int x, y;}
class ColoredPoint extends Point implements
   Colorable {
      byte r, g, b;
      public void setColor(byte rv, byte gv, byte
   bv) {
            r = rv; g = gv; b = bv;
      }
}
class Test {
      public static void main(String[] args) {
            Point p = new Point();
            ColoredPoint cp = new ColoredPoint();
            p = cp;
Colorable c = cp;
}
}
```

In this example:

- The local variable p of the method main of class Test has type Point and is initially assigned a reference to a new instance of class Point.
- The local variable cp similarly has as its type ColoredPoint, and is initially assigned a reference to a new instance of class ColoredPoint.
- The assignment of the value of cp to the variable p causes p to hold a reference to a ColoredPoint object. This is permitted because ColoredPoint is a subclass of Point, so the class ColoredPoint is assignment compatible with the type Point. A ColoredPoint object includes support for all the methods of a Point.

In addition to its particular fields r, g, and b, it has the fields of class Point, namely x and y.

- The local variable c has as its type the interface type Colorable, so it can hold a reference to any object whose class implements Colorable; specifically, it can hold a reference to a ColoredPoint.

Discussion

Note that an expression such as **new Colorable()** is not valid because it is not possible to create an instance of an interface, only of a class.

Every array also has a class; the method **getClass,** when invoked for an array object, will return a class object (of class **Class**) that represents the class of the array.

The classes for arrays have strange names that are not valid identifiers; for example, the class for an array of **int** components has the name "**[I**" and so the value of the expression:

```
new int[10].getClass().getName()
```

is the string **"[I"**; see the specification of **Class.getName** for details.

CONVERSIONS AND PROMOTIONS

Every expression written in the Java programming language has a type that can be deduced from the structure of the expression and the types of the literals, variables, and methods mentioned in the expression. It is possible, however, to write an expression in a context where the type of the expression is not appropriate. In some cases, this leads to an error at compile time. In other cases, the context may be able to accept a type that is related to the type of the expression; as a convenience, rather than requiring the programmer to indicate a type conversion explicitly, the language performs an implicit *conversion* from the type of the expression to a type acceptable for its surrounding context.

A specific conversion from type *S* to type *T* allows an expression of type *S* to be treated at compile time as if it had type *T* instead. In some cases this will require a corresponding action at run time to check the validity of the conversion or to translate the run-time value of the expression into a form appropriate for the new type *T*.

For example:

- *A conversion from type*: Object to type thread requires a run-time check to make sure that the run-time value is actually an instance of class Thread or one of its subclasses; if it is not, an exception is thrown.
- *A conversion from type*: Thread to type Object requires no run-time action; Thread is a subclass of Object, so any reference produced by an expression of type Thread is a valid reference value of type Object.
- A conversion from type int to type long requires run-time sign-extension of a 32-bit integer value to the 64-bit long representation. No information is lost.

A conversion from type **double** to type **long** requires a nontrivial translation from a 64-bit floating-point value to the 64-bit integer representation. Depending on the actual run-time value, information may be lost.

In every conversion context, only certain specific conversions are permitted. For convenience of description, the specific conversions that are possible in the Java programming language are grouped into several broad categories:

- Identity conversions
- Widening primitive conversions
- Narrowing primitive conversions
- Widening reference conversions
- Narrowing reference conversions
- Boxing conversions
- Unboxing conversions
- Unchecked conversions
- Capture conversions
- String conversions
- Value set conversions

There are five *conversion contexts* in which conversion of expressions may occur. Each context allows conversions in some of the categories named above but not others. The term "conversion" is also used to describe the process of choosing a specific conversion for such a context. For example, we say that an expression that is an actual argument in a method invocation is subject to "method invocation conversion," meaning that a specific conversion will be implicitly chosen for that expression according to the rules for the method invocation argument context.

One conversion context is the operand of a numeric operator such as + or *. The conversion process for such operands is called *numeric promotion*. Promotion is special in that, in the case of binary operators, the conversion chosen for one operand may depend in part on the type of the other operand expression. This chapter first describes the eleven categories of conversions, including the special conversions to **String** allowed for the string concatenation operator +.

Then the five conversion contexts are described:

- Assignment conversion converts the type of an expression to the type of a specified variable. Assignment conversion may cause a Out Of Memory Error (as a result of boxing conversion), a Null Pointer Exception (as a result of unboxing conversion), or a ClassCastException (as a result of an unchecked conversion) to be thrown at run time.
- Method invocation conversion is applied to each argument in a method or constructor invocation and, except in one case, performs the same conversions that assignment conversion does. Method invocation conversion may cause a OutOfMemoryError (as a result of boxing conversion), a NullPointerException (as a result of unboxing conversion), or a ClassCastException (as a result of an unchecked conversion) to be thrown at run time.
- Casting conversion converts the type of an expression to a type explicitly specified by a cast operator. It is more inclusive than assignment or method invocation conversion, allowing any specific conversion other than a string conversion, but certain casts to a reference type may cause an exception at run time.
- String conversion allows any type to be converted to type String.

- Numeric promotion brings the operands of a numeric operator to a common type so that an operation can be performed.

Here are some examples of the various contexts for conversion:

```
class Test {
    public static void main(String[] args) {
        // Casting conversion of a float
    literal to
        // type int. Without the cast operator,
    this would
        // be a compile-time error, because
    this is a
        // narrowing conversion:
        int i = (int)12.5f;
        // String conversion of i's int value:
        System.out.println("(int)12.5f==" +
    i);
        // Assignment conversion of i's value
    to type
        // float. This is a widening
    conversion:
        float f = i;
        // String conversion of f's float
    value:
        System.out.println("after float
    widening: " + f);
        // Numeric promotion of i's value to
    type
        // float. This is a binary numeric
    promotion.
        // After promotion, the operation is
    float*float:
        System.out.print(f);
        f = f * i;
        // Two string conversions of i and f:
        System.out.println("*" + i + "==" +
    f);
        // Method invocation conversion of
```

```
  f's value
         // to type double, needed because the
  method Math.sin
         // accepts only a double argument:
         double d = Math.sin(f);
         // Two string conversions of f and d:
         System.out.println("Math.sin(" + f +
  ")==" + d);
    }
}
which produces the output:
(int)12.5f==12
after float widening: 12.0
12.0*12==144.0
Math.sin(144.0)==-0.49102159389846934
```

KINDS OF CONVERSION

Specific type conversions in the Java programming language are divided into the following categories.

IDENTITY CONVERSIONS

A conversion from a type to that same type is permitted for any type. This may seem trivial, but it has two practical consequences.

First, it is always permitted for an expression to have the desired type to begin with, thus allowing the simply stated rule that every expression is subject to conversion, if only a trivial identity conversion. Second, it implies that it is permitted for a programme to include redundant cast operators for the sake of clarity.

Widening Primitive Conversion

The following 19 specific conversions on primitive types are called the *widening primitive conversions*:

- Byte to short, int, long, float, or double
- Short to int, long, float, or double
- Char to int, long, float, or double
- Int to long, float, or double

- Long to float or double
- Float to double

Widening primitive conversions do not lose information about the overall magnitude of a numeric value. Indeed, conversions widening from an integral type to another integral type do not lose any information at all; the numeric value is preserved exactly. Conversions widening from **float** to **double** in **strictfp** expressions also preserve the numeric value exactly; however, such conversions that are not **strictfp** may lose information about the overall magnitude of the converted value.

Conversion of an **int** or a **long** value to **float**, or of a **long** value to **double**, may result in *loss of precision*-that is, the result may lose some of the least significant bits of the value. In this case, the resulting floating-point value will be a correctly rounded version of the integer value, using IEEE 754 round-to-nearest mode.

A widening conversion of a signed integer value to an integral type *T* simply sign-extends the two's-complement representation of the integer value to fill the wider format. A widening conversion of a **char** to an integral type *T* zero-extends the representation of the **char** value to fill the wider format. Despite the fact that loss of precision may occur, widening conversions among primitive types never result in a run-time exception.

Here is an example of a widening conversion that loses precision:

```
class Test {
    public static void main(String[] args) {
        int big = 1234567890;
        float approx = big;
        System.out.println(big - (int)approx);
    }
}
```

which prints:

```
-46
```

thus indicating that information was lost during the conversion from type **int** to type **float** because values of type **float** are not precise to nine significant digits.

NARROWING PRIMITIVE CONVERSIONS

The following 22 specific conversions on primitive types are called the *narrowing primitive conversions*:

- Short to byte or char
- Char to byte or short
- Int to byte, short, or char
- Long to byte, short, char, or int
- Float to byte, short, char, int, or long
- Double to byte, short, char, int, long, or float

Narrowing conversions may lose information about the overall magnitude of a numeric value and may also lose precision.

A narrowing conversion of a signed integer to an integral type *T* simply discards all but the *n* lowest order bits, where *n* is the number of bits used to represent type *T*. In addition to a possible loss of information about the magnitude of the numeric value, this may cause the sign of the resulting value to differ from the sign of the input value.

A narrowing conversion of a **char** to an integral type *T* likewise simply discards all but the *n* lowest order bits, where *n* is the number of bits used to represent type *T*. In addition to a possible loss of information about the magnitude of the numeric value, this may cause the resulting value to be a negative number, even though **char**s represent 16-bit unsigned integer values.

A narrowing conversion of a floating-point number to an integral type *T* takes two steps:

1. In the first step, the floating-point number is converted either to a long, if *T* is long, or to an int, if *T* is byte, short, char, or int, as follows:
   - If the floating-point number is NaN, the result of the first step of the conversion is an int or long 0.
   - Otherwise, if the floating-point number is not an infinity, the floating-point value is rounded to an integer value *V*, rounding toward zero using IEEE 754 round-toward-zero mode. Then there are two cases:
     – If *T* is long, and this integer value can be

represented as a long, then the result of the first step is the long value *V*.
  - Otherwise, if this integer value can be represented as an int, then the result of the first step is the int value *V*.
- Otherwise, one of the following two cases must be true:
  - The value must be too small (a negative value of large magnitude or negative infinity), and the result of the first step is the smallest representable value of type int or long.
  - The value must be too large (a positive value of large magnitude or positive infinity), and the result of the first step is the largest representable value of type int or long.

2. In the second step:
   - If *T* is int or long,the result of the conversion is the result of the first step.
   - If *T* is byte, char, or short, the result of the conversion is the result of a narrowing conversion to type *T* of the result of the first step.

The example:

```
class Test {
    public static void main(String[] args) {
        float fmin = Float.NEGATIVE_INFINITY;
        float fmax = Float.POSITIVE_INFINITY;
        System.out.println("long: " +
    (long)fmin +
                "..” + (long)fmax);
        System.out.println("int: " + (int)fmin
    +
                "..” + (int)fmax);
        System.out.println("short: " +
    (short)fmin +
                "..” + (short)fmax);
        System.out.println("char: " +
    (int)(char)fmin +
                "..” + (int)(char)fmax);
```

```
        System.out.println("byte:  " +
   (byte)fmin +
                     ".." + (byte)fmax);
    }
}
produces the output:
long: -9223372036854775808..9223372036854775807
int: -2147483648..2147483647
short: 0..-1
char: 0..65535
byte: 0..-1
```

The results for char, int, and long are unsurprising, producing the minimum and maximum representable values of the type. The results for byte and short lose information about the sign and magnitude of the numeric values and also lose precision. The results can be understood by examining the low order bits of the minimum and maximum int.

The minimum int is, in hexadecimal, 0 × 80000000, and the maximum int is 0 × 7ffffff. This explains the short results, which are the low 16 bits of these values, namely, 0 × 0000 and 0xffff; it explains the char results, which also are the low 16 bits of these values, namely, '\u0000' and '\uffff'; and it explains the byte results, which are the low 8 bits of these values, namely, 0 × 00 and 0 × ff. Despite the fact that overflow, underflow, or other loss of information may occur, narrowing conversions among primitive types never result in a run-time exception. Here is a small test programme that demonstrates a number of narrowing conversions that lose information:

```
class Test {
    public static void main(String[] args) {
            // A narrowing of int to short loses
   high bits:
System.out.println("(short)0x12345678==0x" +
            Integer.toHexString((short)0
   x12345678));
            // A int value not fitting in byte
   changes sign and magnitude:
            System.out.println("(byte)255==" +
```

```
    (byte)255);
            // A float value too big to fit gives
    largest int value:
            System.out.println("(int)1e20f==" +
    (int)1e20f);
            // A NaN converted to int yields zero:
            System.out.println("(int)NaN==" +
    (int)Float.NaN);
// A double value too large for float yields
    infinity:
            System.out.println("(float)-1e100=="
    + (float)-1e100);
            // A double value too small for float
    underflows to zero:
            System.out.println("(float)1e-50==" +
    (float)1e-50);
        }
}
```

This test programme produces the following output:

```
(short)0x12345678==0x5678
(byte)255==-1
(int)1e20f==2147483647
(int)NaN==0
(float)-1e100==-Infinity
(float)1e-50==0.0
```

WIDENING AND NARROWING PRIMITIVE CONVERSIONS

The following conversion combines both widening and narrowing primitive convesions:

Byte to Char

First, the **byte** is converted to an **int** via widening primitive conversion, and then the resulting **int** is converted to a **char** by narrowing primitive conversion.

WIDENING REFERENCE CONVERSIONS

A *widening reference* conversion exists from any type *S* to any type *T*, provided *S* is a subtype of *T*. Widening reference conversions never require a special action at run time and therefore never throw an exception at run time. They consist simply in regarding a reference as having some other type in a manner that can be proved correct at compile time.

for the detailed specifications for classes, for interfaces, and for arrays.

NARROWING REFERENCE CONVERSIONS

The following conversions are called the *narrowing reference conversions:*

- From any reference type *S* to any reference type *T*, provided that *S* is a proper supertype of *T*. (An important special case is that there is a narrowing conversion from the class type Object to any other reference type.)
- From any class type C to any non-parameterized interface type *K*, provided that C is not final and does not implement *K*.
- From any interface type *J* to any non-parameterized class type *C* that is not final.
- From the interface types Cloneable and java.io.Serializable to any array type *T*[].
- From any interface type *J* to any non-parameterized interface type *K*, provided that *J* is not a subinterface of *K*.
- From any array type *SC*[] to any array type *TC*[], provided that *SC* and *TC* are reference types and there is a narrowing conversion from *SC* to *TC*.

Such conversions require a test at run time to find out whether the actual reference value is a legitimate value of the new type. If not, then a **ClassCastException** is thrown.

BOXING CONVERSION

Boxing conversion converts values of primitive type to corresponding values of reference type. Specifically, the following 8 conversion are called the *boxing conversions*:

- From type boolean to type Boolean

- From type byte to type Byte
- From type char to type Character
- From type short to type Short
- From type int to type Integer
- From type long to type Long
- From type float to type Float
- From type double to type Double

At run time, boxing conversion proceeds as follows:

- If *p* is a value of type boolean, then boxing conversion converts *p* into a reference *r* of class and type Boolean, such that *r*.booleanValue() == *p*
- If *p* is a value of type byte, then boxing conversion converts *p* into a reference *r* of class and type Byte, such that *r*.byteValue() == *p*
- If *p* is a value of type char, then boxing conversion converts *p* into a reference *r* of class and type Character, such that *r*.charValue() == *p*
- If *p* is a value of type short, then boxing conversion converts *p* into a reference *r* of class and type Short, such that *r*.shortValue() == *p*
- If *p* is a value of type int, then boxing conversion converts *p* into a reference *r* of class and type Integer, such that *r*.intValue() == *p*
- If *p* is a value of type long, then boxing conversion converts *p* into a reference *r* of class and type Long, such that *r*.longValue() == *p*
- If *p* is a value of type float then:
  - If *p* is not NaN, then boxing conversion converts *p* into a reference *r* of class and type Float, such that *r*.floatValue() evaluates to *p*
  - Otherwise, boxing conversion converts *p* into a reference *r* of class and type Float such that *r*.isNaN() evaluates to true.
- If *p* is a value of type double, then
  - If *p* is not NaN, boxing conversion converts *p* into a reference *r* of class and type Double, such that *r*.doubleValue() evaluates to *p*
  - Otherwise, boxing conversion converts *p* into a

reference *r* of class and type Double such that *r*.isNaN() evaluates to true.

- If *p* is a value of any other type, boxing conversion is equivalent to an identity conversion (5.1.1).

If the value *p* being boxed is **true, false**, a **byte**, a **char** in the range \u0000 to \u007f, or an **int** or **short** number between -128 and 127, then let *r1* and *r2* be the results of any two boxing conversions of *p*. It is always the case that *r1* == *r2*.

Discussion: Ideally, boxing a given primitive value p, would always yield an identical reference. In practice, this may not be feasible using existing implementation techniques. The rules above are a pragmatic compromise. The final clause above requires that certain common values always be boxed into indistinguishable objects. The implementation may cache these, lazily or eagerly. For other values, this formulation disallows any assumptions about the identity of the boxed values on the programmer's part. This would allow (but not require) sharing of some or all of these references.

This ensures that in most common cases, the behaviour will be the desired one, without imposing an undue performance penalty, especially on small devices. Less memory-limited implementations might, for example, cache all characters and shorts, as well as integers and longs in the range of –32K – +32K.

A boxing conversion may result in an OutOfMemoryError if a new instance of one of the wrapper classes (Boolean, Byte, Character, Short, Integer, Long, Float, or Double) needs to be allocated and insufficient storage is available.

UNBOXING CONVERSION

Unboxing conversion converts values of reference type to corresponding values of primitive type. Specifically, the following 8 conversion are called the *unboxing conversions*:

- From type Boolean to type boolean
- From type Byte to type byte
- From type Character to type char
- From type Short to type short
- From type Integer to type int

- From type Long to type long
- From type Float to type float
- From type Double to type double

At run time, unboxing conversion proceeds as follows:

- If *r* is a reference of type Boolean, then unboxing conversion converts *r* into *r*.booleanValue()
- If *r* is a reference of type Byte, then unboxing conversion converts *r* into *r*.byteValue()
- If *r* is a reference of type Character, then unboxing conversion converts *r* into *r*.charValue()
- If *r* is a reference of type Short, then unboxing conversion converts *r* into *r*.shortValue()
- If *r* is a reference of type Integer, then unboxing conversion converts *r* into *r*.intValue()
- If *r* is a reference of type Long, then unboxing conversion converts *r* into r.longValue()
- If *r* is a reference of type Float, unboxing conversion converts *r* into *r*.floatValue()
- If *r* is a reference of type Double, then unboxing conversion converts *r* into *r*.doubleValue()
- If *r* is null, unboxing conversion throws a NullPointerException

A type is said to be *convertible to a numeric type* if it is a numeric type, or it is a reference type that may be converted to a numeric type by unboxing conversion. A type is said to be *convertible to an integral type* if it is an integral type, or it is a reference type that may be converted to an integral type by unboxing conversion.

UNCHECKED CONVERSION

Let *G* name a generic type declaration with n formal type parameters. There is an *unchecked conversion* from the raw type *G* to any parameterized type of the form $G<T_1 \ldots T_n>$. Use of an unchecked conversion generates a mandatory compile-time warning (which can only be suppressed using the **SuppressWarnings** annotation) unless the parameterized type *G* is a parameterized type in which all type arguments are unbounded wildcards.

Discussion: Unchecked conversion is used to enable a smooth interoperation of legacy code, written before the introduction of generic types, with libraries that have undergone a conversion to use genericity (a process we call *generification*).

In such circumstances (most notably, clients of the collections framework in **java.util**), legacy code uses raw types (e.g., **Collection** instead of **Collection<String>**). Expressions of raw types are passed as arguments to library methods that use parameterized versions of those same types as the types of their corresponding formal parameters.

Such calls cannot be shown to be statically safe under the type system using generics. Rejecting such calls would invalidate large bodies of existing code, and prevent them from using newer versions of the libraries. This in turn, would discourage library vendors from taking advantage of genericity.

To prevent such an unwelcome turn of events, a raw type may be converted to an arbitrary invocation of the generic type declaration the raw type refers to. While the conversion is unsound, it is tolerated as a concession to practicality. A warning (known as an *unchecked warning*) is issued in such cases.

CAPTURE CONVERSION

Let G name a generic type declaration with n formal type parameters $A_1 \ldots A_n$ with corresponding bounds $U_1 \ldots U_n$. There exists a capture conversion from $G<T_1 \ldots T_n>$ to $G<S_1 \ldots S_n>$, where, for $1 \leq i \leq n$:

- If T_i is a wildcard type argument of the form ? then S_i is a fresh type variable whose upper bound is $U_i[A_1 := S_1 \ldots, A_n := S_n]$ and whose lower bound is the null type.
- If T_i is a wildcard type argument of the form ? extends B_i, then S_i is a fresh type variable whose upper bound is $glb(B_i, U_i[A_1 := S_1 \ldots, A_n := S_n])$ and whose lower bound is the null type, where $glb(V_1 \ldots, V_m)$ is V_1 & ... & V_m. It is a compile-time error

if for any two classes (not interfaces) V_i and V_j, V_i is not a subclass of V_j or vice versa.

- If T_i is a wildcard type argument of the form ? super B_i, then S_i is a fresh type variable whose upper bound is $U_i[A_1 := S_1 ..., A_n := S_n]$ and whose lower bound is B_i.
- Otherwise, $S_i = T_i$.

Capture conversion on any type other than a parameterized type acts as an identity conversion. Capture conversions never require a special action at run time and therefore never throw an exception at run time. Capture conversion is not applied recursively.

Discussion: Capture conversion is designed to make wildcards more useful. To understand the motivation, let's begin by looking at the method **java.util.Collections.reverse()**:

```
public static void reverse(List<?> list);
```

The method reverses the list provided as a parameter. It works for any type of list, and so the use of the wildcard type **List<?>** as the type of the formal parameter is entirely appropriate.

Now consider how one would implement reverse().

```
public static void reverse(List<?> list)
   {rev(list);}
private static <T> void rev(List<T> list) {
    List<T> tmp = new ArrayList<T>(list);
    for (int i = 0; i < list.size(); i++) {
    list.set(i, tmp.get(list.size() - i - 1));
    }
}
```

The implementation needs to copy the list, extract elements from the copy, and insert them into the original. To do this in a type safe manner, we need to give a name, **T**, to the element type of the incoming list. We do this in the private service method **rev()**. This requires us to pass the incoming argument list, of type **List<?>**, as an argument to **rev()**. Note that in general, **List<?>** is a list of unknown type. It is not a subtype of **List<T>**, for any type **T**. Allowing such a subtype relation would be unsound.

Given the method:

```
public static <T> void fill(List<T> l, T obj)
a call
List<String> ls = new ArrayList<String>();
List<?> l = ls;
Collections.fill(l, new Object());// not really
    legal - but assume
                                        // it was
String s = ls.get(0);// ClassCastException - ls
    contains Objects,
          //not Strings.
```

would undermine the type system.

So, without some special dispensation, we can see that the call from **reverse()** to **rev()** would be disallowed. If this were the case, the author of **reverse()** would be forced to write its signature as:

```
public static <T> void reverse(List<T> list)
```

This is undesirable, as it exposes implementation information to the caller. Worse, the designer of an API might reason that the signature using a wildcard is what the callers of the API require, and only later realise that a type safe implementation was precluded. The call from **reverse()** to **rev()** is in fact harmless, but it cannot be justified on the basis of a general subtyping relation between **List<?>** and **List<T>**. The call is harmless, because the incoming argument is doubtless a list of some type (albeit an unknown one). If we can capture this unknown type in a type variable **X**, we can infer **T** to be **X**. That is the essence of capture conversion. The specification of course must cope with complications, like non-trivial (and possibly recursively defined) upper or lower bounds, the presence of multiple arguments etc.

Discussion: Mathematically sophisticated readers will want to relate capture conversion to established type theory. Readers unfamiliar with type theory can skip this discussion - or else study a suitable text, such as *Types and Programming Languages* by Benjamin Pierce, and then revisit this section.

Here then is a brief summary of the relationship of capture conversion to established type theoretical notions.

Wildcard types are a restricted form of existential types. Capture conversion corresponds loosely to an opening of a value of existential type. A capture conversion of an expression **e**, can be thought of as an open of **e** in a scope that comprises the top-level expression that encloses **e**.

The classical **open** operation on existentials requires that the captured type variable must not escape the opened expression. The **open** that corresponds to capture conversion is always on a scope sufficiently large that the captured type variable can never be visible outside that scope.

String Conversions

There is a string conversion to type **String** from every other type, including the null type.

Forbidden Conversions

Any conversion that is not explicitly allowed is forbidden.

Value Set Conversion

Value set conversion is the process of mapping a floating-point value from one value set to another without changing its type.

Within an expression that is not FP-strict, value set conversion provides choices to an implementation of the Java programming language:

- If the value is an element of the float-extended-exponent value set, then the implementation may, at its option, map the value to the nearest element of the float value set. This conversion may result in overflow (in which case the value is replaced by an infinity of the same sign) or underflow (in which case the value may lose precision because it is replaced by a denormalized number or zero of the same sign).
- If the value is an element of the double-extended-exponent value set, then the implementation may, at its option, map the value to the nearest element of the double value set. This conversion may result in overflow (in which case the value is replaced by an

infinity of the same sign) or underflow (in which case the value may lose precision because it is replaced by a denormalized number or zero of the same sign). Within an FP-strict expression, value set conversion does not provide any choices; every implementation must behave in the same way:

- If the value is of type float and is not an element of the float value set, then the implementation must map the value to the nearest element of the float value set. This conversion may result in overflow or underflow.
- If the value is of type double and is not an element of the double value set, then the implementation must map the value to the nearest element of the double value set. This conversion may result in overflow or underflow.

Within an FP-strict expression, mapping values from the float-extended-exponent value set or double-extended-exponent value set is necessary only when a method is invoked whose declaration is not FP-strict and the implementation has chosen to represent the result of the method invocation as an element of an extended-exponent value set.

Whether in FP-strict code or code that is not FP-strict, value set conversion always leaves unchanged any value whose type is neither **float** nor **double**.

ASSIGNMENT CONVERSION

Assignment conversion occurs when the value of an expression is assigned to a variable: the type of the expression must be converted to the type of the variable. Assignment contexts allow the use of one of the following:

- An identity conversion
- A widening primitive conversion
- A widening reference conversion
- A boxing conversion optionally followed by a widening reference conversion
- An unboxing conversion optionally followed by a widening primitive conversion.

If, after the conversions listed above have been applied, the resulting type is a raw type, unchecked conversion may then be applied. It is a compile time error if the chain of conversions contains two parameterized types that are not not in the subtype relation.

Discussion: An example of such an illegal chain would be:

```
Integer, Comparable<Integer>, Comparable,
        Comparable<String>
```

The first three elements of the chain are related by widening reference conversion, while the last entry is derived from its predecessor by unchecked conversion. However, this dis not a valid assignment conversion, because the chain contains two parameterized types, **Comparable<Integer>** and **Comparable<String>**, that are not subtypes.

In addition, if the expression is a constant expression of type **byte, short, char** or **int**:

- A narrowing primitive conversion may be used if the type of the variable is byte, short, or char, and the value of the constant expression is representable in the type of the variable.
- A narrowing primitive conversion followed by a boxing conversion may be used if the type of the variable is:
  - Byte and the value of the constant expression is representable in the type byte.
  - Short and the value of the constant expression is representable in the type short.
  - Character and the value of the constant expression is representable in the type char.

If the type of the expression cannot be converted to the type of the variable by a conversion permitted in an assignment context, then a compile-time error occurs.

If the type of the variable is **float** or **double**, then value set conversion is applied to the value v that is the results of the type conversion:

- If v is of type float and is an element of the float-extended-exponent value set, then the implementation must map v to the nearest element of the float of the float value set. This conversion may result in overflow or underflow.

- If v is of type double and is an element of the double-extended-exponent value set, then the implementation must map v to the nearest element of the double value set. This conversion may result in overflow or underflow.

If the type of an expression can be converted to the type of a variable by assignment conversion, we say the expression (or its value) is *assignable to* the variable or, equivalently, that the type of the expression is *assignment compatible with* the type of the variable.

If, after the type conversions above have been applied, the resulting value is an object which is not an instance of a subclass or subinterface of the erasure of the type of the variable, then a **ClassCastException** is thrown.

Discussion: This circumstance can only arise as a result of heap pollution. In practice, implementations need only perfom casts when accessing a field or method of an object of parametized type, when the erased type of the field, or the erased result type of the method differ from their unerased type.

The only exceptions that an assignment conversion may cause are:

- An OutOfMemoryError as a result of a boxing conversion.
- A ClassCastException in the special circumstances indicated above.
- A NullPointerException as a result of an unboxing conversion on a null reference.

Note, however, that an assignment may result in an exception in special cases involving array elements or field access. The compile-time narrowing of constants means that code such as:

```
byte theAnswer = 42;
```

is allowed. Without the narrowing, the fact that the integer literal **42** has type **int** would mean that a cast to **byte** would be required:

```
byte theAnswer = (byte)42;// cast is permitted
but not required
```

The following test programme contains examples of assignment conversion of primitive values:

```
class Test {
    public static void main(String[] args) {
        short s = 12;// narrow 12 to short
        float f = s;// widen short to float
        System.out.println("f=" + f);
        char c = '\u0123';
        long l = c;// widen char to long
        System.out.println("l=0x" +
    Long.toString(l,16));
        f = 1.23f;
        double d = f;// widen float to double
    System.out.println("d=" + d);
    }
}
```

It produces the following output:

```
f=12.0
l=0x123
d=1.2300000190734863
```

The following test, however, produces compile-time errors:

```
class Test {
    public static void main(String[] args) {
        short s = 123;
        char c = s;// error: would require
    cast
        s = c;// error: would require cast
    }
}
```

because not all **short** values are **char** values, and neither are all **char** values **short** values.

A value of the null type (the null reference is the only such value) may be assigned to any reference type, resulting in a null reference of that type.

Here is a sample programme illustrating assignments of references:

```
public class Point {int x, y;}
public class Point3D extends Point {int z;}
public interface Colorable {
     void setColor(int colour);
}
public class ColoredPoint extends Point implements
   Colorable
{
     int colour;
     public  void  setColor(int  colour)
   {this.colour = colour;}
}
class Test {
     public static void main(String[] args) {
            // Assignments to variables of class
   type:
            Point p = new Point();
            p  =  new  Point3D();//  ok:  because
   Point3D is a
                        // subclass of Point
     Point3D p3d = p;  // error: will require a
   cast because a
                  // Point might not be a Point3D
                  //  (even  though  it  is,
   dynamically,
                  // in this example.)
// Assignments to variables of type Object:
     Object o = p;// ok: any object to Object
     int[] a = new int[3];
     Object o2 = a;// ok: an array to Object
     // Assignments  to  variables  of  interface
   type:
     ColoredPoint cp = new ColoredPoint();
     Colorable  c  =  cp;//  ok:  ColoredPoint
   implements
                        // Colorable
  // Assignments to variables of array type:
  byte[] b = new byte[4];
```

```
   a = b;// error: these are not arrays
                                          // of the
same primitive type
      Point3D[] p3da = new Point3D[3];
      Point[] pa = p3da;// ok: since we can assign
    a
            // Point3D to a Point
      p3da = pa;// error: (cast needed) since a
    Point
            // can't be assigned to a Point3D
}
}
```

The following test programme illustrates assignment conversions on reference values, but fails to compile, as described in its comments. This example should be compared to the preceding one.

```
public class Point {int x, y;}
public interface Colorable {void setColor(int
    colour);}
public class ColoredPoint extends Point implements
    Colorable
{
      int colour;
      public void setColor(int colour)
    {this.colour = colour;}
}
class Test {
      public static void main(String[] args) {
            Point p = new Point();
            ColoredPoint cp = new ColoredPoint();
            // Okay because ColoredPoint is a
    subclass of Point:
            p = cp;
            // Okay because ColoredPoint
    implements Colorable:
            Colorable c = cp;
            // The following cause compile-time
    errors because
```

```
        // we cannot be sure they will succeed,
    depending on
        // the run-time type of p; a run-time
    check will be
        // necessary for the needed narrowing
    conversion and
        // must be indicated by including a
    cast:
        cp = p;// p might be neither a
    ColoredPoint
        // nor a subclass of ColoredPoint
        c = p;// p might not implement
    Colorable
    }
}
```

Here is another example involving assignment of array objects:

```
class Point {int x, y;}
class ColoredPoint extends Point {int colour;}
class Test {
    public static void main(String[] args) {
        long[] veclong = new long[100];
        Object o = veclong;// okay
        Long l = veclong;// compile-time error
        short[] vecshort = veclong;// compile-
    time error
        Point[] pvec = new Point[100];
        ColoredPoint[] cpvec = new
    ColoredPoint[100];
        pvec = cpvec;// okay
        pvec[0] = new Point();// okay at
    compile time,
                    // but would throw an
                    // exception at run time
        cpvec = pvec;// compile-time error
    }
}
```

In this example:

- The value of veclong cannot be assigned to a Long variable, because Long is a class type other than Object. An array can be assigned only to a variable of a compatible array type, or to a variable of type Object, Cloneable or java.io.Serializable.
- The value of veclong cannot be assigned to vecshort, because they are arrays of primitive type, and short and long are not the same primitive type.
- The value of cpvec can be assigned to pvec, because any reference that could be the value of an expression of type ColoredPoint can be the value of a variable of type Point. The subsequent assignment of the new Point to a component of pvec then would throw an ArrayStoreException (if the programme were otherwise corrected so that it could be compiled), because a ColoredPoint array can't have an instance of Point as the value of a component.
- The value of pvec cannot be assigned to cpvec, because not every reference that could be the value of an expression of type ColoredPoint can correctly be the value of a variable of type Point. If the value of pvec at run time were a reference to an instance of Point[], and the assignment to cpvec were allowed, a simple reference to a component of cpvec, say, cpvec[0], could return a Point, and a Point is not a ColoredPoint. Thus to allow such an assignment would allow a violation of the type system. A cast may be used to ensure that pvec references a ColoredPoint[]:
- cpvec = (ColoredPoint[])pvec;// okay, but may throw an

```
// exception at run time
```

METHOD INVOCATION CONVERSION

Method invocation conversion is applied to each argument value in a method or constructor invocation: the type of the argument expression must be converted to the type of the corresponding parameter.

Method invocation contexts allow the use of one of the following:

- An identity conversion
- A widening primitive conversion
- A widening reference conversion
- A boxing conversion optionally followed by widening reference conversion
- An unboxing conversion optionally followed by a widening primitive conversion.

If, after the conversions listed above have been applied, the resulting type is a raw type, an unchecked conversion may then be applied. It is a compile time error if the chain of conversions contains two parameterized types that are not not in the subtype relation.

If the type of an argument expression is either **float** or **double**, then value set conversion is applied after the type conversion:

- If an argument value of type float is an element of the float-extended-exponent value set, then the implementation must map the value to the nearest element of the float value set. This conversion may result in overflow or underflow.
- If an argument value of type double is an element of the double-extended-exponent value set, then the implementation must map the value to the nearest element of the double value set. This conversion may result in overflow or underflow.

If, after the type conversions above have been applied, the resulting value is an object which is not an instance of a subclass or subinterface of the erasure of the corresponding formal parameter type, then a **ClassCastException** is thrown.

Discussion: This circumstance can only arise as a result of heap pollution. Method invocation conversions specifically do not include the implicit narrowing of integer constants which is part of assignment conversion.

The designers of the Java programming language felt that including these implicit narrowing conversions would add additional complexity to the overloaded method matching resolution process.

Thus, the example:

```
class Test {
    static int m(byte a, int b){return a+b;}
    static int m(short a, short b){return a-
  b;}
    public static void main(String[] args) {
          System.out.println(m(12, 2));//
  compile-time error
    }
}
```

causes a compile-time error because the integer literals **12** and **2** have type **int**, so neither method **m** matches under the rules of.A language that included implicit narrowing of integer constants would need additional rules to resolve cases like this example.

STRING CONVERSION

String conversion applies only to the operands of the binary + operator when one of the arguments is a **String**. In this single special case, the other argument to the + is converted to a **String**, and a new **String** which is the concatenation of the two strings is the result of the +. String conversion is specified in detail within the description of the string concatenation + operator.

CASTING CONVERSION

Casting conversion is applied to the operand of a cast operator: the type of the operand expression must be converted to the type explicitly named by the cast operator. Casting contexts allow the use of:

- An identity conversion
- A widening primitive conversion
- A narrowing primitive conversion
- A widening reference conversion optionally followed by an unchecked conversion
- A narrowing reference conversion optionally followed by an unchecked conversion
- A boxing conversion

- An unboxing conversion.

Thus casting conversions are more inclusive than assignment or method invocation conversions: a cast can do any permitted conversion other than a string conversion or a capture conversion. Value set conversion is applied after the type conversion. Some casts can be proven incorrect at compile time; such casts result in a compile-time error.

A value of a primitive type can be cast to another primitive type by identity conversion, if the types are the same, or by a widening primitive conversion or a narrowing primitive conversion.

A value of a primitive type can be cast to a reference type by boxing conversion. A value of a reference type can be cast to a primitive type by unboxing conversion.

The remaining cases involve conversion of a compile-time reference type *S* (source) to a compile-time reference type *T* (target). A cast from a type *S* to a type *T* is *statically known to be correct* if and only if $S <: T$. A cast from a type *S* to a parameterized type *T* is *unchecked* unless at least one of the following conditions hold:

- $S <: T$.
- All of the type arguments of *T* are unbounded wildcards.
- $T <: S$ and *S* has no subtype $X \neq T$, such that the erasures of *X* and *T* are the same.

A cast to a type variable is always unchecked.

An unchecked cast from *S* to *T* is *completely unchecked* if the cast from $|S|$ to $|T|$ is statically known to be correct. Otherwise it is *partially unchecked*. An unchecked cast causes an unchecked warning to occur (unless it is suppressed using the **SuppressWarnings** annotation).

A cast is a *checked cast* if it is not statically known to be correct and it is not unchecked.

The detailed rules for compile-time legality of a casting conversion of a value of compile-time reference type *S* to a compile-time reference type *T* are as follows:

- If *S* is a class type:
  - If *T* is a class type, then either $|S| <: |T|$, or $|T|$

<: |*S*|; otherwise a compile-time error occurs. Furthermore, if there exists a supertype *X* of *T*, and a supertype *Y* of *S*, such that both *X* and *Y* are provably distinct parameterized types, and that the erasures of *X* and *Y* are the same, a compile-time error occurs.

– If *T* is an interface type:

- If *S* is not a final class, then, if there exists a supertype *X* of *T*, and a supertype *Y* of *S*, such that both *X* and *Y* are provably distinct parameterized types, and that the erasures of *X* and *Y* are the same, a compile-time error occurs. Otherwise, the cast is always legal at compile time (because even if *S* does not implement *T*, a subclass of *S* might).
- If *S* is a final class, then *S* must implement *T*, or a compile-time error occurs.

– If *T* is a type variable, then this algorithm is applied recursively, using the upper bound of *T* in place of *T*.

– If *T* is an array type, then *S* must be the class Object, or a compile-time error occurs.

- If *S* is an interface type:

– If *T* is an array type, then *T* must implement *S*, or a compile-time error occurs.

– If *T* is a type that is not final, then if there exists a supertype *X* of *T*, and a supertype *Y* of *S*, such that both *X* and *Y* are provably distinct parameterized types, and that the erasures of *X* and *Y* are the same, a compile-time error occurs. Otherwise, the cast is always legal at compile time (because even if *T* does not implement *S*, a subclass of *T* might).

– If *T* is a type that is final, then:

- If *S* is not a parameterized type or a raw type, then *T* must implement *S*, and the cast is statically known to be correct, or a compile-time error occurs.
- Otherwise, *S* is either a parameterized type that is an invocation of some generic type declaration *G*, or

a raw type corresponding to a generic type declaration *G*. Then there must exist a supertype *X* of *T*, such that *X* is an invocation of *G*, or a compile-time error occurs. Furthermore, if *S* and *X* are provably distinct parameterized types then a compile-time error occurs.

- If *S* is a type variable, then this algorithm is applied recursively, using the upper bound of *S* in place of *S*.
- If *S* is an array type *SC*[], that is, an array of components of type *SC*:
  - If *T* is a class type, then if *T* is not Object, then a compile-time error occurs (because Object is the only class type to which arrays can be assigned).
  - If *T* is an interface type, then a compile-time error occurs unless *T* is the type java.io. Serializable or the type Cloneable, the only interfaces implemented by arrays.
  - If *T* is a type variable, then:
- If the upper bound of *T* is Object or the type java.io.Serializable or the type Cloneable, or a type variable that *S* could legally be cast to by recursively applying these rules, then the cast is legal (though unchecked).
- If the upper bound of *T* is an array type *TC[]*, then a compile-time error occurs unless the type *SC[]* can be cast to *TC[]* by a recursive application of these compile-time rules for casting.
- Otherwise, a compile-time error occurs.
  - If *T* is an array type *TC*[], that is, an array of components of type *TC*, then a compile-time error occurs unless one of the following is true:
- *TC* and *SC* are the same primitive type.
- *TC* and *SC* are reference types and type *SC* can be cast to *TC* by a recursive application of these compile-time rules for casting.

If a cast to a reference type is not a compile-time error, there are several cases:

- The cast is statically known to be correct. No run time action is performed for such a cast.
- The cast is a completely unchecked cast. No run time action is performed for such a cast.
- The cast is a partially unchecked cast. Such a cast requires a run-time validity check. The check is performed as if the cast had been a checked cast between |*S*| and |*T*|, as described below.
- The cast is a checked cast. Such a cast requires a run-time validity check. If the value at run time is null, then the cast is allowed. Otherwise, let *R* be the class of the object referred to by the run-time reference value, and let *T* be the erasure of the type named in the cast operator. A cast conversion must check, at run time, that the class *R* is assignment compatible with the type *T*. (Note that *R* cannot be an interface when these rules are first applied for any given cast, but *R* may be an interface if the rules are applied recursively because the run-time reference value may refer to an array whose element type is an interface type.) The algorithm for performing the check is shown here:

– If *R* is an ordinary class (not an array class):

- If *T* is a class type, then *R* must be either the same class as *T* or a subclass of *T*, or a run-time exception is thrown.
- If *T* is an interface type, then *R* must implement interface *T*, or a run-time exception is thrown.
- If *T* is an array type, then a run-time exception is thrown.

– If *R* is an interface:

- If *T* is a class type, then *T* must be Object, or a run-time exception is thrown.
- If *T* is an interface type, then *R* must be either the same interface as *T* or a subinterface of *T*, or a run-time exception is thrown.
- If *T* is an array type, then a run-time exception is thrown.

– If *R* is a class representing an array type *RC*[]- that is, an array of components of type *RC*:

- If *T* is a class type, then *T* must be Object, or a run-time exception is thrown.
- If *T* is an interface type, then a run-time exception is thrown unless *T* is the type java.io.Serializable or the type Cloneable, the only interfaces implemented by arrays (this case could slip past the compile-time checking if, for example, a reference to an array were stored in a variable of type Object).
- If *T* is an array type *TC*[], that is, an array of components of type *TC*, then a run-time exception is thrown unless one of the following is true:
- *TC* and *RC* are the same primitive type.
- *TC* and *RC* are reference types and type *RC* can be cast to *TC* by a recursive application of these run-time rules for casting.

If a run-time exception is thrown, it is a **ClassCast Exception**

Here are some examples of casting conversions of reference types, similar to the example in:

```
public class Point {int x, y;}
public interface Colorable {void setColor(int
   colour);}
public class ColoredPoint extends Point implements
   Colorable
{
     int colour;
     public void setColor(int colour)
   {this.colour = colour;}
}
final class EndPoint extends Point {}
class Test {
     public static void main(String[] args) {
          Point p = new Point();
          ColoredPoint cp = new ColoredPoint();
          Colorable c;
          // The following may cause errors at
```

```
run time because
        // we cannot be sure they will succeed;
this possibility
        // is suggested by the casts:
        cp = (ColoredPoint)p;// p might not
reference an
              // object which is a
ColoredPoint
              // or a subclass of ColoredPoint
        c = (Colorable)p;// p might not be
Colorable
        // The following are incorrect at
compile time because
        // they can never succeed as explained
in the text:
        Long l = (Long)p;// compile-time error
#1
        EndPoint e = new EndPoint();
        c = (Colorable)e;// compile-time error
#2
  }
}
```

Here the first compile-time error occurs because the class types **Long** and **Point** are unrelated (that is, they are not the same, and neither is a subclass of the other), so a cast between them will always fail.

The second compile-time error occurs because a variable of type **EndPoint** can never reference a value that implements the interface **Colorable**. This is because **EndPoint** is a **final** type, and a variable of a **final** type always holds a value of the same run-time type as its compile-time type. Therefore, the run-time type of variable **e** must be exactly the type **EndPoint**, and type **EndPoint** does not implement **Colorable**.

Here is an example involving arrays:

```
class Point {
  int x, y;
  Point(int x, int y) {this.x = x; this.y = y;}
  public String toString() {return
```

```
    "("+x+","+y+")";}
}
public interface Colorable {void setColor(int
    colour);}
public class ColoredPoint extends Point implements
    Colorable
{
    int colour;
    ColoredPoint(int x, int y, int colour) {
        super(x, y); setColor(colour);
    }
    public void setColor(int colour)
    {this.colour = colour;}
    public String toString() {
        return super.toString() + "@" +
    colour;
    }
}
class Test {
    public static void main(String[] args) {
        Point[] pa = new ColoredPoint[4];
        pa[0] = new ColoredPoint(2, 2, 12);
        pa[1] = new ColoredPoint(4, 5, 24);
        ColoredPoint[] cpa =
    (ColoredPoint[])pa;
        System.out.print("cpa: {");
        for (int i = 0; i < cpa.length; i++)
            System.out.print((i == 0 ? " ":
    ", ") + cpa[i]);
        System.out.println("}");
    }
}
```

This example compiles without errors and produces the output:

```
cpa: {(2,2)@12, (4,5)@24, null, null}
```

The following example uses casts to compile, but it throws exceptions at run time, because the types are incompatible:

```
public class Point {int x, y;}
public interface Colorable {void setColor(int
```

```
  colour);}
public class ColoredPoint extends Point implements
  Colorable
{
     int colour;
     public void setColor(int colour)
  {this.colour = colour;}
}
class Test {
     public static void main(String[] args) {
          Point[] pa = new Point[100];
          // The following line will throw a
  ClassCastException:
          ColoredPoint[] cpa =
  (ColoredPoint[])pa;
          System.out.println(cpa[0]);
          int[] shortvec = new int[2];
          Object o = shortvec;
          // The following line will throw a
  ClassCastException:
          Colorable c = (Colorable)o;
          c.setColor(0);
     }
}
```

NUMERIC PROMOTIONS

Numeric promotion is applied to the operands of an arithmetic operator. Numeric promotion contexts allow the use of an identity conversion a widening primitive conversion, or an unboxing conversion. Numeric promotions are used to convert the operands of a numeric operator to a common type so that an operation can be performed. The two kinds of numeric promotion are unary numeric promotion and binary numeric promotion.

UNARY NUMERIC PROMOTION

Some operators apply *unary numeric promotion* to a single operand, which must produce a value of a numeric type:

- If the operand is of compile-time type Byte, Short, Character, or Integer it is subjected to unboxing conversion. The result is then promoted to a value of type int by a widening conversion (§5.1.2) or an identity conversion.
- Otherwise, if the operand is of compile-time type Long, Float, or Double it is subjected to unboxing conversion.
- Otherwise, if the operand is of compile-time type byte, short, or char, unary numeric promotion promotes it to a value of type int by a widening conversion.
- Otherwise, a unary numeric operand remains as is and is not converted.

In any case, value set conversion is then applied.

Unary numeric promotion is performed on expressions in the following situations:

- Each dimension expression in an array creation expression
- The index expression in an array access expression
- The operand of a unary plus operator +
- The operand of a unary minus operator -
- The operand of a bitwise complement operator ~
- Each operand, separately, of a shift operator >>, >>>, or <<; therefore a long shift distance (right operand) does not promote the value being shifted (left operand) to long

Here is a test programme that includes examples of unary numeric promotion:

```
class Test {
   public static void main(String[] args) {
         byte b = 2; int a[] = new int[b];//
  dimension expression promotion
         char c = '\u0001';
         a[c] = 1;// index expression promotion
         a[0] = -c;// unary - promotion
         System.out.println("a: " + a[0] + ","
  + a[1]);
```

```
        b = -1;
        int i = ~b;// bitwise complement
promotion
        System.out.println("~0x" +
Integer.toHexString(b)
        + "==0x" + Integer.toHexString(i));
        i = b << 4L;// shift promotion (left
operand)
        System.out.println("0x" +
Integer.toHexString(b)
        +              "<<4L==0x"             +
Integer.toHexString(i));
    }
}
```

This test programme produces the output:

```
a: -1,1
~0xffffffff==0x0
0xffffffff<<4L==0xfffffff0
```

BINARY NUMERIC PROMOTION

When an operator applies *binary numeric promotion* to a pair of operands, each of which must denote a value that is convertible to a numeric type, the following rules apply, in order, using widening conversion to convert operands as necessary:

- If any of the operands is of a reference type, unboxing conversion is performed.
  Then:
- If either operand is of type double, the other is converted to double.
- Otherwise, if either operand is of type float, the other is converted to float.
- Otherwise, if either operand is of type long, the other is converted to long.
- Otherwise, both operands are converted to type int.

After the type conversion, if any, value set conversion is applied to each operand. Binary numeric promotion is performed on the operands of certain operators:

- The multiplicative operators *,/ and %
- The addition and subtraction operators for numeric types + and -
- The numerical comparison operators <, <=, >, and >=
- The numerical equality operators == and !=
- The integer bitwise operators &, ^, and |
- In certain cases, the conditional operator ?:

An example of binary numeric promotion appears above in. *Here is another*:

```
class Test {
    public static void main(String[] args) {
        int i = 0;
        float f = 1.0f;
        double d = 2.0;
        // First int*float is promoted to
  float*float, then
        // float==double is promoted to
  double==double:
        if (i * f == d)
            System.out.println("oops");
// A char&byte is promoted to int&int:
        byte b = 0x1f;
        char c = 'G';
        int control = c & b;
    System.out.println(Integer.to
  HexString(control));
    // Here int:float is promoted to float:float:
        f = (b==0) ? i: 4.0f;
        System.out.println(1.0/f);
    }
}
```

which produces the output:

```
7
  0.25
```

The example converts the ASCII character G to the ASCII control-G (BEL), by masking off all but the low 5 bits of the character. The 7 is the numeric value of this control character.

Chapter 3

Names and Packages

ENTITIES

Names are used to refer to entities declared in a programme. A declared entity is a package, class type (normal or enum), interface type (normal or annotation type), member (class, interface, field, or method) of a reference type, type parameter (of a class, interface, method or constructor), parameter (to a method, constructor, o'r exception handler), or local variable.

Names in programmes are either simple, consisting of a single identifier, or qualified, consisting of a sequence of identifiers separated by "." tokens.

Every declaration that introduces a name has a *scope*, which is the part of the programme text within which the declared entity can be referred to by a simple name.

Packages and reference types (that is, class types, interface types, and array types) have members. A member can be referred to using a qualified name *N.x*, where *N* is a simple or qualified name and *x* is an identifier. If *N* names a package, then *x* is a member of that package, which is either a class or interface type or a subpackage. If *N* names a reference type or a variable of a reference type, then *x* names a member of that type, which is either a class, an interface, a field, or a method.

In determining the meaning of a name, the context of the occurrence is used to disambiguate among packages, types, variables, and methods with the same name.

Access control can be specified in a class, interface, method, or field declaration to control when *access* to a member is allowed. Access is a different concept from scope; access specifies the part of the programme text within which the declared entity can be referred to by a qualified name, a field access expression, or a method invocation expression in which the method is not specified by a simple name. The default access is that a member can be accessed anywhere within the package that contains its declaration; other possibilities are **public**, **protected**, and **private.**

Fully qualified and canonical names and naming conventions.

The name of a field, parameter, or local variable may be used as an expression.The name of a method may appear in an expression only as part of a method invocation expression. The name of a class or interface type may appear in an expression only as part of a class literal, a qualified this expression, a class instance creation expression, an array creation expression, a cast expression, an **instanceof** expression, an enum constant, or as part of a qualified name for a field or method. The name of a package may appear in an expression only as part of a qualified name for a class or interface type.

DECLARATIONS

A *declaration* introduces an entity into a programme and includes an identifier that can be used in a name to refer to this entity.

A declared entity is one of the following:

- A package, declared in a package declaration
- An imported type, declared in a single-type-import declaration or a type-import-on-demand declaration
- A class, declared in a class type declaration
- An interface, declared in an interface type declaration
- A type variable, declared as a formal type parameter of a generic class, interface, method or constructor.
- A member of a reference type one of the following:
  - A member class.
  - A member interface.
  - an enum constant.

– A field, one of the following:

- A field declared in a class type
- A constant field declared in an interface type
- The field length, which is implicitly a member of every array type
  – A method, one of the following:
- A method (abstract or otherwise) declared in a class type
- A method (always abstract) declared in an interface type
- A parameter, one of the following:
  – A parameter of a method or constructor of a class
  – A parameter of an abstract method of an interface
  – A parameter of an exception handler declared in a catch clause of a try statement
- A local variable, one of the following:
  – A local variable declared in a block
  – A local variable declared in a for statement

Constructors are also introduced by declarations, but use the name of the class in which they are declared rather than introducing a new name.

NAMES AND IDENTIFIERS

A *name* is used to refer to an entity declared in a programme. There are two forms of names: simple names and qualified names. A *simple name* is a single identifier. A *qualified name* consists of a name, a "." token, and an identifier.

In determining the meaning of a name, the context in which the name appears is taken into account. The rules of distinguish among contexts where a name must denote (refer to) a package, a type, a variable or value in an expression, or a method. Not all identifiers in programmes are a part of a name.

Identifiers are also used in the following situations:

- In declarations, where an identifier may occur to specify the name by which the declared entity will be known
- In field access expressions, where an identifier occurs

after a "." token to indicate a member of an object that is the value of an expression or the keyword super that appears before the "." token

- In some method invocation expressions, where an identifier may occur after a "." token and before a "(" token to indicate a method to be invoked for an object that is the value of an expression or the keyword super that appears before the "." token
- In qualified class instance creation expressions, where an identifier occurs immediately to the right of the leftmost new token to indicate a type that must be a member of the compile-time type of the primary expression preceding the "." preceding the leftmost new token.
- As labels in labeled statements and in break and continue statements that refer to statement labels.

In the example:

```
class Test {
     public static void main(String[] args) {
           Class c = System.out.getClass();
     System.out.println(c.toString().length() +
                 args[0].length()          +
    args.length);
     }
}
```

the identifiers **Test**, **main**, and the first occurrences of **args** and **c** are not names; rather, they are used in declarations to specify the names of the declared entities. The names **String**, **Class**, **System.out.getClass**, **System.out.println**, **c.toString**, **args**, and **args.length** appear in the example. The first occurrence of **length** is not a name, but rather an identifier appearing in a method invocation expression. The second occurrence of **length** is not a name, but rather an identifier appearing in a method invocation expression.

The identifiers used in labeled statements and their associated **break** and **continue** statements are completely separate from those used in declarations. Thus, the following code is valid:

```
class TestString {
    char[] value;
    int offset, count;
    int indexOf(TestString str, int fromIndex)
  {
        char[] v1 = value, v2 = str.value;
        int max = offset + (count - str.count);
        int start = offset + ((fromIndex < 0)
  ? 0: fromIndex);
    i:
        for (int i = start; i <= max; i++)
        {
        int  n  =  str.count,  j  =  i,  k  =
  str.offset;
        while (n– != 0) {
        if (v1[j++] != v2[k++])
                            continue i;
                }
                return i - offset;
        }
        return -1;
    }
}
```

This code was taken from a version of the class String and its method indexOf, where the label was originally called test. Changing the label to have the same name as the local variable i does not obscure the label in the scope of the declaration of i. The identifier max could also have been used as the statement label; the label would not obscure the local variable max within the labeled statement.

SCOPE OF DECLARATION

The *scope* of a declaration is the region of the programme within which the entity declared by the declaration can be referred to using a simple name (provided it is visible). A declaration is said to be *in scope* at a particular point in a programme if and only if the declaration's scope includes that point.

The scoping rules for various constructs are given in the sections that describe those constructs. For convenience, the rules are repeated here:

The scope of the declaration of an observable top level package is all observable compilation units. The declaration of a package that is not observable is never in scope. Subpackage declarations are never in scope.

The scope of a type imported by a single-type-import declaration or a type-import-on-demand declaration is all the class and interface type declarations in the compilation unit in which the import declaration appears. The scope of a member imported by a single-static-import declaration or a static-import-on-demand declaration is all the class and interface type declarations in the compilation unit in which the import declaration appears.

The scope of a top level type is all type declarations in the package in which the top level type is declared. The scope of a declaration of a member *m* declared in or inherited by a class type *C* is the entire body of *C*, including any nested type declarations. The scope of the declaration of a member *m* declared in or inherited by an interface type *I* is the entire body of *I*, including any nested type declarations. The scope of a parameter of a method or constructor is the entire body of the method or constructor.

The scope of an interface's type parameter is the entire declaration of the interface including the type parameter section itself. Therefore, type parameters can appear as parts of their own bounds, or as bounds of other type parameters declared in the same section. The scope of a method's type parameter is the entire declaration of the method, including the type parameter section itself. Therefore, type parameters can appear as parts of their own bounds, or as bounds of other type parameters declared in the same section.

The scope of a constructor's type parameter is the entire declaration of the constructor, including the type parameter section itself. Therefore, type parameters can appear as parts of their own bounds, or as bounds of other type parameters declared in the same section.

The scope of a local variable declaration in a block is the rest of the block in which the declaration appears, starting with its own initializer and including any further declarators to the right in the local variable declaration statement.

The scope of a local class immediately enclosed by a block is the rest of the immediately enclosing block, including its own class declaration.

The scope of a local class immediately enclosed by in a switch block statement group is the rest of the immediately enclosing switch block statement group, including its own class declaration.

The scope of a local variable declared in the *forInit* part of a basic **for** statement includes all of the following:

- Its own initializer
- Any further declarators to the right in the *ForInit* part of the for statement
- The *Expression* and *ForUpdate* parts of the for statement
- The contained *Statement*

The scope of a local variable declared in the *FormalParameter* part of an enhanced **for** statement is the contained *Statement*. The scope of a parameter of an exception handler that is declared in a **catch** clause of a **try** statement is the entire block associated with the **catch**.

These rules imply that declarations of class and interface types need not appear before uses of the types.

```
In the example:
package points;
class Point {
int x, y;
PointList list;
Point next;
}
class PointList {
Point first;
}
```

the use of **PointList** in class **Point** is correct, because the scope of the class declaration **PointList** includes both class **Point** and class **PointList**, as well as any other type declarations in other compilation units of package **points**.

SHADOWING DECLARATIONS

Some declarations may be *shadowed* in part of their scope by another declaration of the same name, in which case a simple name cannot be used to refer to the declared entity.

A declaration *d* of a type named *n* shadows the declarations of any other types named *n* that are in scope at the point where *d* occurs throughout the scope of *d*.

A declaration *d* of a field, local variable, method parameter, constructor parameter or exception handler parameter named *n* shadows the declarations of any other fields, local variables, method parameters, constructor parameters or exception handler parameters named *n* that are in scope at the point where *d* occurs throughout the scope of *d*. A declaration *d* of a method named *n* shadows the declarations of any other methods named *n* that are in an enclosing scope at the point where *d* occurs throughout the scope of *d*.

A package declaration never shadows any other declaration. A single-type-import declaration *d* in a compilation unit *c* of package *p* that imports a type named *n* shadows the declarations of:

- Any top level type named *n* declared in another compilation unit of *p*.
- Any type named *n* imported by a type-import-on-demand declaration in *c*.
- Any type named *n* imported by a static-import-on-demand declaration in *c*.

`throughout c.`

A single-static-import declaration *d* in a compilation unit *c* of package *p* that imports a field named *n* shadows the declaration of any static field named *n* imported by a static-import-on-demand declaration in *c*, throughout *c*.

A single-static-import declaration *d* in a compilation unit *c* of package *p* that imports a method named *n* with signature s shadows the declaration of any static method named *n* with signature *s* imported by a static-import-on-demand declaration in *c*, throughout *c*.

A single-static-import declaration *d* in a compilation unit *c* of package *p* that imports a type named *n* shadows the declarations of:

- Any static type named *n* imported by a static-import-on-demand declaration in *c*.
- Any top level type named *n* declared in another compilation unit of *p*.
- Any type named *n* imported by a type-import-on-demand declaration in *c*.

throughout *c*.

A type-import-on-demand declaration never causes any other declaration to be shadowed. A static-import-on-demand declaration never causes any other declaration to be shadowed.

A declaration *d* is said to be *visible at point p in a programme* if the scope of *d* includes *p*, and *d* is not shadowed by any other declaration at *p*. When the programme point we are discussing is clear from context, we will often simply say that a declaration is *visible*.

Note that shadowing is distinct from hiding. Hiding, in the technical sense defined in this specification, applies only to members which would otherwise be inherited but are not because of a declaration in a subclass. Shadowing is also distinct from obscuring. Here is an example of shadowing of a field declaration by a local variable declaration:

```
class Test {
      static int x = 1;
      public static void main(String[] args) {
            int x = 0;
            System.out.print("x=" + x);
            System.out.println(", Test.x=" +
    Test.x);
      }
}
```

produces the output:

```
x=0, Test.x=1
```

This example declares:

- A class Test
- A class (static) variable x that is a member of the class Test
- A class method main that is a member of the class Test
- A parameter args of the main method.
- A local variable x of the main method

Since the scope of a class variable includes the entire body of the class the class variable **x** would normally be available throughout the entire body of the method **main**. In this example, however, the class variable **x** is shadowed within the body of the method **main** by the declaration of the local variable **x**. A local variable has as its scope the rest of the block in which it is declared; in this case this is the rest of the body of the **main** method, namely its initializer **"0"** and the invocations of **print and println**.

This means that:

- The expression "x" in the invocation of print refers to (denotes) the value of the local variable x.
- The invocation of println uses a qualified name Test.x, which uses the class type name Test to access the class variable x, because the declaration of Test.x is shadowed at this point and cannot be referred to by its simple name.

The following example illustrates the shadowing of one type declaration by another:

```
import java.util.*;
class Vector {
     int val[] = {1, 2};
}
class Test {
     public static void main(String[] args) {
           Vector v = new Vector();
           System.out.println(v.val[0]);
     }
}
compiles and prints:
1
```

using the class **Vector** declared here in preference to the generic class **java.util.Vector** that might be imported on demand.

OBSCURED DECLARATIONS

A simple name may occur in contexts where it may potentially be interpreted as the name of a variable, a type or a package. In these situations, the rules of specify that a variable will be chosen in preference to a type, and that a type will be chosen in preference to a package. Thus, it is may sometimes be impossible to refer to a visible type or package declaration via its simple name. We say that such a declaration is *obscured*. Obscuring is distinct from shadowing and hiding. The naming conventions of help reduce obscuring.

MEMBERS AND INHERITANCE

Packages and reference types have *members*.

This section provides an overview of the members of packages and reference types here, as background for the discussion of qualified names and the determination of the meaning of names. For a complete description of membership.

TYPE VARIABLES, PARAMETERIZED TYPES, RAW TYPES AND INTERSECTION TYPES

The members of a type variable were specified in, the members of a parameterized type in, those of a raw type in, and the members of an intersection type were specified in.

THE MEMBERS OF A PACKAGE

The members of a package are specified in. For convenience, we repeat that specification here:

The members of a package are its subpackages and all the top level class types and top level interface types declared in all the compilation units of the package.

In general, the subpackages of a package are determined by the host system. However, the package **java** always includes the subpackages **lang** and **io** and may include other subpackages. No two distinct members of the same package may have the same simple name, but members of different packages may have the same simple name.

For example, it is possible to declare a package:

```
package vector;
public class Vector {Object[] vec;}
```

that has as a member a **public** class named **Vector**, even though the package **java.util** also declares a class named **Vector**. These two class types are different, reflected by the fact that they have different fully qualified names.The fully qualified name of this example **Vector** is **vector.Vector,** whereas **java.util.Vector** is the fully qualified name of the **Vector** class usually included in the Java platform. Because the package **vector** contains a class named **Vector**, it cannot also have a subpackage named **Vector**.

MEMBERS OF A CLASS TYPE

The members of a class type are classes, interfaces, fields, and methods. Members are either declared in the type, or *inherited* because they are accessible members of a superclass or superinterface which are neither private nor hidden nor overridden.

The members of a class type are all of the following:

- Members inherited from its direct superclass, if it has one (the class Object has no direct superclass)
- Members inherited from any direct superinterfaces
- Members declared in the body of the class

Constructors and type variables are not members.

There is no restriction against a field and a method of a class type having the same simple name. Likewise, there is no restriction against a member class or member interface of a class type having the same simple name as a field or method of that class type.

A class may have two or more fields with the same simple name if they are declared in different interfaces and inherited. An attempt to refer to any of the fields by its simple name results in a compile-time error.

In the example:

```
interface Colors {
```

```
    int WHITE = 0, BLACK = 1;
}
interface Separates {
    int CYAN = 0, MAGENTA = 1, YELLOW = 2, BLACK
  = 3;
}
class Test implements Colors, Separates {
    public static void main(String[] args) {
            System.out.println(BLACK);// compile-
  time error: ambiguous
    }
}
```

the name **BLACK** in the method **main** is ambiguous, because class **Test** has two members named **BLACK**, one inherited from **Colors** and one from **Separates.**

A class type may have two or more methods with the same simple name if the methods have signatures that are not override-equivalent.Such a method member name is said to be *overloaded*. A class type may contain a declaration for a method with the same name and the same signature as a method that would otherwise be inherited from a superclass or superinterface. In this case, the method of the superclass or superinterface is not inherited. If the method not inherited is **abstract**, then the new declaration is said to *implement* it; if the method not inherited is not **abstract**, then the new declaration is said to *override* it.

In the example:

```
class Point {
    float x, y;
    void move(int dx, int dy) {x += dx; y +=
  dy;}
    void move(float dx, float dy) {x += dx; y
  += dy;}
    public String toString() {return
  "("+x+","+y+")";}
}
```

the class **Point** has two members that are methods with the same name, **move**. The overloaded **move** method of class **Point** chosen for any particular method invocation is determined at compile time by the overloading resolution procedure given in.

In this example, the members of the class **Point** are the **float** instance variables **x** and **y** declared in **Point**, the two declared **move** methods, the declared **toString** method, and the members that **Point** inherits from its implicit direct superclass **Object**, such as the method **hashCode**. Note that **Point** does not inherit the **toString** method of class **Object** because that method is overridden by the declaration of the **toString** method in class **Point**.

MEMBERS OF AN INTERFACE TYPE

The members of an interface type may be classes, interfaces, fields, and methods.

The members of an interface are:

- Those members declared in the interface.
- Those members inherited from direct superinterfaces.
- If an interface has no direct superinterfaces, then the interface implicitly declares a public abstract member method *m* with signature *s*, return type *r*, and throws clause *t* corresponding to each public instance method *m* with signature *s*, return type *r*, and throws clause *t* declared in Object, unless a method with the same signature, same return type, and a compatible throws clause is explicitly declared by the interface. It is a compile-time error if the interface explicitly declares such a method *m* in the case where *m* is declared to be final in Object.

Type variables are not members.

An interface may have two or more fields with the same simple name if they are declared in different interfaces and inherited. An attempt to refer to any such field by its simple name results in a compile-time error.

In the example:

```
interface Colors {
   int WHITE = 0, BLACK = 1;
}
```

```
interface Separates {
    int CYAN = 0, MAGENTA = 1, YELLOW = 2, BLACK
  = 3;
}
interface ColorsAndSeparates extends Colors,
  Separates {
        int DEFAULT = BLACK;// compile-time
  error: ambiguous
}
```

the members of the interface **ColorsAndSeparates** include those members inherited from **Colors** and those inherited from **Separates**, namely **WHITE, BLACK** (first of two), **CYAN, MAGENTA, YELLOW**, and **BLACK** (second of two). The member name **BLACK** is ambiguous in the interface **ColorsAndSeparates.**

MEMBERS OF AN ARRAY TYPE

The members of an array type are specified in. For convenience, we repeat that specification here.

The members of an array type are all of the following:

- The public final field length, which contains the number of components of the array (length may be positive or zero).
- The public method clone, which overrides the method of the same name in class Object and throws no checked exceptions. The return type of the clone method of an array type *T[]* is *T[]*.
- All the members inherited from class Object; the only method of Object that is not inherited is its clone method.

The example:

```
class Test {
    public static void main(String[] args) {
        int[] ia = new int[3];
        int[] ib = new int[6];
        System.out.println(ia.getClass() ==
  ib.getClass());
        System.out.println("ia has length="
```

```
    + ia.length);
    }
}
```

```
produces the output:
true
ia has length=3
```

This example uses the method **getClass** inherited from class **Object** and the field **length**. The result of the comparison of the **Class** objects in the first **println** demonstrates that all arrays whose components are of type **int** are instances of the same array type, which is **int[]**.

DEFINITION OF NAME

The meaning of a name depends on the context in which it is used. The determination of the meaning of a name requires three steps. First, context causes a name syntactically to fall into one of six categories: *PackageName, TypeName, ExpressionName, MethodName, PackageOrTypeName,* or *AmbiguousName.* Second, a name that is initially classified by its context as an *AmbiguousName* or as a *PackageOrTypeName* is then reclassified to be a *PackageName, TypeName,* or *ExpressionName.* Third, the resulting category then dictates the final determination of the meaning of the name (or a compilation error if the name has no meaning).

```
PackageName:
    Identifier
    PackageName. Identifier
TypeName:
    Identifier
    PackageOrTypeName. Identifier
ExpressionName:
    Identifier
    AmbiguousName. Identifier
MethodName:
    Identifier
    AmbiguousName. Identifier
PackageOrTypeName:
    Identifier
```

```
    PackageOrTypeName. Identifier
AmbiguousName:
    Identifier
    AmbiguousName. Identifier
```

The use of context helps to minimize name conflicts between entities of different kinds. Such conflicts will be rare if the naming conventions described in are followed. Nevertheless, conflicts may arise unintentionally as types developed by different programmers or different organizations evolve. For example, types, methods, and fields may have the same name. It is always possible to distinguish between a method and a field with the same name, since the context of a use always tells whether a method is intended.

CLASSIFICATION OF A NAME ACCORDING TO CONTEXT

A name is syntactically classified as a PackageName in these contexts:

- In a package declaration
- To the left of the "." in a qualified *PackageName*

A name is syntactically classified as a TypeName in these contexts:

- In a single-type-import declaration
- To the left of the "." in a single static import declaration
- To the left of the "." in a static import-on-demand declaration
- To the left of the "<" in a parameterized type
- In an actual type argument list of a parameterized type
- In an explicit actual type argument list in a generic method or constructor invocation
- In an extends clause in a type variable declaration
- In an extends clause of a wildcard type argument
- In a super clause of a wildcard type argument
- In an extends clause in a class declaration
- In an implements clause in a class declaration
- In an extends clause in an interface declaration

- After the "@" sign in an annotation
- As a *Type* (or the part of a *Type* that remains after all brackets are deleted) in any of the following contexts:
  - In a field declaration
  - As the result type of a method
  - As the type of a formal parameter of a method or constructor
  - As the type of an exception that can be thrown by a method or constructor
  - As the type of a local variable
  - As the type of an exception parameter in a catch clause of a try statement
  - As the type in a class literal
  - As the qualifying type of a qualified this expression.
  - As the class type which is to be instantiated in an unqualified class instance creation expression
  - As the direct superclass or direct superinterface of an anonymous class which is to be instantiated in an unqualified class instance creation expression
  - As the element type of an array to be created in an array creation expression
  - As the qualifying type of field access using the keyword super
  - As the qualifying type of a method invocation using the keyword super
  - As the type mentioned in the cast operator of a cast expression
  - As the type that follows the instanceof relational operator

A name is syntactically classified as an *ExpressionName* in these contexts:

- As the qualifying expression in a qualified superclass constructor invocation
- As the qualifying expression in a qualified class instance creation expression
- As the array reference expression in an array access

expression

- As a *PostfixExpression*
- As the left-hand operand of an assignment operator

A name is syntactically classified as a MethodName in these contexts:

- Before the "(" in a method invocation expression
- To the left of the "=" sign in an annotation's element value pair

A name is syntactically classified as a *PackageOrTypeName* in these contexts:

- To the left of the "." in a qualified TypeName
- In a type-import-on-demand declaration

A name is syntactically classified as an *AmbiguousName* in these contexts:

- To the left of the "." in a qualified *ExpressionName*
- To the left of the "." in a qualified *MethodName*
- To the left of the "." in a qualified *AmbiguousName*
- In the default value clause of an annotation type element declaration
- To the right of an "=" in an an element value pair

CONTEXTUALLY AMBIGUOUS NAMES

An AmbiguousName is then reclassified as follows:

- If the *AmbiguousName* is a simple name, consisting of a single *Identifier*:
  - If the *Identifier* appears within the scope of a local variable declaration or parameter declaration or field declaration with that name, then the *AmbiguousName* is reclassified as an *ExpressionName.*
  - Otherwise, if a field of that name is declared in the compilation unit containing the *Identifier* by a single-static-import declaration, or by a static-import-on-demand declaration then the *AmbiguousName* is reclassified as an *ExpressionName.*
  - Otherwise, if the *Identifier* appears within the scope of a top level class or interface type

declaration, a local class declaration or member type declaration with that name, then the *AmbiguousName* is reclassified as a *TypeName*.

- Otherwise, if a type of that name is declared in the compilation unit containing the *Identifier*, either by a single-type-import declaration, or by a type-import-on-demand declaration, or by a single-static-import declaration, or by a static-import-on-demand declaration, then the *AmbiguousName* is reclassified as a *TypeName*.
- Otherwise, the *AmbiguousName* is reclassified as a *PackageName*. A later step determines whether or not a package of that name actually exists.

• If the *AmbiguousName* is a qualified name, consisting of a name, a ".", and an *Identifier*, then the name to the left of the "." is first reclassified, for it is itself an *AmbiguousName*.

There is then a choice:

- If the name to the left of the "." is reclassified as a *PackageName*, then if there is a package whose name is the name to the left of the "." and that package contains a declaration of a type whose name is the same as the *Identifier*, then this *AmbiguousName* is reclassified as a *TypeName*. Otherwise, this *AmbiguousName* is reclassified as a *PackageName*. A later step determines whether or not a package of that name actually exists.
- If the name to the left of the "." is reclassified as a *TypeName*, then if the *Identifier* is the name of a method or field of the type denoted by TypeName, this *AmbiguousName* is reclassified as an *ExpressionName*. Otherwise, if the Identifier is the name of a member type of the type denoted by TypeName, this AmbiguousName is reclassified as a TypeName. Otherwise, a compile-time error results.
- If the name to the left of the "." is reclassified as an *ExpressionName*, then let T be the type of the

expression denoted by ExpressionName. If the Identifier is the name of a method or field of the type denoted by T, this *AmbiguousName* is reclassified as an *ExpressionName.* Otherwise, if the Identifier is the name of a member type of the type denoted by T, then this Ambiguous Name is reclassified as a TypeName. Otherwise, a compile-time error results.

As an example, consider the following contrived "library code":

```
package org.rpgpoet;
import java.util.Random;
interface Music {Random[] wizards = new
Random[4];}
```

and then consider this example code in another package:

```
package bazola;
class Gabriel {
static int n = org.rpgpoet.Music.
wizards.length;
}
```

First of all, the name org.rpgpoet.Music.wizards.length is classified as an *ExpressionName* because it functions as a *PostfixExpression.* Therefore, each of the names:

```
org.rpgpoet.Music.wizards
org.rpgpoet.Music
org.rpgpoet
org
```

is initially classified as an *AmbiguousName.* These are then reclassified:

- The simple name org is reclassified as a *PackageName* (since there is no variable or type named org in scope).
- Next, assuming that there is no class or interface named rpgpoet in any compilation unit of package org (and we know that there is no such class or interface because package org has a subpackage named rpgpoet), the qualified name org.rpgpoet is reclassified as a *PackageName.*
- Next, because package org.rpgpoet has an interface

type named Music, the qualified name org.rpgpoet. Music is reclassified as a *TypeName.*

- Finally, because the name org.rpgpoet.Music is a *TypeName,* the qualified name org.rpgpoet.Music. wizards is reclassified as an *ExpressionName.*

PACKAGE NAMES

The meaning of a name classified as a *ΓackageName* is determined as follows.

SIMPLE PACKAGE NAMES

If a package name consists of a single *Identifier,* then this identifier denotes a top level package named by that identifier. If no top level package of that name is in scope, then a compile-time error occurs.

QUALIFIED PACKAGE NAMES

If a package name is of the form *Q.Id,* then *Q* must also be a package name. The package name *Q.Id* names a package that is the member named *Id* within the package named by *Q*. If *Q* does not name an observable package, or *Id* is not the simple name an observable subpackage of that package, then a compile-time error occurs.

TYPENAMES

SIMPLE PACKAGEORTYPENAMES

If the *Package Or Type Name, Q,* occurs in the scope of a type named KQ, then the *Package Or Type Name* is reclassified as a *TypeName*. Otherwise, the *PackageOrTypeName* is reclassified as a *PackageName*. The meaning of the *PackageOrTypeName* is the meaning of the reclassified name.

PACKAGE OR TYPENAMES

Given a qualified *Package Or Type Name* of the form *Q.Id,* if the type or package denoted by *Q* has a member type named *Id,* then the qualified *PackageOrType Name* name is reclassified as a *TypeName*. Otherwise, it is reclassified as a *PackageName.*

The meaning of the qualified *PackageOrTypeName* is the meaning of the reclassified name.

TYPE NAMES

The meaning of a name classified as a *TypeName* is determined as follows.

SIMPLE TYPE NAMES

If a type name consists of a single *Identifier*, then the identifier must occur in the scope of exactly one visible declaration of a type with this name, or a compile-time error occurs. The meaning of the type name is that type.

QUALIFIED TYPE NAMES

If a type name is of the form *Q.Id*, then *Q* must be either a type name or a package name. If *Id* names exactly one type that is a member of the type or package denoted by *Q*, then the qualified type name denotes that type. If *Id* does not name a member type within *Q*, or the member type named *Id* within *Q* is not accessible, or *Id* names more than one member type within *Q*, then a compile-time error occurs.

The example:

```
package wnj.test;
class Test {
      public static void main(String[] args) {
            java.util.Date date =
            new  java.util.Date(System.current
  TimeMillis());

  System.out.println(date.toLocaleString());
      }
}
```

produced the following output the first time it was run:

```
Sun Jan 21 22:56:29 1996
```

In this example the name **java.util.Date** must denote a type, so we first use the procedure recursively to determine if **java.util** is an accessible type or a package, which it is, and then look to see if the type **Date** is accessible in this package.

Type names are distinct from type declaration specifiers.A type name is always qualified by meas of another type name. In some cases, it is necessary to access an inner class that is a member of a parameterized type:

```
class GenericOuter<T extends Number> {
      public class Inner<S extends Comparable<S>>
    {
            T getT() {return null;}
            S getS() {return null;}
     }
};
GenericOuter<Integer>.Inner<Double> x1 = null;
Integer i = x1.getT();
Double d = x1.getS();
If we accessed Inner by qualifying it with a type
   name, as in:
GenericOuter.Inner x2 = null;
```

we would force its use as a raw type, losing type information.

EXPRESSION NAMES

The meaning of a name classified as an *ExpressionName* is determined as follows.

SIMPLE EXPRESSION NAMES

If an expression name consists of a single *Identifier*, then there must be exactly one visible declaration denoting either a local variable, parameter or field in scope at the point at which the the *Identifier* occurs. Otherwise, a compile-time error occurs.

If the declaration declares a final field, the meaning of the name is the value of that field. Otherwise, the meaning of the expression name is the variable declared by the declaration.

If the field is an instance variable, the expression name must appear within the declaration of an instance method, constructor, instance initializer, or instance variab'e initializer. If it appears within a **static** method, static initializer,or initializer for a **static** variable, then a compile-time error occurs.

The type of the expression name is the declared type of the field, local variable or parameter after capture conversion.

In the example:

```
class Test {
    static int v;
    static final int f = 3;
    public static void main(String[] args) {
        int i;
        i = 1;
        v = 2;
        f = 33;// compile-time error
    System.out.println(i + " " + v + " " + f);
    }
}
```

the names used as the left-hand-sides in the assignments to **i**, **v**, and **f** denote the local variable **i**, the field **v**, and the value of **f** (not the variable **f**, because **f** is a **final** variable). The example therefore produces an error at compile time because the last assignment does not have a variable as its left-hand side.

If the erroneous assignment is removed, the modified code can be compiled and it will produce the output:

```
1 2 3
```

QUALIFIED EXPRESSION NAMES

If an expression name is of the form *Q.Id*, then *Q* has already been classified as a package name, a type name, or an expression name:

- If *Q* is a package name, then a compile-time error occurs.
- If *Q* is a type name that names a class type, then:
  - If there is not exactly one accessible member of the class type that is a field named *Id*, then a compile-time error occurs.
  - Otherwise, if the single accessible member field is not a class variable (that is, it is not declared static), then a compile-time error occurs.
  - Otherwise, if the class variable is declared final,

then *Q.Id* denotes the value of the class variable. The type of the expression *Q.Id* is the declared type of the class variable after capture conversion. If *Q.Id* appears in a context that requires a variable and not a value, then a compile-time error occurs.

- Otherwise, *Q.Id* denotes the class variable. The type of the expression *Q.Id* is the declared type of the class variable after capture conversion. Note that this clause covers the use of enum constants, since these always have a corresponding final class variable.

- If *Q* is a type name that names an interface type, then:
  - If there is not exactly one accessible member of the interface type that is a field named *Id*, then a compile-time error occurs.
  - Otherwise, *Q.Id* denotes the value of the field. The type of the expression *Q.Id* is the declared type of the field after capture conversion. If *Q.Id* appears in a context that requires a variable and not a value, then a compile-time error occurs.
- If *Q* is an expression name, let *T* be the type of the expression *Q*:
  - If *T* is not a reference type, a compile-time error occurs.
  - If there is not exactly one accessible member of the type *T* that is a field named *Id*, then a compile-time error occurs.
  - Otherwise, if this field is any of the following:
- A field of an interface type
- A final field of a class type (which may be either a class variable or an instance variable)
- The final field length of an array type

then *Q.Id* denotes the value of the field. The type of the expression *Q.Id* is the declared type of the field after capture conversion. If *Q.Id* appears in a context that requires a variable and not a value, then a compile-time error occurs.

– Otherwise, *Q.Id* denotes a variable, the field *Id* of class *T*, which may be either a class variable or an instance variable. The type of the expression *Q.Id* is the type of the field member after capture conversion.

The example:

```
class Point {
      int x, y;
      static int nPoints;
}
class Test {
      public static void main(String[] args) {
            int i = 0;
            i.x++;// compile-time error
            Point p = new Point();
            p.nPoints();// compile-time error
      }
}
```

encounters two compile-time errors, because the **int** variable **i** has no members, and because **nPoints** is not a method of class **Point**.

Note that expression names may be qualified by type names, but not by types in general. A consequence is that it is not possible to access a class variable through a parameterized type

```
class Foo<T> {
      public static int classVar = 42;
}
Foo<String>.classVar = 91;// illegal
Instead, one writes
Foo.classVar = 91;
```

This does not restrict the language in any meaningful :vay. Type parameters may not be used in the types of static variables, and so the actual parameters of a parameterized type can never influence the type of a static variable.

Therefore, no expressive power is lost. Technically, the type name **Foo** above is a raw type, but this use of raw types is harmless, and does not give rise to warnings.

METHOD NAMES

A *MethodName* can appear only in a method invocation expression or as an element name in an element-value pair. The meaning of a name classified as a *MethodName* is determined as follows.

SIMPLE METHOD NAMES

A simple method name may appear as the element name in an element-value pair. The *Identifier* in an *ElementValuePair* must be the simple name of one of the elements of the annotation type identified by *TypeName* in the containing annotation.

Otherwise, a compile-time error occurs. (In other words, the identifier in an element-value pair must also be a method name in the interface identified by *TypeName*.)

Otherwise, a simple method name necessarily appears in the context of a method invocation expression. In that case, if a method name consists of a single *Identifier*, then *Identifier* is the method name to be used for method invocation. The *Identifier* must name at least one visible method that is in scope at the point where the *Identifier* appear or a method imported by a single-static-import declaration or static-import-on-demand declaration within the compilation unit within which the *Identifier* appears.

QUALIFIED METHOD NAMES

A qualified method name can only appear in the context of a method invocation expression. If a method name is of the form *Q.Id*, then *Q* has already been classified as a package name, a type name, or an expression name. If *Q* is a package name, then a compile-time error occurs. Otherwise, *Id* is the method name to be used for method invocation. If *Q* is a type name, then *Id* must name at least one **static** method of the type *Q*. If *Q* is an expression name, then let *T* be the type of the expression *Q*; *Id* must name at least one method of the type *T*.

Discussion: Like expression names, method names may be qualified by type names, but not by types in general. The implications are similar to those for expression names.

ACCESS CONTROL

The Java programming language provides mechanisms for *access control,* to prevent the users of a package or class from depending on unnecessary details of the implementation of that package or class. If access is permitted, then the accessed entity is said to be *accessible.*

Note that accessibility is a static property that can be determined at compile time; it depends only on types and declaration modifiers. Qualified names are a means of access to members of packages and reference types; related means of access include field access expressions and method invocation expressions. All three are syntactically similar in that a "." token appears, preceded by some indication of a package, type, or expression having a type and followed by an *Identifier* that names a member of the package or type. These are collectively known as constructs for *qualified access.*

Access control applies to qualified access and to the invocation of constructors by class instance creation expressions and explicit constructor invocations. Accessibility also effects inheritance of class members, including hiding and method overriding.

DETERMINING ACCESSIBILITY

- A package is always accessible.
- If a class or interface type is declared public, then it may be accessed by any code, provided that the compilation unit in which it is declared is observable. If a top level class or interface type is not declared public, then it may be accessed only from within the package in which it is declared.
- An array type is accessible if and only if its element type is accessible.
- A member (class, interface, field, or method) of a reference (class, interface, or array) type or a constructor of a class type is accessible only if the type is accessible and the member or constructor is declared to permit access:
  - If the member or constructor is declared public,

then access is permitted. All members of interfaces are implicitly public.

– Otherwise, if the member or constructor is declared protected, then access is permitted only when one of the following is true:
  - Access to the member or constructor occurs from within the package containing the class in which the protected member or constructor is declared.
  - Access is correct as described in.
– Otherwise, if the member or constructor is declared private, then access is permitted if and only if it occurs within the body of the top level class that encloses the declaration of the member or constructor.
– Otherwise, we say there is default access, which is permitted only when the access occurs from within the package in which the type is declared.

PROTECTED ACCESS

A **protected** member or constructor of an object may be accessed from outside the package in which it is declared only by code that is responsible for the implementation of that object.

ACCESS TO A PROTECTED MEMBER

Let C be the class in which a **protected** member m is declared. Access is permitted only within the body of a subclass S of C. In addition, if *Id* denotes an instance field or instance method, then:

- If the access is by a qualified name *Q.Id*, where *Q* is an *ExpressionName*, then the access is permitted if and only if the type of the expression *Q* is *S* or a subclass of *S*.
- If the access is by a field access expression *E.Id*, where *E* is a *Primary* expression, or by a method invocation expression *E.Id*(...), where *E* is a *Primary* expression, then the access is permitted if and only if the type of *E* is *S* or a subclass of *S*.

ACCESS TO A PROTECTED CONSTRUCTOR

Let *C* be the class in which a **protected** constructor is declared and let *S* be the innermost class in whose declaration the use of the **protected** constructor occurs. Then:

- If the access is by a superclass constructor invocation super(...) or by a qualified superclass constructor invocation of the form *E*.super(...), where *E* is a *Primary* expression, then the access is permitted.
- If the access is by an anonymous class instance creation expression of the form new *C*(...){...} or by a qualified class instance creation expression of the form *E*.new *C*(...){...}, where *E* is a *Primary* expression, then the access is permitted.
- Otherwise, if the access is by a simple class instance creation expression of the form new C(...) or by a qualified class instance creation expression of the form *E*.new *C*(...), where *E* is a *Primary* expression, then the access is not permitted. A protected constructor can be accessed by a class instance creation expression (that does not declare an anonymous class) only from within the package in which it is defined.

EXAMPLE OF ACCESS CONTROL

For examples of access control, consider the two compilation units:

```
package points;
class PointVec {Point[] vec;}
```

and:

```
package points;
public class Point {
    protected int x, y;
    public void move(int dx, int dy) {x += dx;
  y += dy;}
    public int getX() {return x;}
    public int getY() {return y;}
}
```

It declare two class types in the package ***points***:

- The class type PointVec is not public and not part of the public interface of the package points, but rather can be used only by other classes in the package.
- The class type Point is declared public and is available to other packages. It is part of the public interface of the package points.
- The methods move, getX, and getY of the class Point are declared public and so are available to any code that uses an object of type Point.
- The fields x and y are declared protected and are accessible outside the package points only in subclasses of class Point, and only when they are fields of objects that are being implemented by the code that is accessing them.

EXAMPLE: ACCESS TO PUBLIC AND NON-PUBLIC CLASSES

If a class lacks the **public** modifier, access to the class declaration is limited to the package in which it is declared.

In the example:

```
package points;
public class Point {
    public int x, y;
    public void move(int dx, int dy) {x += dx;
  y += dy;}
}
class PointList {
    Point next, prev;
}
```

two classes are declared in the compilation unit. The class **Point** is available outside the package **points**, while the class **PointList** is available for access only within the package.

Thus a compilation unit in another package can access **points.**

Point*, either by using its fully qualified name*:

```
package pointsUser;
class Test {
```

```
    public static void main(String[] args) {
        points.Point p = new points.Point();
        System.out.println(p.x + " " + p.y);
    }
}
```

By using a single-type-import declaration that mentions the fully qualified name, so that the simple name may be used thereafter:

```
package pointsUser;
import points.Point;
class Test {
    public static void main(String[] args) {
        Point p = new Point();
        System.out.println(p.x + " " + p.y);
    }}
```

However, this compilation unit cannot use or import **points.PointList**, which is not declared **public** and is therefore inaccessible outside package **points**.

DEFAULT-ACCESS FIELDS, METHODS, AND CONSTRUCTORS

If none of the access modifiers **public**, **protected**, or **private** are specified, a class member or constructor is accessible throughout the package that contains the declaration of the class in which the class member is declared, but the class member or constructor is not accessible in any other package.

If a **public** class has a method or constructor with default access, then this method or constructor is not accessible to or inherited by a subclass declared outside this package.

For example, if we have:

```
package points;
public class Point {
    public int x, y;
    void move(int dx, int dy) {x += dx; y +=
  dy;}
    public void moveAlso(int dx, int dy)
  {move(dx, dy);}
}
```

Then a subclass in another package may declare an unrelated **move** method, with the same signature and return type. Because the original **move** method is not accessible from package **morepoints, super** may not be used:

```
package morepoints;
public class PlusPoint extends points.Point {
    public void move(int dx, int dy) {
    super.move(dx, dy);// compile-time error
    moveAlso(dx, dy);
    }
}
```

Because move of **Point** is not overridden by **move** in **PlusPoint**, the method **moveAlso** in **Point** never calls the method move in **PlusPoint**.

Thus if you delete the **super.move** call from **PlusPoint** and execute the test programme:

```
import points.Point;
import morepoints.PlusPoint;
class Test {
    public static void main(String[] args) {
        PlusPoint pp = new PlusPoint();
        pp.move(1, 1);
    }
}
```

It terminates normally. If move of **Point** were overridden by **move** in **PlusPoint**, then this programme would recurse infinitely, until a **StackoverflowError** occurred.

PUBLIC FIELDS, METHODS, AND CONSTRUCTORS

A **public** class member or constructor is accessible throughout the package where it is declared and from any other package, provided the package in which it is declared is observable. For example, in the compilation unit:

```
package points;
public class Point {
    int x, y;
    public void move(int dx, int dy) {
```

```
            x += dx; y += dy;
            moves++;
        }
        public static int moves = 0;
}
```

The **public** class **Point** has as **public** members the **move** method and the **moves** field. These **public** members are accessible to any other package that has access to package **points**. The fields **x** and **y** are not **public** and therefore are accessible only from within the package **points**.

PROTECTED FIELDS, METHODS, AND CONSTRUCTORS

Consider this example, where the **points** package declares:

```
  package points;
public class Point {
        protected int x, y;
        void warp(threePoint.Point3d a) {
        if (a.z > 0)// compile-time error: cannot
      access a.z
            a.delta(this);
        }
}
```

and the threePoint package declares:

```
package threePoint;
import points.Point;
public class Point3d extends Point {
        protected int z;
        public void delta(Point p) {
        p.x += this.x;// compile-time error: cannot
      access p.x
        p.y += this.y;// compile-time error: cannot
      access p.y
        }
        public void delta3d(Point3d q) {
            q.x += this.x;
            q.y += this.y;
            q.z += this.z;
```

```
        }
}
```

It defines a class **Point3d**. A compile-time error occurs in the method **delta** here: it cannot access the protected members x and **y** of its parameter **p**, because while **Point3d** (the class in which the references to fields x and **y** occur) is a subclass of **Point** (the class in which x and **y** are declared), it is not involved in the implementation of a **Point** (the type of the parameter **p**). The method **delta3d** can access the protected members of its parameter **q**, because the class **Point3d** is a subclass of **Point** and is involved in the implementation of a **Point3d**. The method **delta** could try to cast its parameter to be a **Point3d**, but this cast would fail, causing an exception, if the class of **p** at run time were not **Point3d**.

A compile-time error also occurs in the method warp: it cannot access the protected member **z** of its parameter **a**, because while the class **Point** (the class in which the reference to field **z** occurs) is involved in the implementation of a **Point3d** (the type of the parameter **a**), it is not a subclass of **Point3d** (the class in which **z** is declared).

FIELDS, METHODS, AND CONSTRUCTORS

A private class member or constructor is accessible only within the body of the top level class that encloses the declaration of the member or constructor. It is not inherited by subclasses. In the example:

```
class Point {
      Point() {setMasterID();}
      int x, y;
      private int ID;
      private static int masterID = 0;
      private void setMasterID() {ID = masterID++;}
}
```

The **private** members **ID**, **masterID**, and **setMasterID** may be used only within the body of class **Point**. They may not be accessed by qualified names, field access expressions, or method invocation expressions outside the body of the declaration of **Point**.

QUALIFIED AND CANONICAL NAMES

Every package, top level class, top level interface, and primitive type has a *fully qualified name*. An array type has a fully qualified name if and only if its element type has a fully qualified name.

- The fully qualified name of a primitive type is the keyword for that primitive type, namely boolean, char, byte, short, int, long, float, or double.
- The fully qualified name of a named package that is not a subpackage of a named package is its simple name.
- The fully qualified name of a named package that is a subpackage of another named package consists of the fully qualified name of the containing package, followed by ".", followed by the simple (member) name of the subpackage.
- The fully qualified name of a top level class or top level interface that is declared in an unnamed package is the simple name of the class or interface.
- The fully qualified name of a top level class or top level interface that is declared in a named package consists of the fully qualified name of the package, followed by ".", followed by the simple name of the class or interface.
- A member class or member interface *M* of another class *C* has a fully qualified name if and only if *C* has a fully qualified name. In that case, the fully qualified name of *M* consists of the fully qualified name of *C*, followed by ".", followed by the simple name of *M*.
- The fully qualified name of an array type consists of the fully qualified name of the component type of the array type followed by "[]".

Examples:

- The fully qualified name of the type long is "long".
- The fully qualified name of the package java.lang is "java.lang" because it is subpackage lang of package java.

- The fully qualified name of the class Object, which is defined in the package java.lang, is "java.lang. Object".
- The fully qualified name of the interface Enumeration, which is defined in the package java.util, is "java.util.Enumeration".
- The fully qualified name of the type "array of double" is "double[]".
- The fully qualified name of the type "array of array of array of array of String" is "java.lang.String[][][][]".

In the example:

```
package points;
class Point {int x, y;}
class PointVec {
    Point[] vec;
}
```

the fully qualified name of the type **Point** is **"points.Point"**; the fully qualified name of the type **PointVec** is **"points.PointVec"**; and the fully qualified name of the type of the field **vec** of class **PointVec** is **"points.Point[]"**.

Every package, top level class, top level interface, and primitive type has a *canonical name*. An array type has a canonical name if and only if its element type has a canonical name. A member class or member interface *M* declared in another class *C* has a canonical name if and only if *C* has a canonical name. In that case, the canonical name of *M* consists of the canonical name of *C*, followed by ".", followed by the simple name of *M*. For every package, top level class, top level interface and primitive type, the canonical name is the same as the fully qualified name. The canonical name of an array type is defined only when the component type of the array has a canonical name. In that case, the canonical name of the array type consists of the canonical name of the component type of the array type followed by **"[]"**.

The difference between a fully qualified name and a canonical name can be seen in examples such as:

```
package p;
class O1 {class I{}}
```

```
class O2 extends O1{};
```

In this example both **p.O1.I** and **p.O2.I** are fully qualified names that denote the same class, but only **p.O1.I** is its canonical name.

NAMING CONVENTIONS

The class libraries of the Java platform attempt to use, whenever possible, names chosen according to the conventions presented here.

These conventions help to make code more readable and avoid certain kinds of name conflicts. We recommend these conventions for use in all programs written in the Java programming language.

However, these conventions should not be followed slavishly if long-held conventional usage dictates otherwise. So, for example, the **sin** and **cos** methods of the class **java.lang.Math** have mathematically conventional names, even though these method names flout the convention suggested here because they are short and are not verbs.

PACKAGE NAMES

Names of packages that are to be made widely available should be formed as described in. Such names are always qualified names whose first identifier consists of two or three lowercase letters that name an Internet domain, such as **com**, **edu**, **gov**, **mil**, **net**, **org**, or a two-letter ISO country code such as **uk** or **jp**. Here are examples of hypothetical unique names that might be formed under this convention:

```
com.JavaSoft.jag.Oak
org.npr.pledge.driver
uk.ac.city.rugby.game
```

Names of packages intended only for local use should have a first identifier that begins with a lowercase letter, but that first identifier specifically should not be the identifier **java**; package names that start with the identifier **java** are reserved by Sun for naming Java platform packages.

When package names occur in expressions:

- If a package name is obscured by a field declaration,

then import declarations can usually be used to make available the type names declared in that package.

- If a package name is obscured by a declaration of a parameter or local variable, then the name of the parameter or local variable can be changed without affecting other code.

The first component of a package name is normally not easily mistaken for a type name, as a type name normally begins with a single uppercase letter. (The Java programming language does not actually rely on case distinctions to determine whether a name is a package name or a type name.)

CLASS AND INTERFACE TYPE NAMES

Names of class types should be descriptive nouns or noun phrases, not overly long, in mixed case with the first letter of each word capitalized.

For example:

- ClassLoader
- SecurityManager
- Thread
- Dictionary

BUFFER INPUT STREAM

Likewise, names of interface types should be short and descriptive, not overly long, in mixed case with the first letter of each word capitalized. The name may be a descriptive noun or noun phrase, which is appropriate when an interface is used as if it were an abstract superclass, such as interfaces **java.io.DataInput** and **java.io. DataOutput**; or it may be an adjective describing a behaviour, as for the interfaces **Runnable** and **Cloneable**. Obscuring involving class and interface type names is rare. Names of fields, parameters, and local variables normally do not obscure type names because they conventionally begin with a lowercase letter whereas type names conventionally begin with an uppercase letter.

TYPE VARIABLE NAMES

Type variable names should be pithy (single character if

possible) yet evocative, and should not include lower case letters.

Discussion: This makes it easy to distinguish formal type parameters from ordinary classes and interfaces.

Container types should use the name **E** for their element type. Maps should use **K** for the type of their keys and **V** for the type of their values.

The name **X** should be used for arbitrary exception types. We use **T** for type, whenever there isn't anything more specific about the type to distinguish it.

Discussion: This is often the case in generic methods.

If there are multiple type parameters that denote arbitrary types, one should use letters that neighbour **T** in the alphabet, such as **S**. Alternately, it is acceptable to use numeric subscripts (e.g., **T1, T2**) to distinguish among the different type variables. In such cases, all the variables with the same prefix should be subscripted.

Discussion: If a generic method appears inside a generic class, it's a good idea to avoid using the same names for the type parameters of the method and class, to avoid confusion. The same applies to nested generic classes.

Discussion: These conventions are illustrated in the code snippets below:

```
public class HashSet<E> extends AbstractSet<E>
{...}
public class HashMap<K,V> extends
AbstractMap<K,V> {...}
public class ThreadLocal<T> {...}
public interface Functor<T, X extends
Throwable> {
T eval() throws X;
}
```

When type parameters do not fall conveniently into one of the categories mentioned, names should be chosen to be as meaningful as possible within the confines of a single letter. The names mentioned above (**E, K, T, V, X**) should not be used for type parameters that do not fall into the designated categories.

METHOD NAMES

Method names should be verbs or verb phrases, in mixed case, with the first letter lowercase and the first letter of any subsequent words capitalized. Here are some additional specific conventions for method names:

- Methods to get and set an attribute that might be thought of as a variable *V* should be named get*V* and set*V*. An example is the methods getPriority and setPriority of class Thread.
- A method that returns the length of something should be named length, as in class String.
- A method that tests a boolean condition *V* about an object should be named is*V*. An example is the method isInterrupted of class Thread.
- A method that converts its object to a particular format *F* should be named to*F*. Examples are the method toString of class Object and the methods toLocaleString and toGMTString of class java.util.Date.

Whenever possible and appropriate, basing the names of methods in a new class on names in an existing class that is similar, especially a class from the Java Application Programming Interface classes, will make it easier to use. Method names cannot obscure or be obscured by other names.

FIELD NAMES

Names of fields that are not final should be in mixed case with a lowercase first letter and the first letters of subsequent words capitalized.

Note that well-designed classes have very few public or protected fields, except for fields that are constants (final static fields).

Fields should have names that are nouns, noun phrases, or abbreviations for nouns. Examples of this convention are the fields buf, pos, and count of the class java.io.ByteArray InputStream and the field bytesTransferred of the class java.io.Interrupted IO Exception.

Obscuring involving field names is rare.

- If a field name obscures a package name, then an import declaration can usually be used to make available the type names declared in that package.
- If a field name obscures a type name, then a fully qualified name for the type can be used unless the type name denotes a local class.
- Field names cannot obscure method names.
- If a field name is shadowed by a declaration of a parameter or local variable, then the name of the parameter or local variable can be changed without affecting other code.

CONSTANT NAMES

The names of constants in interface types should be, and **final** variables of class types may conventionally be, a sequence of one or more words, acronyms, or abbreviations, all uppercase, with components separated by underscore "_" characters.

Constant names should be descriptive and not unnecessarily abbreviated. Conventionally they may be any appropriate part of speech. Examples of names for constants include **MIN_VALUE, MAX_VALUE, MIN_RADIX**, and **MAX_RADIX** of the class **Character**.

A group of constants that represent alternative values of a set, or, less frequently, masking bits in an integer value, are sometimes usefully specified with a common acronym as a name prefix, as in:

```
interface ProcessStates {
int PS_RUNNING = 0;
int PS_SUSPENDED = 1;
}
```

Obscuring involving constant names is rare:

- Constant names normally have no lowercase letters, so they will not normally obscure names of packages or types, nor will they normally shadow fields, whose names typically contain at least one lowercase letter.
- Constant names cannot obscure method names, because they are distinguished syntactically.

LOCAL VARIABLE AND PARAMETER NAMES

Local variable and parameter names should be short, yet meaningful. They are often short sequences of lowercase letters that are not words.

For example:

- Acronyms, that is the first letter of a series of words, as in cp for a variable holding a reference to a ColoredPoint
- Abbreviations, as in buf holding a pointer to a buffer of some kind
- Mnemonic terms, organized in some way to aid memory and understanding, typically by using a set of local variables with conventional names patterned after the names of parameters to widely used classes. *For example*:
  - In and out, whenever some kind of input and output are involved, patterned after the fields of System
  - Off and len, whenever an offset and length are involved, patterned after the parameters to the read and write methods of the interfaces DataInput and DataOutput of java.io

One-character local variable or parameter names should be avoided, except for temporary and looping variables, or where a variable holds an undistinguished value of a type.

Conventional one-character names are:

- b for a byte
- c for a char
- d for a double
- e for an Exception
- f for a float
- i, j, and k for integers
- l for a long
- o for an Object
- s for a String
- v for an arbitrary value of some type

Local variable or parameter names that consist of only two or three lowercase letters should not conflict with the initial country codes and domain names that are the first component of unique package names.

PACKAGES

Programs are organized as sets of packages. Each package has its own set of names for types, which helps to prevent name conflicts. A top level type is accessible outside the package that declares it only if the type is declared **public**.

The naming structure for packages is hierarchical.The members of a package are class and interface types, which are declared in compilation units of the package, and subpackages, which may contain compilation units and subpackages of their own. A package can be stored in a file system or in a database. Packages that are stored in a file system may have certain constraints on the organization of their compilation units to allow a simple implementation to find classes easily.

A package consists of a number of compilation units. A compilation unit automatically has access to all types declared in its package and also automatically imports all of the public types declared in the predefined package **java.lang.**

For small programs and casual development, a package can be unnamed or have a simple name, but if code is to be widely distributed, unique package names should be chosen.This can prevent the conflicts that would otherwise occur if two development groups happened to pick the same package name and these packages were later to be used in a single programme.

PACKAGE MEMBERS

The members of a package are its subpackages and all the top level class types and top level interface types declared in all the compilation units of the package.

For example, in the Java Application Programming Interface:

- The package java has subpackages **awt, applet, io, lang, net,** and **util,** but no compilation units.
- The package **java.awt** has a subpackage named **image,** as well as a number of compilation units containing declarations of class and interface types.

If the fully qualified name of a package is *P*, and *Q* is a subpackage of *P*, then *P.Q* is the fully qualified name of the subpackage. A package may not contain two members of the same name, or a compile-time error results.

Here are some examples:

- Because the package **java.awt** has a subpackage **image**, it cannot (and does not) contain a declaration of a class or interface type named **image**.
  If **com.sun.java.jag** is the fully qualified name of a type, then there cannot be any package whose fully qualified name is either **com.sun.java.jag** or **com.sun.java.jag.scrabble**.

The hierarchical naming structure for packages is intended to be convenient for organizing related packages in a conventional manner, but has no significance in itself other than the prohibition against a package having a subpackage with the same simple name as a top level type declared in that package. There is no special access relationship between a package named **oliver** and another package named **oliver.twist**, or between packages named **evelyn.wood** and **evelyn.waugh**. For example, the code in a package named **oliver.twist** has no better access to the types declared within package **oliver** than code in any other package.

HOST SUPPORT FOR PACKAGES

Each host determines how packages, compilation units, and subpackages are created and stored, and which compilation units are observable in a particular compilation.

The observability of compilation units in turn determines which packages are observable, and which packages are in scope. The packages may be stored in a local file system in simple implementations of the Java platform. Other implementations may use a distributed file system or some form of database to store source and/or binary code.

STORING PACKAGES IN A FILE SYSTEM

As an extremely simple example, all the packages and source and binary code on a system might be stored in a single directory and its subdirectories. Each immediate subdirectory of this directory would represent a top level package, that is, one whose fully qualified name consists of a single simple name. The directory might contain the following immediate subdirectories:

```
com
gls
jag
java
wnj
```

where directory **java** would contain the Java Application Programming Interface packages; the directories **jag**, **gls**, and **wnj** might contain packages that three of the authors of this specification created for their personal use and to share with each other within this small group; and the directory **com** would contain packages procured from companies that used the conventions described in to generate unique names for their packages.

Continuing the example, the directory **java** would contain, among others, the following subdirectories:

```
applet
awt
io
lang
net
util
```

corresponding to the packages **java.applet**, **java.awt**, **java.io**, **java.lang**, **java.net**, and **java.util** that are defined as part of the Java Application Programming Interface.

Still continuing the example, if we were to look inside the directory **util**, we might see the following files:

```
BitSet.java     Observable.java
BitSet.class    Observable.class
Date.java       Observer.java
Date.class      Observer.class
...
```

where each of the.**java** files contains the source for a compilation unit that contains the definition of a class or interface whose binary compiled form is contained in the corresponding.**class** file.

Under this simple organization of packages, an implementation of the Java platform would transform a package name into a pathname by concatenating the components of the package name, placing a file name separator (directory indicator) between adjacent components.

For example, if this simple organization were used on a UNIX system, where the file name separator is/, the package name:

```
jag.scrabble.board
would be transformed into the directory name:
jag/scrabble/board
and:
com.sun.sunsoft.DOE
would be transformed to the directory name:
com/sun/sunsoft/DOE
```

A package name component or class name might contain a character that cannot correctly appear in a host file system's ordinary directory name, such as a Unicode character on a system that allows only ASCII characters in file names. As a convention, the character can be escaped by using, say, the @ character followed by four hexadecimal digits giving the numeric value of the character, as in the **\u***xxxx* escape, so that the package name:

```
children.activities.crafts.papierM\u00e2ch\u00e9
which can also be written using full Unicode
as:
children.activities.crafts.papierMâché
might be mapped to the directory name:
children/activities/crafts/papierM@00e2ch@00e9
```

If the @ character is not a valid character in a file name for some given host file system, then some other character that is not valid in a identifier could be used instead.

STORING PACKAGES IN A DATABASE

A host system may store packages and their compilation units and subpackages in a database.

Such a database must not impose the optional restrictions on compilation units in file-based implementations. For example, a system that uses a database to store packages may not enforce a maximum of one **public** class or interface per compilation unit.

Systems that use a database must, however, provide an option to convert a programme to a form that obeys the restrictions, for purposes of export to file-based implementations.

COMPILATION UNITS

CompilationUnit is the goal symbol for the syntactic grammar of Java programs.

It is defined by the following productions:

```
CompilationUnit:
      PackageDeclarationopt ImportDeclarationsopt
   TypeDeclarationsopt
ImportDeclarations:
      ImportDeclaration
      ImportDeclarations ImportDeclaration
TypeDeclarations:
      TypeDeclaration
      TypeDeclarations TypeDeclaration
```

Types declared in different compilation units can depend on each other, circularly. A Java compiler must arrange to compile all such types at the same time. A *compilation unit* consists of three parts, each of which is optional:

- A package declaration, giving the fully qualified name of the package to which the compilation unit belongs. A compilation unit that has no package declaration is part of an unnamed package.
- Import declarations that allow types from other packages and static members of types to be referred to using their simple names
- Top level type declarations of class and interface types

Which compilation units are *observable* is determined by the host system. However, all the compilation units of the package java and its subpackages lang and io must always be observable. The observability of a compilation unit influences the observability of its package.

Every compilation unit automatically and implicitly imports every public type name declared by the predefined package java.lang, so that the names of all those types are available as simple names.

PACKAGE DECLARATIONS

A package declaration appears within a compilation unit to indicate the package to which the compilation unit belongs.

NAMED

A *package declaration* in a compilation unit specifies the name of the package to which the compilation unit belongs.

```
PackageDeclaration:
        Annotationsopt package PackageName;
```

The keyword **package** may optionally be preceded by annotation modifiers.If an annotation *a* on a package declaration corresponds to an annotation type *T*, and *T* has a (meta-)annotation *m* that corresponds to **annotation.Target**, then *m* must have an element whose value is **annotation.ElementType.PACKAGE**, or a compile-time error occurs. The package name mentioned in a package declaration must be the fully qualified name of the package.

ANNOTATIONS

Annotations may be used on package declarations, with the restriction that at most one annotated package declaration is permitted for a given package.

Discussion: The manner in which this restriction is enforced must, of necessity, vary from implementation to implementation. The following scheme is strongly recommended for file-system-based implementations: The sole annotated package declaration, if it exists, is placed in a source file called **package-info.java** in the directory containing the source files for the package. This file does not contain the source for a class called package-info.java; indeed it would be illegal for it to do so, as package-info is not a legal identifier. Typically **package-info.java** contains only a package declaration, preceded immediately by the annotations on the package. While the file could technically contain the source code for one or more package-private classes, it would be very bad form.

It is recommended that **package-info.java**, if it is present, take the place of **package.html** for javadoc and other similar documentation generation systems. If this file is present, the documentation generation tool should look for the package documentation comment immediately preceding the (possibly annotated) package declaration in **package-info.java**. In this way, package-info.java becomes the sole repository for package level annotations and documentation. If, in future, it becomes desirable to add any other package-level information, this file should prove a convenient home for this information.

UNNAMED

A compilation unit that has no package declaration is part of an unnamed package.

Note that an unnamed package cannot have subpackages, since the syntax of a package declaration always includes a reference to a named top level package.

```
As an example, the compilation unit:
class FirstCall {
     public static void main(String[] args) {
     System.out.println("Mr. Watson, come here.
  "
     + "I want you.");
     }
}
```

defines a very simple compilation unit as part of an unnamed package. An implementation of the Java platform must support at least one unnamed package; it may support more than one unnamed package but is not required to do so. Which compilation units are in each unnamed package is determined by the host system.

In implementations of the Java platform that use a

hierarchical file system for storing packages, one typical strategy is to associate an unnamed package with each directory; only one unnamed package is observable at a time, namely the one that is associated with the "current working directory." The precise meaning of "current working directory" depends on the host system.

Unnamed packages are provided by the Java platform principally for convenience when developing small or temporary applications or when just beginning development.

OBSERVABILITY OF A PACKAGE

A package is observable if and only if either:

- A compilation unit containing a declaration of the package is observable.
- A subpackage of the package is observable.

One can conclude from the rule above and from the requirements on observable compilation units, that the packages **java**, **java.lang**, and **java.io** are always observable.

SCOPE OF A PACKAGE DECLARATION

The scope of the declaration of an observable top level package is all observable compilation units. The declaration of a package that is not observable is never in scope. Subpackage declarations are never in scope.It follows that the package **java** is always in scope.Package declarations never shadow other declarations.

IMPORT DECLARATIONS

An *import declaration* allows a static member or a named type to be referred to by a simple name that consists of a single identifier. Without the use of an appropriate **import** declaration, the only way to refer to a type declared in another package, or a static member of another type, is to use a fully qualified name.

```
ImportDeclaration:
    SingleTypeImportDeclaration
    TypeImportOnDemandDeclaration
    SingleStaticImportDeclaration
```

```
StaticImportOnDemandDeclaration
```

A single-type-import declaration imports a single named type, by mentioning its canonical name.

A type-import-on-demand declaration imports all the accessible types of a named type or package as needed. It is a compile time error to import a type from the unnamed package.

A single static import declaration imports all accessible static members with a given name from a type, by giving its canonical name.

A static-import-on-demand declaration imports all accessible static members of a named type as needed.

The scope of a type imported by a single-type-import declaration or a type-import-on-demand declaration is all the class and interface type declarations in the compilation unit in which the import declaration appears.

The scope of a member imported by a single-static-import declaration or a static-import-on-demand declaration is all the class and interface type declarations in the compilation unit in which the import declaration appears.

An **import** declaration makes types available by their simple names only within the compilation unit that actually contains the **import** declaration. The scope of the entities(s) it introduces specifically does not include the **package** statement, other **import** declarations in the current compilation unit, or other compilation units in the same package.

SINGLE-TYPE-IMPORT DECLARATION

A *single-type-import declaration* imports a single type by giving its canonical name, making it available under a simple name in the class and interface declarations of the compilation unit in which the single-type import declaration appears.

```
SingleTypeImportDeclaration:
import TypeName;
```

The *TypeName* must be the canonical name of a class or interface type; a compile-time error occurs if the named type does not exist. The named type must be accessible or a compile-time error occurs.

A single-type-import declaration *d* in a compilation unit *c* of package *p* that imports a type named *n* shadows the declarations of:

- Any top level type named *n* declared in another compilation unit of *p*.
- Any type named *n* imported by a type-import-on-demand declaration in *c*.
- Any type named *n* imported by a static-import-on-demand declaration in *c*.

```
throughout c.
```

The example:

```
import java.util.Vector;
```

causes the simple name **Vector** to be available within the class and interface declarations in a compilation unit. Thus, the simple name **Vector** refers to the type declaration **Vector** in the package **java.util** in all places where it is not shadowed or obscured by a declaration of a field, parameter, local variable, or nested type declaration with the same name.

Discussion: Note that **Vector** is declared as a generic type. Once imported, the name **Vector** can be used without qualification in a parameterized type such as **Vector<String>**, or as the raw type **Vector.**

This highlights a limitation of the **import** declaration. A type nested inside a generic type declaration can be imported, but its outer type is always erased.

If two single-type-import declarations in the same compilation unit attempt to import types with the same simple name, then a compile-time error occurs, unless the two types are the same type, in which case the duplicate declaration is ignored. If the type imported by the the single-type-import declaration is declared in the compilation unit that contains the import declaration, the import declaration is ignored. If a compilation unit contains both a single-static-import declaration that imports a type whose simple name is *n*, and a single-type-import declaration that imports a type whose simple name is *n*, a compile-time error occurs.

If another top level type with the same simple name is otherwise declared in the current compilation unit except by a type-import-on-demand declaration or a static-import-on-demand declaration, then a compile-time error occurs.

So the sample programme:

```
import java.util.Vector;
class Vector {Object[] vec;}
```

causes a compile-time error because of the duplicate declaration of **Vector**, as does:

```
import java.util.Vector;
import myVector.Vector;
```

where **myVector** is a package containing the compilation unit:

```
package myVector;
public class Vector {Object[] vec;}
```

The compiler keeps track of types by their binary names.

Note that an import statement cannot import a subpackage, only a type. For example, it does not work to try to import **java.util** and then use the name **util.Random** to refer to the type **java.util.Random**:

```
import java.util;// incorrect: compile-time
error
class Test {util.Random generator;}
```

TYPE-IMPORT-ON-DEMAND DECLARATION

A *type-import-on-demand declaration* allows all accessible types declared in the type or package named by a canonical name to be imported as needed.

```
TypeImportOnDemandDeclaration:
    import PackageOrTypeName. *;
```

It is a compile-time error for a type-import-on-demand declaration to name a type or package that is not accessible. Two or more type-import-on-demand declarations in the same compilation unit may name the same type or package. All but one of these declarations are considered *redundant*; the effect is as if that type was imported only once.

If a compilation unit contains both a static-import-on-demand declaration and a type-import-on-demand declaration that name the same type, the effect is as if the static member types of that type were imported only once. It is not a compile-time error to name the current package or **java.lang** in a type-import-on-demand declaration. The type-import-on-demand declaration is ignored in such cases.

A type-import-on-demand declaration never causes any other declaration to be shadowed.

The example:

```
import java.util.*;
```

causes the simple names of all **public** types declared in the package **java.util** to be available within the class and interface declarations of the compilation unit. Thus, the simple name **Vector** refers to the type **Vector** in the package **java.util** in all places in the compilation unit where that type declaration is not shadowed or obscured. The declaration might be shadowed by a single-type-import declaration of a type whose simple name is **Vector**; by a type named **Vector** and declared in the package to which the compilation unit belongs; or any nested classes or interfaces. The declaration might be obscured by a declaration of a field, parameter, or local variable named **Vector** (It would be unusual for any of these conditions to occur.)

Single Static Import Declaration

A *single-static-import declaration* imports all accessible static members with a given simple name from a type. This makes these static members available under their simple name in the class and interface declarations of the compilation unit in which the single-static import declaration appears.

```
SingleStaticImportDeclaration:
    import static TypeName. Identifier;
```

The *TypeName* must be the canonical name of a class or interface type; a compile-time error occurs if the named type does not exist.

The named type must be accessible or a compile-time error occurs. The Identifier must name at least one static member of the named type; a compile-time error occurs if there is no member of that name or if all of the named members are not accessible.

A single-static-import declaration *d* in a compilation unit *c* of package *p* that imports a field named *n* shadows the declaration of any static field named *n* imported by a static-import-on-demand declaration in *c,* throughout *c.*

A single-static-import declaration *d* in a compilation unit *c* of package *p* that imports a method named *n* with signature s shadows the declaration of any static method named *n* with signature *s* imported by a static-import-on-demand declaration in *c,* throughout *c.*

A single-static-import declaration *d* in a compilation unit *c* of package *p* that imports a type named *n* shadows the declarations of:

- Any static type named *n* imported by a static-import-on-demand declaration in *c.*
- Any top level type named *n* declared in another compilation unit of *p.*
- Any type named *n* imported by a type-import-on-demand declaration in *c.*

`throughout c.`

Note that it is permissable for one single-static-import declaration to import several fields or types with the same name, or several methods with the same name and signature.

If a compilation unit contains both a single-static-import declaration that imports a type whose simple name is *n,* and a single-type-import declaration that imports a type whose simple name is *n,* a compile-time error occurs.

If a single-static-import declaration imports a type whose simple name is *n,* and the compilation unit also declares a top level type whose simple name is *n,* a compile-time error occurs.

STATIC-IMPORT-ON-DEMAND DECLARATION

A *static-import-on-demand declaration* allows all accessible static members declared in the type named by a canonical name to be imported as needed.

```
StaticImportOnDemandDeclaration:
    import static TypeName. *;
```

It is a compile-time error for a static-import-on-demand declaration to name a type that does not exist or a type that is not accessible. Two or more static-import-on-demand declarations in the same compilation unit may name the same type or package; the effect is as if there was exactly one such declaration. Two or more static-import-on-demand declarations in the same compilation unit may name the same member; the effect is as if the member was imported exactly once.

Note that it is permissable for one static-import-on-demand declaration to import several fields or types with the same name, or several methods with the same name and signature. If a compilation unit contains both a static-import-on-demand declaration and a type-import-on-demand declaration that name the same type, the effect is as if the static member types of that type were imported only once. A static-import-on-demand declaration never causes any other declaration to be shadowed.

AUTOMATIC IMPORTS

Each compilation unit automatically imports all of the public type names declared in the predefined package java.lang, as if the declaration:

```
import java.lang.*;
```

appeared at the beginning of each compilation unit, immediately following any **package** statement.

A STRANGE EXAMPLE

Package names and type names are usually different under the naming conventions. Nevertheless, in a contrived example where there is an unconventionally-named package **Vector**, which declares a **public** class whose,

```
name is Mosquito:
package Vector;
public class Mosquito {int capacity;}
and then the compilation unit:
package strange.example;
import java.util.Vector;
import Vector.Mosquito;
class Test {
     public static void main(String[] args) {
```

```
        System.out.println(new
  Vector().getClass());
        System.out.println(new
  Mosquito().getClass());
    }
}
```

the single-type-import declaration importing class **Vector** from package **java.util** does not prevent the package name **Vector** from appearing and being correctly recognized in subsequent **import** declarations.

The example compiles and produces the output:

```
class java.util.Vector
class Vector.Mosquito
```

TYPE DECLARATIONS

A *top level type declaration* declares a top level class type or a top level interface type:

```
TypeDeclaration:
    ClassDeclaration
    InterfaceDeclaration
    ;
```

By default, the top level types declared in a package are accessible only within the compilation units of that package, but a type may be declared to be **public** to grant access to the type from code in other packages. The scope of a top level type is all type declarations in the package in which the top level type is declared. If a top level type named *T* is declared in a compilation unit of a package whose fully qualified name is *P*, then the fully qualified name of the type is *P.T*. If the type is declared in an unnamed package, then the type has the fully qualified name *T*.

Thus in the example:

```
package wnj.points;
class Point {int x, y;}
```

the fully qualified name of class **Point** is **wnj.points.Point**.

An implementation of the Java platform must keep track of types within packages by their binary names. Multiple ways of naming a type must be expanded to binary names to make sure that such names are understood as referring to the same type. For example, if a compilation unit contains the single-type-import declaration:

```
import java.util.Vector;
```

then within that compilation unit the simple name **Vector** and the fully qualified name **java.util.Vector** refer to the same type.

When packages are stored in a file system, the host system may choose to enforce the restriction that it is a compile-time error if a type is not found in a file under a name composed of the type name plus an extension (such as **.java** or **.jav**) if either of the following is true:

- The type is referred to by code in other compilation units of the package in which the type is declared.
- The type is declared public (and therefore is potentially accessible from code in other packages).

This restriction implies that there must be at most one such type per compilation unit. This restriction makes it easy for a compiler for the Java programming language or an implementation of the Java virtual machine to find a named class within a package; for example, the source code for a **public** type **wet.sprocket.Toad** would be found in a file **Toad.java** in the directory **wet/sprocket**, and the corresponding object code would be found in the file **Toad.class** in the same directory.

When packages are stored in a database, the host system must not impose such restrictions. In practice, many programmers choose to put each class or interface type in its own compilation unit, whether or not it is public or is referred to by code in other compilation units.

A compile-time error occurs if the name of a top level type appears as the name of any other top level class or interface type declared in the same package.

A compile-time error occurs if the name of a top level type is also declared as a type by a single-type-import declaration in the compilation unit containing the type declaration.

In the example:

```
class Point {int x, y;}
```

the class Point is declared in a compilation unit with no package statement, and thus Point is its fully qualified name, whereas in the example:

```
package vista;
class Point {int x, y;}
```

the fully qualified name of the class Point is **vista.Point**. (The package name vista is suitable for local or personal use; if the package were intended to be widely distributed, it would be better to give it a unique package name.)

In the example:

```
package test;
import java.util.Vector;
class Point {
    int x, y;
}
interface Point {
// compile-time error #1
    int getR();
    int getTheta();
}
class Vector {Point[] pts;}
// compile-time error #2
```

the first compile-time error is caused by the duplicate declaration of the name Point as both a class and an **interface** in the same package. A second error detected at compile time is the attempt to declare the name Vector both by a class type declaration and by a single-type-import declaration.

Note, however, that it is not an error for the name of a class to also to name a type that otherwise might be imported by a type-import-on-demand declaration in the compilation unit containing the class declaration.

In the example:

```
package test;
import java.util.*;
class Vector {Point[] pts;}
// not a compile-time error
```

the declaration of the class **Vector** is permitted even though there is also a class **java.util.Vector**. Within this compilation unit, the simple name **Vector** refers to the class **test.Vector**, not to **java.util.Vector** (which can still be referred to by code within the compilation unit, but only by its fully qualified name).

As another example, the compilation unit:

```
package points;
class Point {
     int x, y;// coordinates
     PointColor colour;// colour of this point
     Point next;// next point with this colour
     static int nPoints;
}
class PointColor {
     Point first;// first point with this colour
     PointColor(int colour) {
          this.colour = colour;
     }
     private int colour;// colour components
}
```

defines two classes that use each other in the declarations of their class members. Because the class types **Point** and **PointColor** have all the type declarations in package points, including all those in the current compilation unit, as their scope, this example compiles correctly-that is, forward reference is not a problem. It is a compile-time error if a top level type declaration contains any one of the following access modifiers: **protected, private** or **static**.

PACKAGE NAMES

Developers should take steps to avoid the possibility of two published packages having the same name by choosing *unique package names* for packages that are widely distributed. This allows packages to be easily and automatically installed and catalogued. This section specifies a suggested convention for generating such unique package names. Implementations of the Java platform are encouraged to provide automatic support for converting a set of packages from local and casual package names to the unique name format described here.

If unique package names are not used, then package name conflicts may arise far from the point of creation of either of the conflicting packages. This may create a situation that is difficult or impossible for the user or programmer to resolve. The class **ClassLoader** can be used to isolate packages with the same name from each other in those cases where the packages will have constrained interactions, but not in a way that is transparent to a naïve programme.

You form a unique package name by first having (or belonging to an organization that has) an Internet domain name, such as **sun.com**. You then reverse this name, component by component, to obtain, in this example, **com.sun**, and use this as a prefix for your package names, using a convention developed within your organization to further administer package names.

In some cases, the internet domain name may not be a valid package name. Here are some suggested conventions for dealing with these situations:

- If the domain name contains a hyphen, or any other special character not allowed in an identifier, convert it into an underscore.
- If any of the resulting package name components are keywords then append underscore to them.
- If any of the resulting package name components start with a digit, or any other character that is not allowed as an initial character of an identifier, have an underscore prefixed to the component.

Such a convention might specify that certain directory name components be division, department, project, machine, or login names.

Some possible examples:

```
com..sun.sunsoft.DOE
com.sun.java.jag.scrabble
com.apple.quicktime.v2
edu.cmu.cs.bovik.cheese
gov.whitehouse.socks.mousefinder
```

The first component of a unique package name is always written in all-lowercase ASCII letters and should be one of the top level domain names, currently **com, edu, gov, mil, net, org**, or one of the English two-letter codes identifying countries as specified in ISO Standard 3166, 1981. For more information, refer to the documents stored at **ftp://rs.internic.net/rfc**, for example, **rfc920.txt** and **rfc1032.txt.**

The name of a package is not meant to imply where the package is stored within the Internet; for example, a package named **edu.cmu.cs.bovik.cheese** is not necessarily obtainable from Internet address **cmu.edu** or from **cs.cmu.edu** or from **bovik.cs.cmu.edu**. The suggested convention for generating unique package names is merely a way to piggyback a package naming convention on top of an existing, widely known unique name registry instead of having to create a separate registry for package names.

Chapter 4

Class Declarations

INTRODUCTION

Class declarations define new reference types and describe how they are implemented. A *nested class* is any class whose declaration occurs within the body of another class or interface. A *top level class* is a class that is not a nested class. The common semantics of all classes-top level and nested (including member classes, local classes and anonymous classes). Details that are specific to particular kinds of classes are discussed in the sections dedicated to these constructs.

A named class may be declared abstract and must be declared abstract if it is incompletely implemented; such a class cannot be instantiated, but can be extended by subclasses. A class may be declared final, in which case it cannot have subclasses. If a class is declared public, then it can be referred to from other packages. Each class except Object is an extension of (that is, a subclass of) a single existing class and may implement interfaces. Classes may be generic, that is, they may declare type variables whose bindings may differ among different instances of the class.

Classes may be decorated with annotations just like any other kind of declaration. The body of a class declares members (fields and methods and nested classes and interfaces), instance and static initializers, and constructors.The scope of a member is the entire body of the declaration of the class to which the member belongs. Field, method, member class, member interface, and constructor declarations may include the access modifiers public, protected, or private. The members of a class include both declared and inherited members. Newly declared fields can hide fields declared in a superclass or superinterface. Newly declared class members and interface members can hide class or interface members declared in a superclass or superinterface. Newly declared methods can hide, implement, or override methods declared in a superclass or superinterface.

Field declarations describe class variables, which are incarnated once, and instance variables, which are freshly incarnated for each instance of the class. A field may be declared final, in which case it can be assigned to only once. Any field declaration may include an initializer.

Member class declarations describe nested classes that are members of the surrounding class. Member classes may be static, in which case they have no access to the instance variables of the surrounding class; or they may be inner classes. Member interface declarations describe nested interfaces that are members of the surrounding class.

Method declarations describe code that may be invoked by method invocation expressions.A class method is invoked relative to the class type; an instance method is invoked with respect to some particular object that is an instance of a class type. A method whose declaration does not indicate how it is implemented must be declared abstract.

A method may be declared final, in which case it cannot be hidden or overridden. A method may be implemented by platform-dependent native code.

A synchronized method automatically locks an object before executing its body and automatically unlocks the object on return, as if by use of a synchronized statement, thus allowing its activities to be synchronized with those of other threads.

Method names may be overloaded.Instance initializers are blocks of executable code that may be used to help initialize an instance when it is created.Static initializers are blocks of executable code that may be used to help initialize a class.Constructors are similar to methods, but cannot be invoked directly by a method call; they are used to initialize new class instances. Like methods, they may be overloaded.

REFERENCE TYPE

A *class declaration* specifies a new named reference type. There are two kinds of class declarations - *normal class declarations* and *enum declarations*:

```
ClassDeclaration:
     NormalClassDeclaration
     EnumDeclaration
NormalClassDeclaration:
     ClassModifiersopt class Identifier
   TypeParametersopt Superopt Interfacesopt
ClassBody
```

The rules in this section apply to all class declarations unless this specification explicitly states otherwise. In many cases, special restrictions apply to enum declarations.

The *Identifier* in a class declaration specifies the name of the class. A compile-time error occurs if a class has the same simple name as any of its enclosing classes or interfaces.

CLASS MODIFIERS

A class declaration may include *class modifiers*.

```
ClassModifiers:
     ClassModifier
     ClassModifiers ClassModifier
ClassModifier: one of
     Annotation public protected private
     abstract static final strictfp
```

Not all modifiers are applicable to all kinds of class declarations. The access modifier **public** pertains only to top level classes and to member classes, and is discussed in and. The access modifiers **protected** and **private** pertain only to member classes within a directly enclosing class declaration and are discussed in.The access modifier **static** pertains only to member classes. A compile-time error occurs if the same modifier appears more than once in a class declaration.

If an annotation *a* on a class declaration corresponds to an annotation type *T*, and *T* has a (meta-)annotation *m* that corresponds to **annotation.Target**, then *m* must have an element whose value is **annotation.ElementType.TYPE**, or a compile-time error occurs. Annotation modifiers are described later.

If two or more class modifiers appear in a class declaration, then it is customary, though not required, that they appear in the order consistent with that shown above in the production for *ClassModifier*.

ABSTRACT CLASSES

An abstract class is a class that is incomplete, or to be considered incomplete. Normal classes may have abstract methods, that is methods that are declared but not yet implemented, only if they are abstract classes. If a normal class that is not abstract contains an abstract method, then a compile-time error occurs.

Enum types must not be declared abstract; doing so will result in a compile-time error. It is a compile-time error for an enum type *E* to have an abstract method *m* as a member unless *E* has one or more enum constants, and all of *E*'s enum constants have class bodies that provide concrete implementations of *m*. It is a compile-time error for the class body of an enum constant to declare an abstract method.

A class C has ***abstract*** *methods if any of the following is true*:

- C explicitly contains a declaration of an abstract method.
- Any of C's superclasses has an abstract method and C neither declares nor inherits a method that implements it.
- A direct superinterface of C declares or inherits a method (which is therefore necessarily abstract) and C neither declares nor inherits a method that implements it.

In the example:

```
abstract class Point {
    int x = 1, y = 1;
    void move(int dx, int dy) {
        x += dx;
        y += dy;
```

```
            alert();
        }
        abstract void alert();
}
abstract class ColoredPoint extends Point {
        int colour;
}
class SimplePoint extends Point {
        void alert() {}
}
```

a class **Point** is declared that must be declared **abstract**, because it contains a declaration of an **abstract** method named **alert**. The subclass of **Point** named **ColoredPoint** inherits the **abstract** method **alert**, so it must also be declared **abstract**. On the other hand, the subclass of **Point** named **SimplePoint** provides an implementation of **alert**, so it need not be **abstract**.

A compile-time error occurs if an attempt is made to create an instance of an **abstract** class using a class instance creation expression.

Thus, continuing the example just shown, the statement:

```
Point p = new Point();
```

would result in a compile-time error; the class **Point** cannot be instantiated because it is **abstract**. However, a **Point** variable could correctly be initialized with a reference to any subclass of **Point**, and the class **SimplePoint** is not **abstract**, so the statement:

```
Point p = new SimplePoint();
```

would be correct. A subclass of an **abstract** class that is not itself **abstract** may be instantiated, resulting in the execution of a constructor for the **abstract** class and, therefore, the execution of the field initializers for instance variables of that class. Thus, in the example just given, instantiation of a **SimplePoint** causes the default constructor and field initializers for **x** and **y** of **Point** to be executed.

It is a compile-time error to declare an **abstract** class type such that it is not possible to create a subclass that implements all of its **abstract** methods.

This situation can occur if the class would have as

members two **abstract** methods that have the same method signature but incompatible return types.

As an example, the declarations:

```
interface Colorable {void setColor(int colour);}
abstract class Colored implements Colorable {
     abstract int setColor(int colour);
}
```

result in a compile-time error: it would be impossible for any subclass of class **Colored** to provide an implementation of a method named **setColor**, taking one argument of type **int**, that can satisfy both **abstract** method specifications, because the one in interface **Colorable** requires the same method to return no value, while the one in class **Colored** requires the same method to return a value of type **int**.

A class type should be declared **abstract** only if the intent is that subclasses can be created to complete the implementation. If the intent is simply to prevent instantiation of a class, the proper way to express this is to declare a constructor of no arguments, make it **private**, never invoke it, and declare no other constructors. A class of this form usually contains class methods and variables. The class **Math** is an example of a class that cannot be instantiated; its declaration looks like this:

```
public final class Math {
     private Math() {}// never instantiate this
   class
     ... declarations of class variables and
   methods...
}
```

FINAL CLASSES

A class can be declared **final** if its definition is complete and no subclasses are desired or required. A compile-time error occurs if the name of a **final** class appears in the **extends** clause of another **class** declaration; this implies that a **final** class cannot have any subclasses. A compile-time error occurs if a class is declared both **final** and **abstract**, because the implementation of such a class could never be completed.

Because a **final** class never has any subclasses, the methods of a **final** class are never overridden.

STRICTFP CLASSES

The effect of the **strictfp** modifier is to make all **float** or **double** expressions within the class declaration be explicitly FP-strict.This implies that all methods declared in the class, and all nested types declared in the class, are implicitly strictfp.

Note also that all **float** or **double** expressions within all variable initializers, instance initializers, static initializers and constructors of the class will also be explicitly FP-strict.

Generic Classes and Type Parameters

A class is *generic* if it declares one or more type variables. These type variables are known as the *type parameters* of the class. The type parameter section follows the class name and is delimited by angle brackets. It defines one or more type variables that act as parameters. A generic class declaration defines a set of parameterized types, one for each possible invocation of the type parameter section. All of these parameterized types share the same class at runtime.

For instance, executing the code

```
Vector<String> x = new Vector<String>();
Vector<Integer> y = new Vector<Integer>();
boolean b = x.getClass() == y.getClass();
```

will result in the variable **b** holding the value **true**.

```
TypeParameters::= < TypeParameterList >
TypeParameterList   ::=  TypeParameterList,
TypeParameter
                        | TypeParameter
```

It is a compile-time error if a generic class is a direct or indirect subclass of **Throwable**.

This restriction is needed since the **catch** mechanism of the Java virtual machine works only with non-generic classes.

The scope of a class' type parameter is the entire declaration of the class including the type parameter section itself. Therefore, type parameters can appear as parts of their own bounds, or as bounds of other type parameters declared in the same section. It is a compile-time error to refer to a type parameter of a class *C* anywhere in the declaration of a static member of *C* or the declaration of a static member of any type declaration nested within C. It is a compile-time error to refer to a type parameter of a class C within a static initializer of C or any class nested within C.

Example

Mutually recursive type variable bounds.

```
interface ConvertibleTo<T> {
    T convert();
}
class ReprChange<T implements ConvertibleTo<S>,
    S implements ConvertibleTo<T>> {
    T t;
    void set(S s) {t = s.convert();}
    S get() {return t.convert();}
}
```

Parameterized class declarations can be nested inside other declarations.

This is illustrated in the following example:

```
class Seq<T> {
    T head;
    Seq<T> tail;
    Seq() {this(null, null);}
    boolean isEmpty() {return tail == null;}
    Seq(T head, Seq<T> tail) {this.head = head;
  this.tail = tail;}
    class Zipper<S> {
            Seq<Pair<T,S>> zip(Seq<S> that) {
                if  (this.isEmpty()  ||
  that.isEmpty())
                return new Seq<Pair<T,S>>();
                else
                return new Seq<Pair<T,S>>(
                      new Pair<T,S>(this.head,
  that.head),
    this.tail.zip(that.tail));
```

```
            }
        }
}
class Pair<T, S> {
        T fst; S Snd;
        Pair(T f, S s) {fst = f; snd = s;}
}
class Client {
        {
                Seq<String> strs =
                new    Seq<String>("a",    new
    Seq<String>("b",
                    new Seq<String>()));
        Seq<Number> nums =
                    new Seq<Number>(new Integer(1),
                    new       Seq<Number>(new
    Double(1.5),
                    new Seq<Number>()));
        Seq<String>.Zipper<Number> zipper =
                    strs.new Zipper<Number>();
        Seq<Pair<String,Number>> combined =
    zipper.zip(nums);
        }
}
```

INNER CLASSES AND ENCLOSING INSTANCES

An *inner class* is a nested class that is not explicitly or implicitly declared **static**. Inner classes may not declare static initializers or member interfaces. Inner classes may not declare static members, unless they are compile-time constant fields.

To illustrate these rules, consider the example below:

```
class HasStatic{
        static int j = 100;
}
class Outer{
        class Inner extends HasStatic{
                static final int x = 3;// ok - compile-
    time constant
```

```
            static int y = 4;// compile-time error,
    an inner class
      }
      static class NestedButNotInner{
      static int z = 5;// ok, not an inner class
      }
      interface NeverInner{}// interfaces are
    never inner
}
```

Inner classes may inherit static members that are not compile-time constants even though they may not declare them. Nested classes that are not inner classes may declare static members freely, in accordance with the usual rules of the Java programming language. Member interfaces are always implicitly static so they are never considered to be inner classes.

A statement or expression *occurs in a static context* if and only if the innermost method, constructor, instance initializer, static initializer, field initializer, or explicit constructor invocation statement enclosing the statement or expression is a static method, a static initializer, the variable initializer of a static variable, or an explicit constructor invocation statement.

An inner class C is a *direct inner class of a class O* if O is the immediately lexically enclosing class of C and the declaration of C does not occur in a static context. A class C is an *inner class of class* O if it is either a direct inner class of O or an inner class of an inner class of O. A class O is the *zeroth lexically enclosing class of itself.* A class O is the *nth lexically enclosing class of a class* C if it is the immediately enclosing class of the *n*-1st lexically enclosing class of C.

An instance *i* of a direct inner class C of a class O is associated with an instance of O, known as the *immediately enclosing instance of i.* The immediately enclosing instance of an object, if any, is determined when the object is created.

An object *o* is the *zeroth lexically enclosing instance of itself.* An object *o* is the *nth lexically enclosing instance of an instance i* if it is the immediately enclosing instance of the *n*-1st lexically enclosing instance of *i.* When an inner class refers to an instance variable that is a member of a lexically enclosing class, the variable of the corresponding lexically enclosing instance is used. A blank final field of a lexically enclosing class may not be assigned within an inner class.

An instance of an inner class *I* whose declaration occurs in a static context has no lexically enclosing instances. However, if *I* is immediately declared within a static method or static initializer then *I* does have an *enclosing block*, which is the innermost block statement lexically enclosing the declaration of *I*.

Furthermore, for every superclass *S* of *C* which is itself a direct inner class of a class *SO*, there is an instance of *SO* associated with *i*, known as the *immediately enclosing instance of i with respect to S*. The immediately enclosing instance of an object with respect to its class' direct superclass, if any, is determined when the superclass constructor is invoked via an explicit constructor invocation statement.

Any local variable, formal method parameter or exception handler parameter used but not declared in an inner class must be declared final. Any local variable, used but not declared in an inner class must be definitely assigned before the body of the inner class. Inner classes include local, anonymous and non-static member classes.

Here are some examples:

```
class Outer {
     int i = 100;
     static void classMethod() {
          final int l = 200;
          class LocalInStaticContext{
               int k = i;// compile-time error
               int m = l;// ok
          }
     }

void foo() {
     class Local {// a local class
          int j = i;
          }
```

```
    }
}
```

The declaration of class **LocalInStaticContext** occurs in a static context-within the static method **classMethod**. Instance variables of class **Outer** are not available within the body of a static method. In particular, instance variables of **Outer** are not available inside the body of **LocalInStaticContext**. However, local variables from the surrounding method may be referred to without error (provided they are marked **final**).

Inner classes whose declarations do not occur in a static context may freely refer to the instance variables of their enclosing class. An instance variable is always defined with respect to an instance. In the case of instance variables of an enclosing class, the instance variable must be defined with respect to an enclosing instance of that class. So, for example, the class **Local** above has an enclosing instance of class **Outer**.

As a further example:

```
class WithDeepNesting{
    boolean toBe;
    WithDeepNesting(boolean b) {toBe = b;}
    class Nested {
        boolean theQuestion;
        class DeeplyNested {
            DeeplyNested(){
            theQuestion = toBe || !toBe;
            }
        }
    }
}
```

Here, every instance of **WithDeepNesting.Nested. DeeplyNested** has an enclosing instance of class **WithDeepNesting.Nested** (its immediately enclosing instance) and an enclosing instance of class **WithDeepNesting** (its 2nd lexically enclosing instance).

SUPERCLASSES AND SUBCLASSES

The optional extends clause in a normal class declaration specifies the *direct superclass* of the current class.

The following is repeated from to make the presentation here clearer:

TYPEDECLSPECIFIER TYPEARGUMENTS$_{OPT}$

A class is said to be a *direct subclass* of its direct superclass. The direct superclass is the class from whose implementation the implementation of the current class is derived. The direct superclass of an enum type E is Enum<E>. The extends clause must not appear in the definition of the class Object, because it is the primordial class and has no direct superclass.

Given a (possibly generic) class declaration for $C<F_1\ldots,F_n>$, $n \geq 0$, $C \neq Object$, the direct superclass of the class type $C<F_1\ldots,F_n>$ is the type given in the extends clause of the declaration of C if an extends clause is present, or Object otherwise.

Let $C<F_1\ldots,F_n>$, $n>0$, be a generic class declaration. The direct superclass of the parameterized class type $C<T_1\ldots,T_n>$, where T_i, $1 \leq i \leq n$, is a type, is $D<U_1$ *theta*..., U_k *theta*>, where $D<U_1\ldots,U_k>$ is the direct superclass of $C<F_1\ldots,F_n>$, and *theta* is the substitution $[F_1 := T_1\ldots, F_n := T_n]$.

The *ClassType* must name an accessible class type, or a compile-time error occurs. If the specified *ClassType* names a class that is final, then a compile-time error occurs; final classes are not allowed to have subclasses. It is a compile-time error if the *ClassType* names the class Enum or any invocation of it. If the TypeName is followed by any type arguments, it must be a correct invocation of the type declaration denoted by TypeName, and none of the type arguments may be wildcard type arguments, or a compile-time error occurs.

In the example:

```
class Point {int x, y;}
final class ColoredPoint extends Point {int
colour;}
class Colored3DPoint extends ColoredPoint {int
z;}// error
```

The relationships are as follows:

- The class Point is a direct subclass of Object.
- The class Object is the direct superclass of the class Point.

- The class ColoredPoint is a direct subclass of class Point.
- The class Point is the direct superclass of class ColoredPoint.

The declaration of class Colored3dPoint causes a compile-time error because it attempts to extend the final class ColoredPoint. The *subclass* relationship is the transitive closure of the direct subclass relationship.

A class A is a subclass of class C if either of the following is true:

- *A* is the direct subclass of *C*.
- There exists a class *B* such that *A* is a subclass of *B*, and *B* is a subclass of *C*, applying this definition recursively.

Class C is said to be a *superclass* of class *A* whenever *A* is a subclass of C.

In the example:

```
class Point {int x, y;}
class ColoredPoint extends Point {int colour;}
final class Colored3dPoint extends
ColoredPoint {int z;}
the relationships are as follows:
```

- The class Point is a superclass of class ColoredPoint.
- The class Point is a superclass of class Colored3dPoint.
- The class ColoredPoint is a subclass of class Point.
- The class ColoredPoint is a superclass of class Colored3dPoint.
- The class Colored3dPoint is a subclass of class ColoredPoint.
- The class Colored3dPoint is a subclass of class Point.

A class *C directly depends* on a type *T* if *T* is mentioned in the extends or implements clause of *C* either as a superclass or superinterface, or as a qualifier of a superclass or superinterface name. A class *C* depends on a reference type *T* if any of the following conditions hold:

- *C* directly depends on *T*.
- *C* directly depends on an interface *I* that depends on *T*.

- C directly depends on a class D that depends on T (using this definition recursively).

It is a compile-time error if a class depends on itself.

For example:

```
class Point extends ColoredPoint {int x, y;}
class ColoredPoint extends Point {int colour;}
```

causes a compile-time error.

If circularly declared classes are detected at run time, as classes are loaded, then a ClassCircularityError is thrown.

SUPERINTERFACES

The optional **implements** clause in a class declaration lists the names of interfaces that are *direct superinterfaces* of the class being declared:

```
Interfaces:
     implements InterfaceTypeList
InterfaceTypeList:
     InterfaceType
     InterfaceTypeList, InterfaceType
```

The following is repeated from to make the presentation here clearer:

```
InterfaceType:
     TypeDeclSpecifier TypeArgumentsopt
```

Given a (possibly generic) class declaration for $C<F_1..., F_n>$, $n \geq 0$, $C \neq Object$, the direct superinterfaces of the class type $C<F_1..., F_n>$ are the types given in the implements clause of the declaration of C if an implements clause is present.

Let $C<F_1..., F_n>$, $n>0$, be a generic class declaration. The direct superinterfaces of the parameterized class type $C<T_1..., T_n>$, where T_i, $1 \leq i \leq n$, is a type, are all types $I<U_1$ *theta*..., U_k *theta*>, where $I<U_1..., U_k>$ is a direct superinterface of $C<F_1..., F_n>$, and *theta* is the substitution $[F_1 := T_1..., F_n := T_n]$.

Each *InterfaceType* must name an accessible interface type, or a compile-time error occurs. If the *TypeName* is followed by any type arguments, it must be a correct invocation of the type declaration denoted by *TypeName*, and none of the type arguments may be wildcard type arguments, or a compile-time error occurs.

A compile-time error occurs if the same interface is mentioned as a direct superinterface two or more times in a single **implements** clause names. This is true even if the interface is named in different ways; for example, the code:

```
class Redundant implements
java.lang.Cloneable, Cloneable {
    int x;
}
```

results in a compile-time error because the names java.lang.**Cloneable** and **Cloneable** refer to the same interface.

An interface type *I* is a *superinterface* of class type *C* if any of the following is true:

- *I* is a direct superinterface of *C*.
- *C* has some direct superinterface *J* for which *I* is a superinterface, using the definition of "superinterface of an interface" given in.
- *I* is a superinterface of the direct superclass of *C*.

A class is said to *implement* all its superinterfaces.

In the example:

```
public interface Colorable {
    void setColor(int colour);
    int getColor();
}
public enum Finish {MATTE, GLOSSY}
public interface Paintable extends Colorable {
    void setFinish(Finish finish);
    Finish getFinish();
}
class Point {int x, y;}
class ColoredPoint extends Point implements
  Colorable {
    int colour;
    public void setColor(int colour)
  {this.colour = colour;}
    public int getColor() {return colour;}
}
class PaintedPoint extends ColoredPoint implements
  Paintable
```

```
{
    Finish finish;
    public void setFinish(Finish finish) {
        this.finish = finish;
    }
    public Finish getFinish() {return finish;}
}
```

the relationships are as follows:

- The interface Paintable is a superinterface of class PaintedPoint.
- The interface Colorable is a superinterface of class ColoredPoint and of class PaintedPoint.
- The interface Paintable is a subinterface of the interface Colorable, and Colorable is a superinterface of Paintable.

A class can have a superinterface in more than one way. In this example, the class **PaintedPoint** has **Colorable** as a superinterface both because it is a superinterface of **ColoredPoint** and because it is a superinterface of **Paintable**. Unless the class being declared is **abstract**, the declarations of all the method members of each direct superinterface must be implemented either by a declaration in this class or by an existing method declaration inherited from the direct superclass, because a class that is not **abstract** is not permitted to have **abstract** methods.

Thus, the example:

```
interface Colorable {
    void setColor(int colour);
    int getColor();
}
class Point {int x, y;};
class ColoredPoint extends Point implements
  Colorable {
    int colour;
}
```

Causes a compile-time error, because **ColoredPoint** is not an **abstract** class but it fails to provide an implementation of methods **setColor** and **getColor** of the interface **Colorable**.

It is permitted for a single method declaration in a class to implement methods of more than one superinterface. For example, in the code:

```
interface Fish {int getNumberOfScales();}
interface Piano {int getNumberOfScales();}
class Tuna implements Fish, Piano {
    // You can tune a piano, but can you tuna fish?
    int getNumberOfScales() {return 91;}
}
```

The method **getNumberOfScales** in class **Tuna** has a name, signature, and return type that matches the method declared in interface **Fish** and also matches the method declared in interface **Piano**; it is considered to implement both. On the other hand, in a situation such as this:

```
interface Fish {int getNumberOfScales();}
interface StringBass {double getNumberOfScales();}
class Bass implements Fish, StringBass {
    // This declaration cannot be correct, no matter what type is used.
    public ??? getNumberOfScales() {return 91;}
}
```

It is impossible to declare a method named **getNumberOfScales** whose signature and return type are compatible with those of both the methods declared in interface **Fish** and in interface **StringBass**, because a class cannot have multiple methods with the same signature and different primitive return types. Therefore, it is impossible for a single class to implement both interface **Fish** and interface **StringBass**.

A class may not at the same time be a subtype of two interface types which are different invocations of the same generic interface, or an invocation of a generic interface and a raw type naming that same generic interface.

Here is an example of an illegal multiple inheritance of an interface:

```
class B implements I<Integer>
class C extends B implements I<String>
```

This requirement was introduced in order to support translation by type erasure.

CLASS BODY AND MEMBER DECLARATIONS

A *class body* may contain declarations of members of the class, that is, fields, classes, interfaces and methods. A class body may also contain instance initializers, static initializers, and declarations of constructors for the class.

```
ClassBody:
    {ClassBodyDeclarationsopt}
ClassBodyDeclarations:
    ClassBodyDeclaration
    ClassBodyDeclarations ClassBodyDeclaration
ClassBodyDeclaration:
    ClassMemberDeclaration
    InstanceInitializer
    StaticInitializer
    ConstructorDeclaration
ClassMemberDeclaration:
    FieldDeclaration
    MethodDeclaration
    ClassDeclaration

    InterfaceDeclaration
    ;
```

The scope of a declaration of a member *m* declared in or inherited by a class type C is the entire body of C, including any nested type declarations. If C itself is a nested class, there may be definitions of the same kind (variable, method, or type) and name as *m* in enclosing scopes. (The scopes may be blocks, classes, or packages.) In all such cases, the member *m* declared or inherited in C shadows the other definitions of the same kind and name.

CLASS MEMBERS

The members of a class type are all of the following:

- Members inherited from its direct superclass, except in class Object, which has no direct superclass

- Members inherited from any direct superinterfaces
- Members declared in the body of the class

Members of a class that are declared **private** are not inherited by subclasses of that class. Only members of a class that are declared **protected** or **public** are inherited by subclasses declared in a package other than the one in which the class is declared.

We use the phrase the type of a member to denote:

- For a field, its type.
- For a method, an ordered 3-tuple consisting of:
  - Argument types: a list of the types of the arguments to the method member.
  - Return type: the return type of the method member.
  - Throws clause: exception types declared in the throws clause of the method member.

Constructors, static initializers, and instance initializers are not members and therefore are not inherited.

The example:

```
class Point {
    int x, y;
    private Point() {reset();}
    Point(int x, int y) {this.x = x; this.y =
  y;}
    private void reset() {this.x = 0; this.y =
  0;}
}
class ColoredPoint extends Point {
    int colour;
    void clear() {reset();}
  // error
}
class Test {
    public static void main(String[] args) {
          ColoredPoint c = new ColoredPoint(0,
  0);     // error
          c.reset();
  // error
```

```
        }
}
```

causes four compile-time errors:

- An error occurs because ColoredPoint has no constructor declared with two integer parameters, as requested by the use in main. This illustrates the fact that ColoredPoint does not inherit the constructors of itr superclass Point.
- Another error occurs because ColoredPoint declares no constructors, and therefore a default constructor for it is automatically created, and this default constructor is equivalent to:
- ColoredPoint() {super();}

which invokes the constructor, with no arguments, for the direct superclass of the class **ColoredPoint**. The error is that the constructor for **Point** that takes no arguments is **private**, and therefore is not accessible outside the class **Point**, even through a superclass constructor invocation.

Two more errors occur because the method **reset** of class **Point is private**, and therefore is not inherited by class **ColoredPoint**. The method invocations in method **clear** of class **ColoredPoint** and in method **main** of class **Test** are therefore not correct.

EXAMPLES OF INHERITANCE

This section illustrates inheritance of class members through several examples.

Example: Inheritance with Default Access

Consider the example where the **points** package declares two compilation units:

```
package points;
public class Point {
        int x, y;
        public void move(int dx, int dy) {x += dx;
     y += dy;}
}
and:
package points;
```

```
public class Point3d extends Point {
      int z;
      public void move(int dx, int dy, int dz) {
            x += dx; y += dy; z += dz;
      }
}
```

and a third compilation unit, in another package, is:

```
import points.Point3d;
class Point4d extends Point3d {
      int w;
      public void move(int dx, int dy, int dz,
    int dw) {
            x += dx; y += dy; z += dz; w += dw;/
    / compile-time errors
      }
}
```

Here both classes in the **points** package compile. The class **Point3d** inherits the fields **x** and **y** of class **Point**, because it is in the same package as **Point**. The class **Point4d**, which is in a different package, does not inherit the fields **x** and **y** of class **Point** or the field **z** of class **Point3d**, and so fails to compile.

A better way to write the third compilation unit would be:

```
import points.Point3d;
class Point4d extends Point3d {
      int w;
      public void move(int dx, int dy, int dz,
    int dw) {
            super.move(dx, dy, dz); w += dw;
      }
}
```

using the **move** method of the superclass **Point3d** to process **dx, dy,** and **dz**. If **Point4d** is written in this way it will compile without errors.

INHERITANCE WITH PUBLIC AND PROTECTED

*Given the class **Point***:

```
package points;
```

```
public class Point {
    public int x, y;
    protected int useCount = 0;
    static protected int totalUseCount = 0;
    public void move(int dx, int dy) {
          x += dx; y += dy; useCount++;
   totalUseCount++;
    }
}
```

the **public** and **protected** fields **x**, **y**, **useCount** and **totalUseCount** are inherited in all subclasses of **Point**. Therefore, this test programme, in another package, can be compiled successfully:

```
class Test extends points.Point {
    public void moveBack(int dx, int dy) {
          x -= dx; y -= dy; useCount++;
   totalUseCount++;
    }
}
```

INHERITANCE WITH PRIVATE

In the example:

```
class Point {
    int x, y;
    void move(int dx, int dy) {
        x += dx; y += dy; totalMoves++;
    }
    private static int totalMoves;
    void                    printMoves()
   {System.out.println(totalMoves);}
}
class Point3d extends Point {
    int z;
    void move(int dx, int dy, int dz) {
          super.move(dx, dy); z += dz;
   totalMoves++;
    }
}
```

the class variable **totalMoves** can be used only within the class **Point**; it is not inherited by the subclass **Point3d**. A compile-time error occurs because method **move** of class **Point3d** tries to increment **totalMoves**.

ACCESSING MEMBERS OF INACCESSIBLE CLASSES

Even though a class might not be declared **public**, instances of the class might be available at run time to code outside the package in which it is declared by means a **public** superclass or superinterface. An instance of the class can be assigned to a variable of such a **public** type. An invocation of a **public** method of the object referred to by such a variable may invoke a method of the class if it implements or overrides a method of the **public** superclass or superinterface. (In this situation, the method is necessarily declared **public**, even though it is declared in a class that is not **public**.)

Consider the compilation unit:

```
package points;
public class Point {
      public int x, y;
      public void move(int dx, int dy) {
            x += dx; y += dy;
      }
}
```

and another compilation unit of another package:

```
package morePoints;
class Point3d extends points.Point {
      public int z;
      public void move(int dx, int dy, int dz) {
            super.move(dx, dy); z += dz;
      }
      public void move(int dx, int dy) {
            move(dx, dy, 0);
      }
}
public class OnePoint {
      public static points.Point getOne() {
```

```
            return new Point3d();
        }
}
```

An invocation **morePoints.OnePoint.getOne()** in yet a third package would return a **Point3d** that can be used as a **Point**, even though the type **Point3d** is not available outside the package **morePoints**.

The two argument version of method **move** could then be invoked for that object, which is permissible because method **move** of **Point3d** is **public** (as it must be, for any method that overrides a **public** method must itself be **public**, precisely so that situations such as this will work out correctly). The fields **x** and **y** of that object could also be accessed from such a third package.

While the field **z** of class **Point3d** is **public**, it is not possible to access this field from code outside the package **morePoints**, given only a reference to an instance of class **Point3d** in a variable **p** of type **Point**. This is because the expression **p.z** is not correct, as **p** has type **Point** and class **Point** has no field named **z**; also, the expression **((Point3d)p).z** is not correct, because the class type **Point3d** cannot be referred to outside package **morePoints**.

The declaration of the field **z as public** is not useless, however. If there were to be, in package **morePoints**, a **public** subclass **Point4d** of the class **Point3d**:

```
package morePoints;
public class Point4d extends Point3d {
    public int w;
    public void move(int dx, int dy, int dz,
  int dw) {
            super.move(dx, dy, dz); w += dw;
    }
}
```

then class **Point4d** would inherit the field **z**, which, being **public**, could then be accessed by code in packages other than **morePoints**, through variables and expressions of the **public** type **Point4d**.

FIELD DECLARATIONS

The variables of a class type are introduced by *field declarations*:

```
FieldDeclaration:
    FieldModifiersopt Type VariableDeclarators;
VariableDeclarators:
    VariableDeclarator
    VariableDeclarators, VariableDeclarator
VariableDeclarator:
    VariableDeclaratorId
    VariableDeclaratorId = VariableInitializer
VariableDeclaratorId:
    Identifier
    VariableDeclaratorId []
VariableInitializer:
    Expression
      ArrayInitializer
```

It is a compile-time error for the body of a class declaration to declare two fields with the same name. Methods, types, and fields may have the same name, since they are used in different contexts and are disambiguated by different lookup procedures.

If the class declares a field with a certain name, then the declaration of that field is said to *hide* any and all accessible declarations of fields with the same name in superclasses, and superinterfaces of the class. The field declaration also shadows declarations of any accessible fields in enclosing classes or interfaces, and any local variables, formal method parameters, and exception handler parameters with the same name in any enclosing blocks.

If a field declaration hides the declaration of another field, the two fields need not have the same type.

A class inherits from its direct superclass and direct superinterfaces all the non-private fields of the superclass and superinterfaces that are both accessible to code in the class and not hidden by a declaration in the class.

Note that a private field of a superclass might be accessible to a subclass (for example, if both classes are members of the same class). Nevertheless, a private field is never inherited by a subclass.

It is possible for a class to inherit more than one field with the same name.Such a situation does not in itself cause a compile-time error. However, any attempt within the body of the class to refer to any such field by its simple name will result in a compile-time error, because such a reference is ambiguous.

There might be several paths by which the same field declaration might be inherited from an interface. In such a situation, the field is considered to be inherited only once, and it may be referred to by its simple name without ambiguity.

A hidden field can be accessed by using a qualified name (if it is **static**) or by using a field access expression that contains the keyword **super** or a cast to a superclass type. A value stored in a field of type **float** is always an element of the float value set; similarly, a value stored in a field of type **double** is always an element of the double value set. It is not permitted for a field of type **float** to contain an element of the float-extended-exponent value set that is not also an element of the float value set, nor for a field of type **double** to contain an element of the double-extended-exponent value set that is not also an element of the double value set.

FIELD MODIFIERS

```
FieldModifiers:
     FieldModifier
     FieldModifiers FieldModifier
FieldModifier: one of
     Annotation public protected private
     static final transient volatile
```

A compile-time error occurs if the same modifier appears more than once in a field declaration, or if a field declaration has more than one of the access modifiers **public, protected,** and **private**.

If an annotation *a* on a field declaration corresponds to an annotation type *T*, and *T* has a (meta-)annotation *m* that corresponds to **annotation.Target**, then *m* must have an element whose value is **annotation.ElementType.FIELD**, or a compile-time error occurs. Annotation modifiers are described later.

If two or more (distinct) field modifiers appear in a field declaration, it is customary, though not required, that they appear in the order consistent with that shown above in the production for *FieldModifier*.

STATIC FIELDS

If a field is declared **static**, there exists exactly one incarnation of the field, no matter how many instances (possibly zero) of the class may eventually be created. A **static** field, sometimes called a *class variable,* is incarnated when the class is initialized.

A field that is not declared **static** (sometimes called a non-**static** field) is called an *instance variable.* Whenever a new instance of a class is created, a new variable associated with that instance is created for every instance variable declared in that class or any of its superclasses. The example programme:

```
class Point {
    int x, y, useCount;
    Point(int x, int y) {this.x = x; this.y =
  y;}
    final static Point origin = new Point(0,
  0);
}
class Test {
    public static void main(String[] args) {
            Point p = new Point(1,1);
            Point q = new Point(2,2);
            p.x = 3; p.y = 3; p.useCount++;
  p.origin.useCount++;
            System.out.println("(" + q.x + "," +
  q.y + ")");
            System.out.println(q.useCount);
            System.out.println(q.origin ==
  Point.origin);

  System.out.println(q.origin.useCount);
```

```
    }
}
prints:
(2,2)
0
true
1
```

showing that changing the fields **x**, **y**, and **useCount** of **p** does not affect the fields of **q**, because these fields are instance variables in distinct objects. In this example, the class variable **origin** of the class **Point** is referenced both using the class name as a qualifier, in **Point.origin**, and using variables of the class type in field access expressions, as in **p.origin** and **q.origin**. These two ways of accessing the **origin** class variable access the same object, evidenced by the fact that the value of the reference equality expression:

q.origin==Point.origin

is `true`. Further evidence is that the incrementation:

```
p.origin.useCount++;
```

causes the value of q.origin.useCount to be 1; this is so because p.origin and q.origin refer to the same variable.

FINAL FIELDS

A field can be declared **final**. Both class and instance variables (**static** and non-**static** fields) may be declared **final**.

It is a compile-time error if a blank final class variable is not definitely assigned by a static initializer of the class in which it is declared.

A blank final instance variable must be definitely assigned at the end of every constructor of the class in which it is declared; otherwise a compile-time error occurs.

TRANSIENT FIELDS

Variables may be marked **transient** to indicate that they are not part of the persistent state of an object.

*If an instance of the class **Point**:*

```
class Point {
```

```
        int x, y;
        transient float rho, theta;
}
```

were saved to persistent storage by a system service, then only the fields x and y would be saved. This specification does not specify details of such services; see the specification of **java.io.Serializable** for an example of such a service.

VOLATILE FIELDS

The Java programming language allows threads to access shared variables. As a rule, to ensure that shared variables are consistently and reliably updated, a thread should ensure that it has exclusive use of such variables by obtaining a lock that, conventionally, enforces mutual exclusion for those shared variables.

The Java programming language provides a second mechanism, volatile fields, that is more convenient than locking for some purposes. A field may be declared **volatile,** in which case the Java memory model ensures that all threads see a consistent value for the variable. If, in the following example, one thread repeatedly calls the method **one** (but no more than **Integer.MAX_VALUE** times in all), and another thread repeatedly calls the method **two**:

```
class Test {
        static int i = 0, j = 0;
        static void one() {i++; j++;}
        static void two() {
                System.out.println("i=" + i + " j=" +
   j);
        }
}
```

then method **two** could occasionally print a value for **j** that is greater than the value of **i**, because the example includes no synchronization and, under the rules explained in, the shared values of **i** and **j** might be updated out of order.

One way to prevent this out-or-order behaviour would be to declare methods **one** and **two** to be **synchronized**:

```
class Test {
```

```
    static int i = 0, j = 0;
    static synchronized void one() {i++; j++;}
    static synchronized void two() {
            System.out.println("i=" + i + " j=" +
  j);
    }
}
```

This prevents method **one** and method **two** from being executed concurrently, and furthermore guarantees that the shared values of **i** and **j** are both updated before method **one** returns. Therefore method **two** never observes a value for **j** greater than that for **i**; indeed, it always observes the same value for **i** and **j**.

Another approach would be to declare ***i*** *and* ***j*** *to be* ***volatile***:

```
class Test {
    static volatile int i = 0, j = 0;
    static void one() {i++; j++;}
    static void two() {
            System.out.println("i=" + i + " j=" +
  j);
    }
}
```

This allows method **one** and method **two** to be executed concurrently, but guarantees that accesses to the shared values for **i** and **j** occur exactly as many times, and in exactly the same order, as they appear to occur during execution of the programme text by each thread.

Therefore, the shared value for **j** is never greater than that for **i**, because each update to **i** must be reflected in the shared value for **i** before the update to **j** occurs.

It is possible, however, that any given invocation of method **two** might observe a value for **j** that is much greater than the value observed for **i**, because method **one** might be executed many times between the moment when method **two** fetches the value of **i** and the moment when method **two** fetches the value of **j**.

A compile-time error occurs if a **final** variable is also declared **volatile**.

INITIALIZATION OF FIELDS

If a field declarator contains a *variable initializer*, then it has the semantics of an assignment to the declared variable, and:

- If the declarator is for a class variable (that is, a static field), then the variable initializer is evaluated and the assignment performed exactly once, when the class is initialized.
- If the declarator is for an instance variable (that is, a field that is not static), then the variable initializer is evaluated and the assignment performed each time an instance of the class is created.

The example:

```
class Point {
    int x = 1, y = 5;
}
class Test {
    public static void main(String[] args) {
        Point p = new Point();
        System.out.println(p.x + ", " + p.y);
    }
}
```

produces the output:

```
1, 5
```

because the assignments to **x** and **y** occur whenever a new **Point** is created. Variable initializers are also used in local variable declaration statements, where the initializer is evaluated and the assignment performed each time the local variable declaration statement is executed.

It is a compile-time error if the evaluation of a variable initializer for a **static** field of a named class (or of an interface) can complete abruptly with a checked exception.

It is compile-time error if an instance variable initializer of a named class can throw a checked exception unless that exception or one of its supertypes is explicitly declared in the throws clause of each constructor of its class and the class has at least one explicitly declared constructor. An instance variable initializer in an anonymous class can throw any exceptions.

INITIALIZERS FOR CLASS VARIABLES

If a reference by simple name to any instance variable occurs in an initialization expression for a class variable, then a compile-time error occurs. If the keyword **this** or the keyword **super** occurs in an initialization expression for a class variable, then a compile-time error occurs. One subtlety here is that, at run time, **static** variables that are **final** and that are initialized with compile-time constant values are initialized first. This also applies to such fields in interfaces. These variables are "constants" that will never be observed to have their default initial values, even by devious programs.

Use of class variables whose declarations appear textually after the use is sometimes restricted, even though these class variables are in scope.The precise rules governing forward reference to class variables.

INITIALIZERS FOR INSTANCE VARIABLES

Initialization expressions for instance variables may use the simple name of any **static** variable declared in or inherited by the class, even one whose declaration occurs textually later.

Thus the example:

```
class Test {
    float f = j;
    static int j = 1;
}
```

compiles without error; it initializes **j** to **1** when class **Test** is initialized, and initializes **f** to the current value of **j** every time an instance of class **Test** is created. Initialization expressions for instance variables are permitted to refer to the current object **this** and to use the keyword **super**. Use of instance variables whose declarations appear textually after the use is sometimes restricted, even though these instance variables are in scope. The precise rules governing forward reference to instance variables.

RESTRICTIONS ON THE USE OF FIELDS DURING INITIALIZATION

The declaration of a member needs to appear textually

before it is used only if the member is an instance (respectively **static**) field of a class or interface C and all of the following conditions hold:

- The usage occurs in an instance (respectively static) variable initializer of *C* or in an instance (respectively static) initializer of C.
- The usage is not on the left hand side of an assignment.
- The usage is via a simple name.
- *C* is the innermost class or interface enclosing the usage.

A compile-time error occurs if any of the four requirements above are not met. This means that a compile-time error results from the test programme:

```
class Test {
        int i = j;  // compile-time error:
    incorrect forward reference
        int j = 1;
}
```

whereas the following example compiles without error:

```
class Test {
        Test() {k = 2;}
        int j = 1;
        int i = j;
        int k;
}
```

even though the constructor for **Test** refers to the field **k** that is declared three lines later. These restrictions are designed to catch, at compile time, circular or otherwise malformed initializations. Thus, both:

```
class Z {
    static int i = j + 2;
    static int j = 4;
}
```

and:

```
class Z {
    static {i = j + 2;}
```

```
    static int i, j;
    static {j = 4;}
}
```

result in compile-time errors. Accesses by methods are not checked in this way, so:

```
class Z {
    static int peek() {return j;}
    static int i = peek();
    static int j = 1;
}
class Test {
    public static void main(String[] args) {
        System.out.println(Z.i);
    }
}
```

produces the output:

```
0
```

because] the variable initializer for **i** uses the class method **peek** to access the value of the variable **j** before **j** has been initialized by its variable initializer, at which point it still has its default value.

A more elaborate example is:

```
class UseBeforeDeclaration {
    static {
        x = 100;// ok - assignment
        int y = x + 1;// error - read before
 declaration
        int v = x = 3;// ok - x at left hand
 side of assignment
        int z = UseBeforeDeclaration.x * 2;
    // ok - not accessed via simple name
        Object o = new Object(){
            void foo(){x++;}// ok - occurs
 in a different class
            {x++;}// ok - occurs in a
 different class
        };
}
```

```
{
        j = 200;// ok - assignment
        j = j + 1;// error - right hand side
reads before declaration
        int k = j = j + 1;
        int n = j = 300;// ok - j at left hand
side of assignment
        int h = j++;// error - read before
declaration
        int l = this.j * 3;// ok - not accessed
via simple name
        Object o = new Object(){
              void foo(){j++;}// ok - occurs
in a different class
              {j = j + 1;}// ok - occurs in a
different class
        };
  }
  int w = x = 3;// ok - x at left hand side of
assignment
  int p = x;// ok - instance initializers may
access static fields
  static int u = (new Object(){int bar(){return
x;}}).bar();
  // ok - occurs in a different class
  static int x;
  int m = j = 4;// ok - j at left hand side of
assignment
  int o = (new Object(){int bar(){return
j;}}).bar();
  // ok - occurs in a different class
  int j;
}
```

EXAMPLES OF FIELD DECLARATIONS

The following examples illustrate some (possibly subtle) points about field declarations.

HIDING OF CLASS VARIABLES

The example:

```
class Point {
    static int x = 2;
}
class Test extends Point {
    static double x = 4.7;
    public static void main(String[] args) {
        new Test().printX();
    }
    void printX() {
        System.out.println(x + " " + super.x);
    }
}
```

produces the output:

```
4.7 2
```

because the declaration of **x** in class **Test** hides the definition of **x** in class **Point**, so class **Test** does not inherit the field **x** from its superclass **Point**. Within the declaration of class **Test**, the simple name **x** refers to the field declared within class **Test**. Code in class **Test** may refer to the field **x** of class **Point** as **super.x** (or, because **x** is **static**, as **Point.x**). If the declaration of **Test.x** is deleted:

```
class Point {
    static int x = 2;
}
class Test extends Point {
    public static void main(String[] args) {
        new Test().printX();
    }
    void printX() {
        System.out.println(x + " " + super.x);
    }
}
```

then the field **x** of class **Point** is no longer hidden within class **Test**; instead, the simple name **x** now refers to the field **Point.x**. Code in class **Test** may still refer to that same field as **super.x**.

Therefore, the output from this variant programme is:

```
2 2
```

HIDING OF INSTANCE VARIABLES

This example is similar to that in the previous section, but uses instance variables rather than static variables.

The code:

```
class Point {
     int x = 2;
}
class Test extends Point {
     double x = 4.7;
     void printBoth() {
          System.out.println(x + " " + super.x);
     }
     public static void main(String[] args) {
          Test sample = new Test();
          sample.printBoth();
          System.out.println(sample.x + " " +

                       ((Point)sample).x);
     }
}
```

produces the output:

```
4.7 2
4.7 2
```

because the declaration of **x** in class **Test** hides the definition of **x** in class **Point**, so class **Test** does not inherit the field **x** from its superclass **Point**. It must be noted, however, that while the field **x** of class **Point** is not *inherited* by class **Test**, it is nevertheless *implemented* by instances of class Test.

In other words, every instance of class **Test** contains two fields, one of type **int** and one of type **double**. Both fields bear the name **x**, but within the declaration of class **Test**, the simple name **x** always refers to the field declared within class **Test**. Code in instance methods of class **Test** may refer to the instance variable **x** of class **Point** as **super.x**.

Code that uses a field access expression to access field **x** will access the field named **x** in the class indicated by the type of reference expression. Thus, the expression **sample.x** accesses a **double** value, the instance variable declared in class **Test**, because the type of the variable sample is **Test**, but the expression **((Point)sample).x** accesses an **int** value, the instance variable declared in class **Point**, because of the cast to type **Point**.

If the declaration of **x** *is deleted from class* **Test**, *as in the programme:*

```
class Point {
      static int x = 2;
}
class Test extends Point {
      void printBoth() {
            System.out.println(x + " " + super.x);
      }
      public static void main(String[] args) {
            Test sample = new Test();
            sample.printBoth();
            System.out.println(sample.x + " " +

                         ((Point)sample).x);
      }
}
```

then the field **x** of class **Point** is no longer hidden within class **Test**. Within instance methods in the declaration of class **Test**, the simple name **x** now refers to the field declared within class **Point**. Code in class **Test** may still refer to that same field as **super.x**. The expression **sample.x** still refers to the field **x** within type **Test**, but that field is now an inherited field, and so refers to the field **x** declared in class **Point**. The output from this variant programme is:

```
2 2
2 2
```

MULTIPLY INHERITED FIELDS

A class may inherit two or more fields with the same name, either from two interfaces or from its superclass and an interface. A compile-time error occurs on any attempt to refer to any ambiguously inherited field by its simple name. A qualified name or a field access expression that contains the keyword **super** may be used to access such fields unambiguously.

In the example:

```
interface Frob {float v = 2.0f;}
class SuperTest {int v = 3;}
class Test extends SuperTest implements Frob {
      public static void main(String[] args) {
            new Test().printV();
      }
      void printV() {System.out.println(v);}
}
```

the class **Test** inherits two fields named **v**, one from its superclass **SuperTest** and one from its superinterface **Frob**. This in itself is permitted, but a compile-time error occurs because of the use of the simple name **v** in method **printV**: it cannot be determined which **v** is intended.

The following variation uses the field access expression **super.v** to refer to the field named **v** declared in class **SuperTest** and uses the qualified name **Frob.v** to refer to the field named **v** declared in interface **Frob**:

```
interface Frob {float v = 2.0f;}
class SuperTest {int v = 3;}
class Test extends SuperTest implements Frob {
     public static void main(String[] args) {
           new Test().printV();
     }
     void printV() {
           System.out.println((super.v + Frob.v)/
   2);
     }
}
It compiles and prints:
2.5
```

Even if two distinct inherited fields have the same type, the same value, and are both **final**, any reference to either field by simple name is considered ambiguous and results in a compile-time error.

In the example:

```
interface Colour {int RED=0, GREEN=1, BLUE=2;}
interface TrafficLight {int RED=0, YELLOW=1,
    GREEN=2;}
class Test implements Colour, TrafficLight {
    public static void main(String[] args) {
        System.out.println(GREEN);// compile-
    time error
        System.out.println(RED);// compile-
    time error
    }
}
```

it is not astonishing that the reference to **GREEN** should be considered ambiguous, because class **Test** inherits two different declarations for **GREEN** with different values. The point of this example is that the reference to **RED** is also considered ambiguous, because two distinct declarations are inherited. The fact that the two fields named **RED** happen to have the same type and the same unchanging value does not affect this judgment.

RE-INHERITANCE OF FIELDS

If the same field declaration is inherited from an interface by multiple paths, the field is considered to be inherited only once. It may be referred to by its simple name without ambiguity.

For example, in the code:

```
public interface Colorable {
    int RED = 0xff0000, GREEN = 0x00ff00, BLUE
    = 0x0000ff;
}
public interface Paintable extends Colorable {
    int MATTE = 0, GLOSSY = 1;
}
class Point {int x, y;}
class ColoredPoint extends Point implements
```

```
    Colorable {
        ...
}
class PaintedPoint extends ColoredPoint implements
    Paintable
{
        ... RED...
}
```

the fields **RED, GREEN,** and **BLUE** are inherited by the class **PaintedPoint** both through its direct superclass **ColoredPoint** and through its direct superinterface **Paintable**. The simple names **RED, GREEN,** and **BLUE** may nevertheless be used without ambiguity within the class **PaintedPoint** to refer to the fields declared in interface **Colorable**.

METHOD DECLARATIONS

A *method* declares executable code that can be invoked, passing a fixed number of values as arguments.

```
MethodDeclaration:
      MethodHeader MethodBody
MethodHeader:
      MethodModifiersopt  TypeParametersopt
    ResultType MethodDeclarator
Throwsopt
ResultType:
      Type
      void
MethodDeclarator:
      Identifier (FormalParameterListopt)
```

A method declaration either specifies the type of value that the method returns or uses the keyword **void** to indicate that the method does not return a value.

The *Identifier* in a *MethodDeclarator* may be used in a name to refer to the method. A class can declare a method with the same name as the class or a field, member class or member interface of the class, but this is discouraged as a matter of style. For compatibility with older versions of the Java platform, a declaration form for a method that returns an array is allowed to place (some or all of) the empty bracket pairs that form the declaration of the array type after the parameter list. This is supported by the obsolescent production:

```
MethodDeclarator:
        MethodDeclarator []
```

but should not be used in new code.

It is a compile-time error for the body of a class to declare as members two methods with override-equivalent signatures (name, number of parameters, and types of any parameters). Methods and fields may have the same name, since they are used in different contexts and are disambiguated by different lookup procedures.

FORMAL PARAMETERS

The *formal parameters* of a method or constructor, if any, are specified by a list of comma-separated parameter specifiers. Each parameter specifier consists of a type (optionally preceded by the **final** modifier and/or one or more annotations) and an identifier (optionally followed by brackets) that specifies the name of the parameter. The last formal parameter in a list is special; it may be a *variable arity parameter*, indicated by an elipsis following the type:

```
FormalParameterList:
        LastFormalParameter
        FormalParameters, LastFormalParameter
FormalParameters:
        FormalParameter
        FormalParameters, FormalParameter
FormalParameter:
        VariableModifiers Type VariableDeclaratorId
VariableModifiers:
        VariableModifier
        VariableModifiers VariableModifier
VariableModifier: one of
        final Annotation
LastFormalParameter:
        VariableModifiers              Type...opt
    VariableDeclaratorId
```

```
        FormalParameter
```

The following is repeated from to make the presentation here clearer:

```
VariableDeclaratorId:
        Identifier
        VariableDeclaratorId []
```

If a method or constructor has no parameters, only an empty pair of parentheses appears in the declaration of the method or constructor. If two formal parameters of the same method or constructor are declared to have the same name (that is, their declarations mention the same *Identifier*), then a compile-time error occurs. If an annotation *a* on a formal parameter corresponds to an annotation type *T*, and *T* has a (meta-)annotation *m* that corresponds to **annotation.Target**, then *m* must have an element whose value is **annotation.ElementType.PARAMETER**, or a compile-time error occurs. It is a compile-time error if a method or constructor parameter that is declared final is assigned to within the body of the method or constructor.

When the method or constructor is invoked, the values of the actual argument expressions initialize newly created parameter variables, each of the declared *Type,* before execution of the body of the method or constructor. The *Identifier* that appears in the *DeclaratorId* may be used as a simple name in the body of the method or constructor to refer to the formal parameter.

If the last formal parameter is a variable arity parameter of type *T*, it is considered to define a formal parameter of type *T[]*. The method is then a *variable arity method*. Otherwise, it is a *fixed arity method*. Invocations of a variable arity method may contain more actual argument expressions than formal parameters. All the actual argument expressions that do not correspond to the formal parameters preceding the variable arity parameter will be evaluated and the results stored into an array that will be passed to the method invocation.

The scope of a parameter of a method or constructor is the entire body of the method or constructor. These parameter names may not be redeclared as local variables of the method, or as exception parameters of catch clauses in a try statement of the method or constructor. However, a parameter of a method or constructor may be shadowed anywhere inside a class declaration nested within that method or constructor. Such a nested class declaration could declare either a local class or an anonymous class.

Formal parameters are referred to only using simple names, never by using qualified names. A method or constructor parameter of type **float** always contains an element of the float value set; similarly, a method or constructor parameter of type **double** always contains an element of the double value set. It is not permitted for a method or constructor parameter of type **float** to contain an element of the float-extended-exponent value set that is not also an element of the float value set, nor for a method parameter of type **double** to contain an element of the double-extended-exponent value set that is not also an element of the double value set.

Where an actual argument expression corresponding to a parameter variable is not FP-strict, evaluation of that actual argument expression is permitted to use intermediate values drawn from the appropriate extended-exponent value sets. Prior to being stored in the parameter variable the result of such an expression is mapped to the nearest value in the corresponding standard value set by method invocation conversion.

Method Signature

It is a compile-time error to declare two methods with override-equivalent signatures (defined below) in a class. Two methods have the *same signature* if they have the same name and argument types.

Two method or constructor declarations M and N have the *same argument types* if all of the following conditions hold:

- They have the same number of formal parameters (possibly zero)
- They have the same number of type parameters (possibly zero)
- Let $<A_1...,A_n>$ be the formal type parameters of M and let $<B_1...,B_n>$ be the formal type parameters of

N. After renaming each occurrence of a B_i in *N*'s type to A_i the bounds of corresponding type variables and the argument types of *M* and *N* are the same.

The signature of a method *m1* is a *subsignature* of the signature of a method *m2* if either

- *m2* has the same signature as *m1*, or
- The signature of *m1* is the same as the erasure of the signature of *m2*.

The notion of subsignature defined here is designed to express a relationship between two methods whose signatures are not identical, but in which one may override the other. Specifically, it allows a method whose signature does not use generic types to override any generified version of that method. This is important so that library designers may freely generify methods independently of clients that define subclasses or subinterfaces of the library.

Consider the example:

```
class CollectionConverter {
List toList(Collection c) {...}
}
class Overrider extends CollectionConverter{
List toList(Collection c) {...}
}
```

Now, assume this code was written before the introduction of genericity, and now the author of class **CollectionConverter** decides to generify the code, thus:

```
class CollectionConverter {
      <T> List<T> toList(Collection<T> c) {...}
}
```

Without special dispensation, **Overrider.toList()** would no longer override **CollectionConverter.toList()**.

Instead, the code would be illegal. This would significantly inhibit the use of genericity, since library writers would hesitate to migrate existing code. Two method signatures *m1* and *m2* are *override-equivalent* iff either *m1* is a subsignature of *m2* or *m2* is a subsignature of *m1*.

The example:

```
class Point implements Move {
```

```
    int x, y;
    abstract void move(int dx, int dy);
    void move(int dx, int dy) {x += dx; y +=
  dy;}
}
```

causes a compile-time error because it declares two **move** methods with the same (and hence, override-equivalent) signature. This is an error even though one of the declarations is **abstract.**

METHOD MODIFIERS

```
MethodModifiers:
    MethodModifier
    MethodModifiers MethodModifier
MethodModifier: one of
    Annotation public protected private abstract
  static
     final synchronized native strictfp
```

A compile-time error occurs if the same modifier appears more than once in a method declaration, or if a method declaration has more than one of the access modifiers **public, protected**, and **private**. A compile-time error occurs if a method declaration that contains the keyword **abstract** also contains any one of the keywords **private, static, final, native, strictfp,** or **synchronized**. A compile-time error occurs if a method declaration that contains the keyword **native** also contains **strictfp.**

If an annotation *a* on a method declaration corresponds to an annotation type *T*, and *T* has a (meta-)annotation *m* that corresponds to **annotation.Target**, then *m* must have an element whose value is **annotation.ElementType.METHOD**, or a compile-time error occurs. If two or more method modifiers appear in a method declaration, it is customary, though not required, that they appear in the order consistent with that shown above in the production for *MethodModifier*.

Abstract Methods

An **abstract** method declaration introduces the method

as a member, providing its signature return type, and **throws** clause (if any), but does not provide an implementation. The declaration of an **abstract** method *m* must appear directly within an **abstract** class (call it *A*) unless it occurs within an enum otherwise a compile-time error results. Every subclass of *A* that is not **abstract** must provide an implementation for *m*, or a compile-time error occurs. It is a compile-time error for a **private** method to be declared **abstract**.

It would be impossible for a subclass to implement a **private abstract** method, because **private** methods are not inherited by subclasses; therefore such a method could never be used. It is a compile-time error for a **static** method to be declared **abstract**. It is a compile-time error for a **final** method to be declared **abstract**. An **abstract** class can override an **abstract** method by providing another **abstract** method declaration.

This can provide a place to put a documentation comment, to refine the return type, or to declare that the set of checked exceptions that can be thrown by that method, when it is implemented by its subclasses, is to be more limited.

For example, consider this code:

```
class BufferEmpty extends Exception {
    BufferEmpty() {super();}
    BufferEmpty(String s) {super(s);}
}
class BufferError extends Exception {
    BufferError() {super();}
    BufferError(String s) {super(s);}
}
public interface Buffer {
    char get() throws BufferEmpty, BufferError;
}
public abstract class InfiniteBuffer implements
  Buffer {
   public abstract char get() throws
  BufferError;
}
```

The overriding declaration of method get in class

InfiniteBuffer states that method get in any subclass of **InfiniteBuffer** never throws a **BufferEmpty** exception, putatively because it generates the data in the buffer, and thus can never run out of data. An instance method that is not **abstract** can be overridden by an **abstract** method. For example, we can declare an **abstract** class **Point** that requires its subclasses to implement **toString** if they are to be complete, instantiable classes:

```
abstract class Point {
    int x, y;
    public abstract String toString();
}
```

This abstract declaration of toString overrides the non-abstract toString method of class Object. (Class Object is the implicit direct superclass of class Point.) Adding the code:

```
class ColoredPoint extends Point {
    int colour;
    public String toString() {
        return super.toString() + ": colour
    " + colour;// error
    }
}
```

results in a compile-time error because the invocation **super.toString()** refers to method **toString** in class **Point**, which is **abstract** and therefore cannot be invoked. Method **toString** of class **Object** can be made available to class **ColoredPoint** only if class **Point** explicitly makes it available through some other method, as in:

```
abstract class Point {
    int x, y;
    public abstract String toString();
    protected String objString() {return
   super.toString();}
}
class ColoredPoint extends Point {
    int colour;
    public String toString(){
```

```
        return objString() + ": colour "+
colour;                              //
correct
    }
}
```

STATIC METHODS

A method that is declared **static** is called a *class method*. A class method is always invoked without reference to a particular object. An attempt to reference the current object using the keyword **this** or the keyword **super** or to reference the type parameters of any surrounding declaration in the body of a class method results in a compile-time error. It is a compile-time error for a **static** method to be declared **abstract**.

A method that is not declared **static** is called an *instance method,* and sometimes called a non-**static** method. An instance method is always invoked with respect to an object, which becomes the current object to which the keywords **this** and **super** refer during execution of the method body.

FINAL METHODS

A method can be declared **final** to prevent subclasses from overriding or hiding it. It is a compile-time error to attempt to override or hide a **final** method. A **private** method and all methods declared immediately within a **final** class behave as if they are **final**, since it is impossible to override them. It is a compile-time error for a **final** method to be declared **abstract**.

At run time, a machine-code generator or optimizer can "inline" the body of a **final** method, replacing an invocation of the method with the code in its body. The inlining process must preserve the semantics of the method invocation. In particular, if the target of an instance method invocation is **null**, then a **NullPointerException** must be thrown even if the method is inlined. The compiler must ensure that the exception will be thrown at the correct point, so that the actual arguments to the method will be seen to have been evaluated in the correct order prior to the method invocation.

Consider the example:

```
final class Point {
    int x, y;
      void move(int dx, int dy) {x += dx; y +=
    dy;}
}
class Test {
      public static void main(String[] args) {
            Point[] p = new Point[100];
            for (int i = 0; i < p.length; i++) {
                  p[i] = new Point();
                  p[i].move(i, p.length-1-i);
            }
      }
}
```

Here, inlining the method move of class Point in method main would transform the for loop to the form:

```
            for (int i = 0; i < p.length; i++) {
                  p[i] = new Point();
                  Point pi = p[i];
                  int j = p.length-1-i;
                  pi.x += i;
                  pi.y += j;
            }
```

The loop might then be subject to further optimizations.

Such inlining cannot be done at compile time unless it can be guaranteed that Test and Point will always be recompiled together, so that whenever Point-and specifically its move method-changes, the code for Test.main will also be updated.

NATIVE METHODS

A method that is **native** is implemented in platform-dependent code, typically written in another programming language such as C, C++, FORTRAN,or assembly language. The body of a native method is given as a semicolon only, indicating that the implementation is omitted, instead of a block.

A compile-time error occurs if a native method is declared abstract. For example, the class RandomAccessFile of the package java.io might declare the following native methods:

```
package java.io;
public class RandomAccessFile
    implements DataOutput, DataInput
{   ...
    public native void open(String name, boolean
  writeable)
        throws IOException;
    public native int readBytes(byte[] b, int
  off, int len)
        throws IOException;
    public native void writeBytes(byte[] b, int
  off, int len)
        throws IOException;
    public native long getFilePointer() throws
  IOException;
    public native void seek(long pos) throws
  IOException;
    public native long length() throws
  IOException;
    public native void close() throws
  IOException;
}
```

STRICTFP METHODS

The effect of the strictfp modifier is to make all float or double expressions within the method body be explicitly FP-strict.

SYNCHRONIZED METHODS

A **synchronized** method acquires a monitor before it executes. For a class **(static)** method, the monitor associated with the **Class** object for the method's class is used. For an instance method, the monitor associated with **this** (the object for which the method was invoked) is used.

These are the same locks that can be used by the synchronized statement; thus, the code:

```
class Test {
      int count;
      synchronized void bump() {count++;}
      static int classCount;
      static synchronized void classBump() {
            classCount++;
      }
}
```

has exactly the same effect as:

```
class BumpTest {
      int count;
      void bump() {
            synchronized (this) {
                  count++;
            }
      }
      static int classCount;
      static void classBump() {
            try {
            s y n c h r o n i z e d
    (Class.forName("BumpTest")) {
                        classCount++;
                  }
            } catch (ClassNotFoundException e) {
                  ...
            }
      }
}
```

The more elaborate example:

```
public class Box {
      private Object boxContents;
      public synchronized Object get() {
            Object contents = boxContents;
            boxContents = null;
            return contents;
      }
```

```
public synchronized boolean put(Object
    contents) {
            if (boxContents != null)
                    return false;
            boxContents = contents;
            return true;
    }
}
```

defines a class which is designed for concurrent use. Each instance of the class Box has an instance variable boxContents that can hold a reference to any object. You can put an object in a Box by invoking put, which returns false if the box is already full. You can get something out of a Box by invoking get, which returns a null reference if the box is empty.

If put and get were not synchronized, and two threads were executing methods for the same instance of Box at the same time, then the code could misbehave. It might, for example, lose track of an object because two invocations to put occurred at the same time.

GENERIC METHODS

A method is *generic* if it declares one or more type variables. These type variables are known as the *formal type parameters* of the method.

The form of the formal type parameter list is identical to a type parameter list of a class or interface. The scope of a method's type parameter is the entire declaration of the method, including the type parameter section itself.

Therefore, type parameters can appear as parts of their own bounds, or as bounds of other type parameters declared in the same section.

Type parameters of generic methods need not be provided explicitly when a generic method is invoked. Instead, they are almost always inferred.

METHOD RETURN TYPE

The return type of a method declares the type of value a method returns, if it returns a value, or states that the method is **void**. A method declaration d_1 with return type R_1 is return-type-substitutable for another method d_2 with return type R_2, if and only if the following conditions hold:

- If R_1 is a primitive type, then R_2 is identical to R_1.
- If R_1 is a reference type then:
  - R_1 is either a subtype of R_2 or R_1 can be converted to a subtype of R_2 by unchecked conversion or
  - $R_1 = | R_2 |$.
- If R_1 is void then R_2 is void.

Discussion: The notion of return-type substitutability summarizes the ways in which return types may vary among methods that override each other.

Note that this definition supports *covariant returns* - that is, the specialization of the return type to a subtype (but only for reference types).

Also note that unchecked conversions are allowed as well. This is unsound, and requires an unchecked warning whenever it is used; it is a special allowance is made to allow smooth migration from non-generic to generic code.

METHOD THROWS

A *throws clause* is used to declare any checked exceptions that can result from the execution of a method or constructor:

```
Throws:
        throws ExceptionTypeList
ExceptionTypeList:
        ExceptionType
        ExceptionTypeList, ExceptionType
ExceptionType:
        ClassType
        TypeVariable
```

A compile-time error occurs if any *ExceptionType* mentioned in a throws clause is not a subtype of Throwable. It is permitted but not required to mention other (unchecked) exceptions in a throws clause.

For each checked exception that can result from execution of the body of a method or constructor, a compile-time error occurs unless that exception type or a supertype of that exception type is mentioned in a throws clause in the declaration of the method or constructor.

The requirement to declare checked exceptions allows the compiler to ensure that code for handling such error conditions has been included.

Methods or constructors that fail to handle exceptional conditions thrown as checked exceptions will normally result in a compile-time error because of the lack of a proper exception type in a throws clause.

The Java programming language thus encourages a programming style where rare and otherwise truly exceptional conditions are documented in this way.

The predefined exceptions that are not checked in this way are those for which declaring every possible occurrence would be unimaginably inconvenient:

- Exceptions that are represented by the subclasses of class Error, for example OutOfMemoryError, are thrown due to a failure in or of the virtual machine. Many of these are the result of linkage failures and can occur at unpredictable points in the execution of a programme. Sophisticated programs may yet wish to catch and attempt to recover from some of these conditions.
- The exceptions that are represented by the subclasses of the class RuntimeException, for example NullPointerException, result from run—time integrity checks and are thrown either directly from the programme or in library routines. It is beyond the scope of the Java programming language, and perhaps beyond the state of the art, to include sufficient information in the programme to reduce to a manageable number the places where these can be proven not to occur.

A method that overrides or hides another method, including methods that implement **abstract** methods defined in interfaces, may not be declared to throw more checked exceptions than the overridden or hidden method.

More precisely, suppose that *B* is a class or interface, and *A* is a superclass or superinterface of *B*, and a method declaration *n* in *B* overrides or hides a method declaration *m* in *A*. If *n* has a **throws** clause that mentions any checked exception types, then *m* must have a **throws** clause, and for every checked exception type listed in the **throws** clause of *n*, that same exception class or one of its supertypes must occur in the erasure of the **throws** clause of *m*; otherwise, a compile-time error occurs.

Chapter 5

JAVA Swings

DEFINITION

The Java Swing provides the multiple platform independent APIs interfaces for interacting between the users and GUIs components. All Java Swing classes imports form the import javax.swing.*; package. Java provides an interactive features for design the GUIs toolkit or components like: labels, buttons, text boxes, checkboxes, combo boxes, panels and sliders etc. All AWT flexible components can be handled by the Java Swing.

The Java Swing supports the plugging between the look and feel features. The look and feel that means the dramatically changing in the component like JFrame, JWindow, JDialog etc. for viewing it into the several types of window.

Here the following APIs interfaces and classes are available:

The following interfaces and it's descriptions to be used by the Java swing.

Interfaces	Descriptions
Action	This interface performed the action with the ActionListener where the multiple controls are used for same purposes.
BoundedRangeModel	This interface defines the data model of components like: sliders and progressBars.
ButtonModel	It defines the state model for the buttons like: radio buttons, check boxes etc.
CellEditor	This interface used by the developer for creating the new editor and it has the new

	components implement interfaces. The CellEditor implements the wrapper based approach.
ComboBoxEditor	In this interface, the editor component used to JComboBox components.
ComboBoxModel	This interface represents the data model in a list model with the selected items.
DesktopManager	This interface has JDesktopPane object. The JInternalFrame implements in the JDesktopPane with the help of DesktopManager.
Icon	This interface used to graphical representation of the components. It has fixed size picture.
JComboBox.Key SelectionManager	This interface has KeySelectionManager and used for the combo box data model.
ListCellRenderer	This interface used for paint the cell in the list with the help of "rubber stamps".
ListModel	This interface used for JList components method. It gets the value of each cell of list.
ListSelectionModel	This interface indicates the components, which are stable or not.
MenuElement	This interface used where the any components are implements in the menu.
MutableCombo BoxModel	This interface extends from the ComboBoxModel. It is a mutable version of ComboBoxModel.
Renderer	It defines the requirements of an object for displaying the values.
RootPaneContainer	This interface uses the RootPane properties and it has the components like: JFrame, JInternalFrame and JWindow etc.
Scrollable	This interface provides the scrolling to show the large amount of data with the help of JScrollPane.
ScrollPaneConstants	This interface used for JScrollPane components.
SingleSelectionModel	This interface used to select the one index in

	a model.
SwingConstants	You can set the components on the screen to own requirements.
UIDefaults.ActiveValue	It constructs the DefaultListCellRenderer.
UIDefaults.LazyValue	This enables one to store an entry in the default table. The entered value is not constructed until first time is a real value is created through it using *LazyValue.createValue()* method.
WindowConstants	This interface has two methods setDefaultCloseOperation and getDefaultCloseOperation and provides the window close opration.

The following classes and it's descriptions to be used by the Java swing.

Classes	Descriptions
AbstractAction	This class handles the any types of action and provides JFC Action interface.
AbstractButton	This class defines the nature of buttons and menu items.
AbstractCellEditor	It provides a list and contents of the data model.
AbstractListModel	This class defines the data model which provides the list with its contents.
ActionMap	This class works with InputMap and performs any action when the key is pressed.
BorderFactory	This class extends from Object and creates the Border instance in the factory.
Box	It provides the fixed spaces between two components and uses the BoxLayout object of the layout manager.
Box.Filler	This class participates in the Layout and uses the lightweight components.
BoxLayout	This class uses the arranging the multiple components either horizontally or vertically. The Box container uses this class.
ButtonGroup	This class used to create the multiple buttons

	in a ButtonGroup object.
CellRandererPane	This class used to insert the components like: JList, JTable and JTree.
ComponentInputMap	This class has ComponentInputMap constructor and creates the components with the help of InpuMap.
DebugGraphics	It extends from the Graphics and used to debug the graphics
DefaultBounded RangeModel	This class provides the implementation of default BoundedRangeModel.
DefaultButtonModel	This class implements the generic ButtonModel.
DefaultCellEditor	It implements the TableCellEditor and TreeCellEditor for the table and tree cells.
DefaultCombo BoxModel	It provides the default model for combo boxes.
DefaultDesktop Manager	It implements the DesktopManager. The DesktopManager has the JInternalFrame for creating the internal fame in a frame.
DefaultFocusManager	It provides the implementing the FocusManager.
DefaultListCell Randerer	It implements the default ListCellRanderer.
DefaultListCell Randerer.UIResource	This extends the DefaultListCellRanderer and implementing in the UIResource.
DefaultListModel	It extends the AbstractListModel and implementing the *java.util.Vector*.
DefaultListSelection Model	This class used for select the list in a data model.
DefaultSingle SelectionModel	This class provides the default SingleSelectionModel.
FocusManager	It handles all focus like: gainedFocus and lostFocus.
GrayFilter	It extends the RGBImageFilter and used for disabling the image through the button.
ImageIcon	This class implements the Icon and paints the icons from the images.
InputMap	This class uses the ActionMap to performed

	the action when you press any key of keyboard. It bounds data between the input event and an object.
InputVerifier	This class helps you when you works with the text fields through the focus.
JApplet	This class extends the Applet and implements the Accessible and RootPaneContainer.
JButton	This class extends the AbstractButton and you can create the new button.
JCheckBox	This class extends the JToggleButton and implements the check box in which buttons are selected or deselected.
JCheckBoxMenuItem	It extends the JMenuItem and determines the items which is selected or deselected.
JColorChooser	It extends the JComponent and implementing the Accessable. Here, you choose and manipulate the colors.
JComboBox	This class extends the JComboBox. It provides the drop-down list where user select only one item or value at a time. But combo box is a combination of multiple text or buttons etc.
JComponent	In java swing, All components are used the JComponent except the top-level containers like: JFrame, JDialog etc.
JDesktopPane	This class extends the JLayeredPane and when you create the object of JInternalFrame to be maintained in the JDesktopPane. The JDesktopPane has DesktopManager.
JDialog	It extends the Dialog. This class used to create the dialog window and when you want to create the custom dialog window with the help of JOptionPane method.
JEditorPane	This class extends the JTextComponent. It edits the component by the EditorKit.
JFileChooser	This class provides the facility to choosing the file.

JFrame	It extends the Frame and supports the swing components architecture.
JInternalFrame	This class extends from the JComponent and provides the facility to dragging, closing, resizing and menu bar of the internal frame. The JInternalFrame added into the
JDesktopPane.	JInternalFrame.JDesktopIcon It displays the desktop icon and create the instance of JInternalFrame and iconify.
JLabel	This class used to show the small text and image.
JLayeredPane	It has JFC/Swing container that can be used to overlap the components to each other.
JList	This class used to create a list where you select the one or more than objects.
JMenu	This class used to create a new menu where you add the JMenuItems. When you select the item then shows the popup menu items in the JMenuBar.
JMenuBar	It used to create a new menu bar where the JMenu objects are added.
JMenuItem	This class used to create new menu items in the mebus.
JOptionPane	It used to create some different types of dialog box like: message dialog box, error dialog box etc.
JPanel	It extends the JComponent and used to create a new panel.
JPassworkField	It provides the single line text editing. Here, don't available the original characters but view type indication characters are available.
JPopupMenu	This class used to create a popup menu. It provides small window where the various types of choices are available.
JPopupMenu.Separator	Here the popup menu and the separator are available.
JProgressBar	It shows the integer types values in per cent within a bounded range to determine the

	working process.
JRadioButton	It implements the radio button and shows the state of an item selected or deselected.
JRadioButtonMenuItem	It extends the JMenuItem and implements the radio button menu item
JRootPane	This class provides the component behind the scenes by JFrame, JWindow, JDialog etc. for providing the task-orientation and functionality.
JScrollBar	This class used to create a scroll bar. It provides the view content area where you show the content to scroll this.
JScrollPane	It provides the scrollable view components.
JSeparator	This class use the separator among the components.
JSlider	This class provides a control to represent a numeric value by dragging the slider.
JSplitPane	This class used to divides the two components graphically like: top and button, left and right.
JTabbedPane	This class provides the tab component through which you can switch from one component to another component regarding to the specific tab button by clicking on that.
JTable	It provides the user interface component and represents the two dimensional data.
JTextArea	It provides the multi line plain text area.
JTextField	It provides the facility to editing the text in a single line.
JTextPane	This class provides the component like JTexArea for multiple lines text with more capabalities.
JToggleButton	It implements two state button that means selected or deselected.
JToggleButton.Toggle ButtonModel	It extends the DefaultButtonModel and provides the ToggleButton model.
JToolBar	It provides set of command buttons icons that performs the different actions or controls.

JToolBar.Separator	It provides the tool bar separator.
JToolTip	It shows the tool tips related to it's components.
JTree	It shows the data in a hierarchical way.
JTree.DynamicUtil TreeNode	This extends the DefaultMutableTreeNode and create children nodes.
JTree.EmptySelection Model	It does not allows the any selection.
JViewPort	It gives you about the underlying information.
JWindow	It extends window and shows the any location or area on the desktop. It couldn't any title bar and window management buttons.
KeyStroke	This class controls the key events on the keyboard for the equivalent device.
LayoutFocusTraversal Policy	This class conducts the sorting objects according to their size, type, position or orientation.
LookAndFeel	It provides the dramatically changes in the component like frame related to the graphics for the application. Through this the application can be done very efficient and easier.
MenuSelectionManager	It has menu selection hierarchy.
OverlayLayout	The layout manager arrange the components.
ProgressMonitor	This class is used to monitoring the progress of any operation to be done.
ProgressMonitorInput Stream	This class creates a progress monitor to monitor the progress of reading input from the input stream. It cleanups all the rights when the stream is closed.
RepaintManager	This class manage and override the repaint requests.
ScrollPaneLayout	It implements the LayoutManager and manage the components like: scroll bar, row header, column header etc.
ScrollPaneLayout.UI	It extends the ScrollPaneLayout and

Resource	implements the UIResource.
SizeRequirements	It calculates the size and positions of components.
SizeSequence	It represents the order list of size and it's positions.
SwingUtilities	This class has utilities methods for swing.
Timer	Actions perform the predefined rate.
ToolTipManager	It manages the all tool tips.
UIDefaults	It extends the Hashtable and you set/get the value with the help of UIManager.
UIDefaults.LazyInput Map	This class creates a Input Map through it's createValue() method. The array of key after binding is passed to the constructor of this. Example of binding of key is array of pressing key information (e.g. ctrl + c or alt + f).
UIDefaults.ProxyLazy Value	This class is used to create a lazy value which is used to delay loading of the class to create instance for that.
UIManager	This class has track of the current look and feel details.
UIManager.LookAnd FeelInfo	This is the nested class of UIManager class i.e. used for getting information about all the look and feels installed with the software development kit.
ViewportLayout	It implements the LayoutManager and defines the policy for the layout.

CREATING A FRAME

The frame in java works like the main window where your components (controls) are added to develop an application. In the Java Swing, top-level windows are represented by the JFrame class. Java supports the look and feel and decoration for the frame.

For creating java standalone application you must provide GUI for a user. The most common way of creating a frame is, using single argument constructor of the JFrame class. The argument of the constructor is the title of the window or frame.

Other user interface are added by constructing and adding it to the container one by one.

The frame initially are not visible and to make it visible the setVisible(true) function is called passing the boolean value *true*. The close button of the frame by default performs the hide operation for the JFrame.

In this example we have changed this behaviour to window close operation by setting the setDefaultClose Operation() to EXIT_ON_CLOSE value.

```
setSize (400, 400):
```

Above method sets the size of the frame or window to width (400) and height (400) pixels.

```
setVisible(true):
```

Above method makes the window visible.

```
setDefaultCloseOperation(JFrame.EXIT_ON_CLOSE):
```

Above code sets the operation of close operation to Exit the application using the System exit method.

CODE FOR THE PROGRAMME

```
import javax.swing.*;
public class Swing_Create_Frame{
  public static void main(String[] args){
   JFrame frame = new JFrame("Frame in Java Swing");
    frame.setSize(400, 400);
    frame.setVisible(true);
    frame.setDefaultCloseOperation(JFrame.EXIT_
   ON_CLOSE);
  }
}
```

DIALOG BOX IN JAVA

Message dialog box is used to display informative messages to the user. In this section we will use JOptionPane class to display the message Dialog box. Our programme display "Click Me" button on the window and when user clicks on it programme displays Message box with "OK" button and message "Roseindia.net". When you run the programme following window will be displayed:

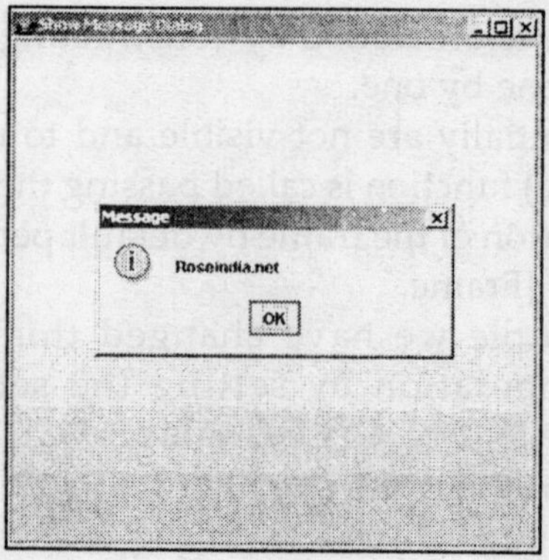

When you click on "Click Me" button, following Message is displayed:

- Programme description
- JOption Pane Class

In non-swing application we were using System.in class for input or output some text or numeric values but now in the swing application we can use Option Pane to show the output or show the message. This way of inputting or outputting works very efficiently in the Swing Applications. The window for showing message for input or output makes your application very innovative. Option Pane class is available in the *javax.swing.*;* package. This class provide various types of message dialog box as follows:

- A simple message dialog box which has only one button i.e. "Ok". This type of message dialog box is used only for showing the appropriate message and user can finish the message dialog box by clicking the "Ok" button.
- A message dialog box which has two or three buttons. You can set several values for viewing several message dialog box as follows:
  1.) "Yes" and "No"
  2.) "Yes", "No" and "Cancel"
  3.) "Ok", and "Cancel"
- A input dialog box which contains two buttons "Ok" and "Cancel".

The JOption Pane class has three methods as follows:

- *ShowMessageDialog()*: First is the showMessageDialog () method which is used to display a simple message.
- *ShowInputDialog()*: Second is the showInputDialog() method which is used to display a prompt for inputting. This method returns a String value which is entered by you.
- *ShowConfirmDialog()*: And the last or third method is the showConfirmDialog() which asks the user for confirmation (Yes/No) by displaying message. This method return a numeric value either 0 or 1. If you click on the "Yes" button then the method returns 1 otherwise 0.

HOW PROGRAMME WORKS

This programme illustrates you how to show a message dialog box when you click on the button.

`showMessageDialog():`

This method is used to show a message dialog box which contains some text messages. This is being used with two arguments in the programme where the first argument is the parent object in which the dialog box opens and another is the message which has to be shown.

CODE FOR PROGRAMME

```
import javax.swing.*;
import java.awt.event.*;
public class ShowDialogBox{
  JFrame frame;
  public static void main(String[] args){
    ShowDialogBox db = new ShowDialogBox();
  }
  public ShowDialogBox(){
    frame = new JFrame("Show Message Dialog");
    JButton button = new JButton("Click Me");
    button.addActionListener(new MyAction());
    frame.add(button);
    frame.setSize(400, 400);
```

```
      frame.setVisible(true);
     frame.setDefaultCloseOperation(JFrame.EXIT_ON_CLOSE);
   }
   public class MyAction implements ActionListener{
     public void actionPerformed(ActionEvent e){
        JOptionPane.showMessageDialog(
           frame,"Roseindia.net");
     }
   }
}
```

METHODS

For this purposes two methods have been used:

- ShowMessageDialog():

Above method shows a simple message dialog box which holds only one button i.e. "Ok" button. This method takes four arguments in which, first is the parent object name, second is the message as string, third is the title of the message dialog box as string and the last is the type of the message dialog box.

- ShowConfirmDialog():

Above method asks from the user by displaying a message dialog box which contains more than one button. Depending on the parameter passed it can be "Ok" and "Cancel" or "Yes", "No" and "Cancel". This method returns the integer value.

Code:

```
import javax.swing.*;
import java.awt.*;
import java.awt.event.*;
public class ShowMessageDialog{
  JButton button;
  public static void main(String[] args){
    ShowMessageDialog md = new ShowMessageDialog();
  }
  public ShowMessageDialog(){
    JFrame frame = new JFrame("Message Dialog Box");
     button = new JButton("Show simple
    message dialog box");
```

```
        button.addActionListener(new MyAction());
        JPanel panel = new JPanel();
        panel.add(button);
         button = new JButton("Show \"Ok/
Cancel\" message
    dialog box");
        button.addActionListener(new MyAction());
        panel.add(button);
        button = new JButton("Show \"Yes/No/
Cancel\" dialog box");
        button.addActionListener(new MyAction());
        panel.add(button);
        frame.add(panel);
        frame.setSize(400, 400);
        frame.setVisible(true);
        frame.setDefaultCloseOperation(JFrame.
        EXIT_ON_CLOSE);
        }
      public class MyAction implements ActionListener{
        public void actionPerformed(ActionEvent ae){
          String str = ae.getActionCommand();
          if(str.equals("Show simple message dialog box")){
            JOptionPane.showMessageDialog(null,
             "This is the simple message
    dialog box.", "Roseindia.net", 1);
          }
            else if(str.equals("Show \"Ok/
Cancel\" message dialog box")){
            if(JOptionPane.showConfirmDialog(null,
             "This is the \"Ok/Cancel\"
    message dialog box.", "Roseindia.net", JOptionPane.
    OK_CANCEL_OPTION) == 0)
              JOptionPane.showMessageDialog(null,
             "You clicked on \"Ok\" button",
     "Roseindia.net", 1);
            else
              JOptionPane.showMessage Dialog(null,
    "You clicked on \"Cancel\" button",
```

```
"Roseindia.net", 1);
        }
        else if(str.equals("Show \"Yes/No/
Cancel\" dialog box")){
          JOptionPane.showConfirmDialog(null, "This
            is the \"Yes/No/Cancel\"
  message dialog box.");
        }
      }
    }
  }
```

In this programme, addActionListener() method has been added to the button to register the action listener and then if you click on the button, the generated action event is captured in the actionPerformed(ActionEvent e) method. In the actionPerformed(ActionEvent e){we check the label of the button. If the label of the button is "Roseindia.net", it will change the button label to "Click Me" otherwise it will change the label to "Roseindia.net".

setText(String):

Above method sets the label of the button.

Code of the programme

```
import javax.swing.*;
import java.awt.event.*;
public class ChangeButtonLabel{
  JButton button;
  public static void main(String[] args){
    ChangeButtonLabel cl = new ChangeButtonLabel();
  }
  public ChangeButtonLabel(){
    JFrame frame = new JFrame("Change JButton Lebel");
    button = new JButton("Click Me");
    button.addActionListener(new MyAction());
    frame.add(button);
    frame.setSize(400, 400);
    frame.setVisible(true);
    frame.setDefaultCloseOperation(JFrame.EXIT_ON_CLOSE);
  }
```

```
    public class MyAction implements ActionListener{
      public void actionPerformed(ActionEvent e){
        String text = (String)e.getActionCommand();
        if (text.equals("Click Me")){
          button.setText("Roseindia.net");
        }
        else{
          button.setText("Click Me");
        }
      }
    }
  }
```

CREATE MENUS AND SUBMENUS

In this, you will learn about creation of menus, submenus and Separators in Java Swing. Menu bar contains a collection of menus. Each menu can have multiple menu items these are called submenu. Similarly, all menus have multiples menu items.

`Menu Items`

The Separator divides the menu items in a separate groups like same types of menu Items are divided into a individual parts. For pictorial representation, the image for the result of the given programme is given below:

This programme shows how to create menu bar, menus, submenus and Separators. Here, all items shows on a frame with the help of following methods and APIs:

`JMenuBar`

This is the class which constructs a menu bar that contains several menus.

`JMenu(String)`

This is the constructor of JMenu class. This constructor constructs the new menu. It takes the string type value which is the name label for the menu.

`JMenuItem(String)`

This is the constructor of JMenuItem class which constructs new menu items for the specific menu. It takes string types value which is the label for the menu item.

```
JSeparator()
```

This is the constructor of JSeparator class which adds an extra line between menu items. This line, only separates the menu items.

```
setJMenuBar()
```

This method is used to set the menu bar to the specified frame. It takes the object of the JMenuBar class.

Code:

```
import javax.swing.*;
public class SwingMenu{
  public static void main(String[] args) {
    SwingMenu s = new SwingMenu();
  }
  public SwingMenu(){
   JFrame frame = new JFrame("Creating a JMenuBar,
   JMenu, JMenuItem and
   seprator Component");
    frame.setDefaultCloseOperation(JFrame.
   EXIT_ON_CLOSE);
    JMenuBar menubar = new JMenuBar();
    JMenu filemenu = new JMenu("File");
    filemenu.add(new JSeparator());
    JMenu editmenu = new JMenu("Edit");
    editmenu.add(new JSeparator());
   JMenuItem fileItem1 = new JMenuItem("New");
   JMenuItem fileItem2 = new JMenuItem("Open");
   JMenuItem fileItem3 = new JMenuItem("Close");
    fileItem3.add(new JSeparator());
   JMenuItem fileItem4 = new JMenuItem("Save");
   JMenuItem editItem1 = new JMenuItem("Cut");
   JMenuItem editItem2 = new JMenuItem("Copy");
   editItem2.add(new JSeparator());
   JMenuItem editItem3 = new JMenuItem("Paste");
   JMenuItem editItem4 = new JMenuItem("Insert");
    filemenu.add(fileItem1);
    filemenu.add(fileItem2);
    filemenu.add(fileItem3);
    filemenu.add(fileItem4);
```

```
        editmenu.add(editItem1);
        editmenu.add(editItem2);
        editmenu.add(editItem3);
        editmenu.add(editItem4);
        menubar.add(filemenu);
        menubar.add(editmenu);
        frame.setJMenuBar(menubar);
        frame.setSize(400,400);
        frame.setVisible(true);
    }
}
```

SYNCHRONIZATION ORDER

Every execution has a *synchronization order*. A synchronization order is a total order over all of the synchronization actions of an execution. For each thread *t*, the synchronization order of the synchronization actions in *t* is consistent with the programme order of *t*.

Synchronization actions induce the *synchronized-with* relation on actions, defined as follows:

- An unlock action on monitor *m* synchronizes-with all subsequent lock actions on *m* (where subsequent is defined according to the synchronization order).
- A write to a volatile variable *v* synchronizes-with all subsequent reads of *v* by any thread (where subsequent is defined according to the synchronization order).
- An action that starts a thread synchronizes-with the first action in the thread it starts.
- The write of the default value (zero, false or null) to each variable synchronizes-with the first action in every thread. Although it may seem a little strange to write a default value to a variable before the object containing the variable is allocated, conceptually every object is created at the start of the programme with its default initialized values.
- The final action in a thread *T1* synchronizes-with any

action in another thread *T2* that detects that *T1* has terminated. *T2* may accomplish this by calling T1.isAlive() or T1.join().

- If thread *T1* interrupts thread *T2*, the interrupt by *T1* synchronizes-with any point where any other thread (including *T2*) determines that *T2* has been interrupted (by having an InterruptedException thrown or by invoking Thread.interrupted or Thread.isInterrupted).

The source of a synchronizes-with edge is called a release, and the destination is called an *acquire.*

HAPPENS-BEFORE ORDER

Two actions can be ordered by a *happens-before* relationship. If one action happens-before another, then the first is visible to and ordered before the second.

If we have two actions x and y, we write $hb(x, y)$ to indicate that x happens-before y.

- If x and y are actions of the same thread and x comes before y in programme order, then $hb(x, y)$.
- There is a happens-before edge from the end of a constructor of an object to the start of a finalizer for that object.
- If an action x synchronizes-with a following action y, then we also have $hb(x, y)$.
- If $hb(x, y)$ and $hb(y, z)$, then $hb(x, z)$.

It should be noted that the presence of a happens-before relationship between two actions does not necessarily imply that they have to take place in that order in an implementation. If the reordering produces results consistent with a legal execution, it is not illegal.

Discussion

For example, the write of a default value to every field of an object constructed by a thread need not happen before the beginning of that thread, as long as no read ever observes that fact. More specifically, if two actions share a happens-before relationship, they do not necessarily have to appear to have happened in that order to any code with which they do not share a happens-before relationship. Writes in one thread that are in a data race with reads in another thread may, for example, appear to occur out of order to those reads.

The **wait** methods of class **Object** have lock and unlock actions associated with them; their happens-before relationships are defined by these associated actions.

The happens-before relation defines when data races take place. A set of synchronization edges, *S*, is *sufficient* if it is the minimal set such that the transitive closure of *S* with the programme order determines all of the happens-before edges in the execution. This set is unique.

Index